Happy 22nd Birthday, Soph
Keep on saving the world ♡

Zoë /xx

# ONLY PLANET

A FLIGHT-FREE ADVENTURE
AROUND THE WORLD

ED GILLESPIE

WILD
THINGS
PUBLISHING

# ONLY
# PLANET

*Murun. Mongolia*

*The world is still large and strange and, thank God,*
*full of empty places that are nothing like home.*

— Paul Theroux —

# CONTENTS

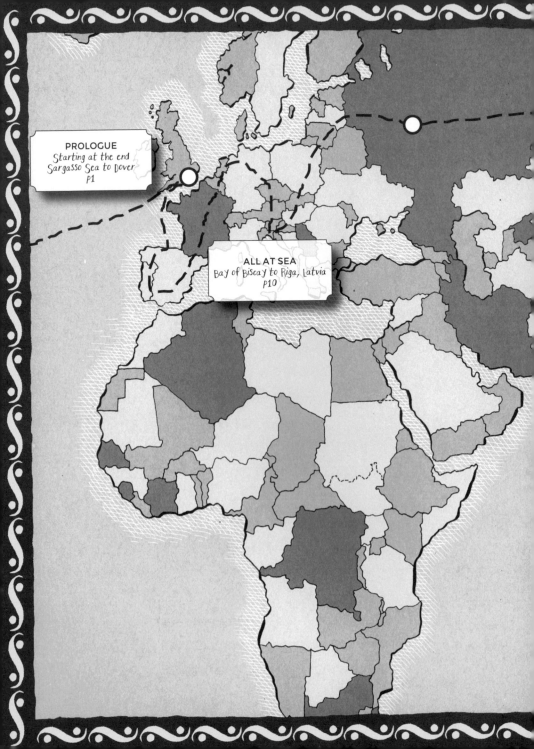

**PROLOGUE**
Starting at the end
Sargasso Sea to Dover
p1

**ALL AT SEA**
Bay of Biscay to Riga, Latvia
p10

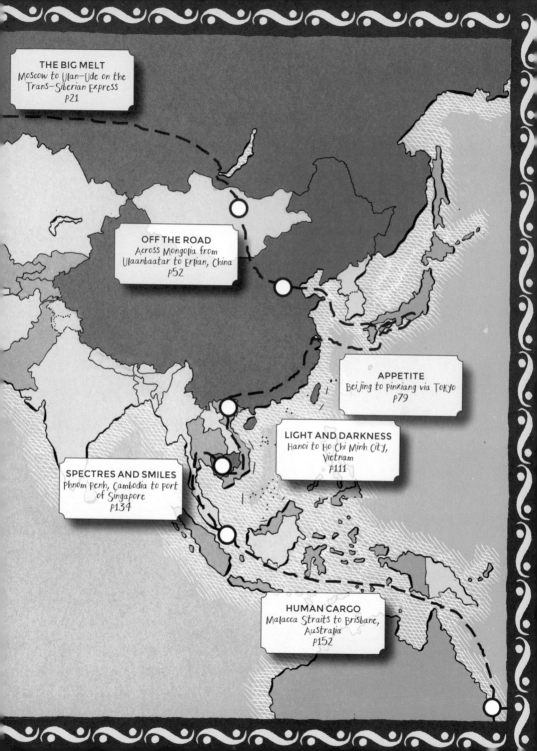

**THE BIG MELT**
Moscow to Ulan-Ude on the Trans-Siberian Express
p21

**OFF THE ROAD**
Across Mongolia from Ulaanbaatar to Erlian, China
p52

**APPETITE**
Beijing to pinxiang via Tokyo
p79

**LIGHT AND DARKNESS**
Hanoi to Ho Chi Minh City, Vietnam
p111

**SPECTRES AND SMILES**
Phnom Penh, Cambodia to port of Singapore
p134

**HUMAN CARGO**
Malacca Straits to Brisbane, Australia
p152

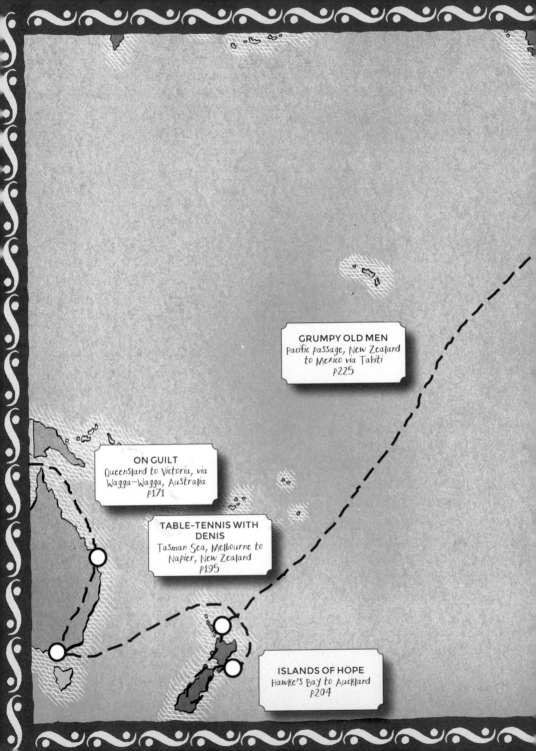

**GRUMPY OLD MEN**
Pacific passage, New Zealand
to Mexico via Tahiti
p225

**ON GUILT**
Queensland to Victoria, via
Wagga-Wagga, Australia
p171

**TABLE-TENNIS WITH
DENIS**
Tasman Sea, Melbourne to
Napier, New Zealand
p195

**ISLANDS OF HOPE**
Hawke's Bay to Auckland
p204

# PROLOGUE

*We are like islands in the sea, separate on the
surface but connected in the deep*

— William James —

Smashed shipping containers spilling bright green melons across the deck. Grotesquely twisted steel gantries. A jagged hole in the ship's hull just above the waterline. These images stuck in my mind.

'I thought it was our last moment of life.' The news report was quoting a woman who'd been aboard MV *Horncliff* when it was struck by three huge freak waves off the Scilly Isles. En route full of fruit from the Caribbean, the Horncliff had lost ninety of its refrigerated containers over the side as the 12,000-tonne, 500-foot-long ship had all but capsized. The ferocity of the Force 10 storm it had encountered at the mouth of the English Channel was unprecedented.

A Royal Navy helicopter performed a heroic rescue of several wounded passengers and the captain, who had suffered severe spinal injuries and internal bleeding after being thrown across the bridge by the impact; all while the ship was reeling in a 45- foot swell, repeatedly lashed by the monstrous waves.

Sitting aboard the *Horncliff's* sister vessel, the *Horncap*, it was hard for me to mentally erase the reports I'd read of this disaster a few short weeks previously. As we had edged out of the harbour in Puerto Limón, Costa Rica, it was in some trepidation of the next fortnight's voyage across a restless spring Atlantic Ocean.

*I have two hobbies: laziness and silliness,* giggled Dietlinde, a slim, retired German woman with a mischievous twinkle in her eye. We were in the bar of the *Horncap* with our fellow passengers, discussing the recent fate of its sibling ship. Dietlinde was a veteran cargo ship cruiser and had experienced a similar, slightly less intense but no less frightening storm on the *Horncliff* the previous year.

*It was all calm and professional at the time,* she smiled ruefully. *But later the Captain admitted it had been touch and go – very dangerous.* A handsome young Swede returning home with his small half-Nicaraguan son observed of our impassive Eastern European crew, *They don't want to tell you anything bad. You get the impression that even if we were sinking they wouldn't tell us.*

*I wasn't scared,* continued Dietlinde philosophically. *When it's your time, it's your time. The problem is that people think they are important,* she flicked her eyes towards the well-padded posteriors of the other German passengers, perched on bar stools behind her, *when really we are all insignificant!* I asked her whether she thought the *Horncliff* incident involved human error or if it was simply an accident caused by the unpredictably huge waves. *Accident?* she scoffed, *in German we say there is no word for 'accident', just a failure of human nature.*

Dietlinde was a brilliant example of the exuberantly eccentric and often devil-may-care people we had met during our travels and who had enriched our experience. Vadim, the ship's steward, was another. An ex-heavyweight boxer, Ukrainian Vadim was a hefty giant of a man with a surprisingly straight nose. I asked, politely, how this could be so following his pugilistic career. *No-one hit nose,* Vadim replied dryly.

*You play table tennis?* Vadim had barked at me one evening. I concurred eagerly, and found myself roped in as his doubles partner in a daily session with two other almost equally burly Slavic seamen. To say they took their table tennis seriously would be a gross understatement, racking up 14 to 15 games an hour of savage swipes, brutal backhands and viciously deviant spin shots. My nerves weren't helped by the fact that every time I fluffed a return shot Vadim would roar in frustrated exasperation. This was highly intimidating in close proximity to such a large man. At the end of one frenzied stint, in which we'd narrowly lost five games to six, a sweating Vadim glowered over me. I was definitely the weaker link in our partnership and was struggling to hold it together. *Last three games. Much better,* he admonished.

My girlfriend Fiona and I were on the final leg of a global circumnavigation of the world without flying. We'd been travelling for just over a year, covering over 40,000 miles and passing through 31 countries. Forsaking planes and their associated destructive carbon emissions, we'd set out to rediscover the joy of travelling *through* the world, not just over it. We'd wanted to experience the intimate transition of landscape, culture, people and language, soak up the sights, sounds and smells of the journey and not just bunny-hop around the globe in an aluminium sausage. By staying grounded we'd hoped, liked the Taoists, to find that the journey is actually the reward.

After all, it's the experience along the way in life that matters, not the ultimate destination. The very nature of our round-the-world-trip meant that our eventual endpoint would also be precisely where we'd started out. This was Brixton in south London which, though I love it dearly, is perhaps not a destination worth travelling all the way round the world to reach. So we'd very much hoped to enjoy ourselves along the way.

And now, just days from reaching home, we were rolling gently in the eerily, oily calm waters of the Sargasso Sea sat atop 10,000 tonnes of bananas and pineapples, ruminating on our adventures. Appropriately I was just finishing reading my sixtieth book of the year – slow travel creates plentiful amounts of reading time – the wonderful *Waterland* by Graham Swift. The Fenland landscapes in the story were a poignant reminder of my East Anglian roots and, despite the dark, bleak plot, made me hanker for home.

*The MV Horncap, with all the manoeuvrability of a tower-block, in the Mid-Atlantic*

The book's eely theme also chimed a chord. The mysterious lifecycle of the European eel is believed to begin here in the Sargasso. The mature Fenland adults swim 4,000 miles across the Atlantic and spawn together in these limpid tropical waters. Their larvae then embark on a 300-day drift back home to the rivers of Europe on the Gulf Stream. It's a fantastic example of the almost magical, miraculous ability of nature to pull off heroic global breeding migrations. For now.

The eel has suffered a catastrophic decline in numbers since the 1970s. Up to 98 percent fewer eels return to Europe now than when chocolate brown was still a fashionable colour. The exact cause is unknown but shifts in ocean currents related to climate change, overfishing and migratory obstructions such as dams and weirs have all been blamed. The eels' slow transatlantic travel and current relative rarity echoed our journey. Like the eel, the number of those who might be described as 'slow travellers', the great overland- and ocean-journeying folk among whom we counted ourselves, has also plummeted. War and political upheaval in Afghanistan and the Middle East had effectively ended the Hippy Trail east. Increased concerns about security and the end of casual labour at sea had done the same for informal cargo-ship voyages. Our flightless trip around the world felt like a dying gasp from a disappearing way of travel, as people buzz and bounce around the planet on ever-cheaper, faster planes. My parents had met whilst working on ocean liners, so in some ways it felt that flightless travel is in my blood.

Flying makes the world *seem* small. But let's face it, it's not. It's a 25,000 mile journey around the equator. That's a bit more than a stroll in the park. Let me assure you: when you bump across every last dusty mile of land from London to Singapore, toss on the crest of each briny wave of the Timor, Tasman and Pacific seas and oceans, rattle through Central America and blow back across the brooding Atlantic to Blighty, the world feels like a mighty *big* place! Slow travel resizes the world in a way that represents reality, not perception.

Rapid, affordable aviation has opened up the planet, meaning it's possible for anyone to twang themselves to the other side of the globe in around 24 hours. In some ways this connectivity has been great: creating the sense of a global village, fostering cultural understanding, opening our eyes to the great diversity of the human family and the wonders of the world and, of course, enhancing international tourism and business markets.

But it's also worth noting what we've lost: the sense of scale, the challenge of travel, the wonderful appreciation of gentle change that overland journeys involve, the slow shifts that reveal the planet and its people's rich and varied delights. Travel certainly has the potential to bring people together; as Mark Twain noted, 'Travel is fatal to prejudice, bigotry, and narrow-mindedness'. Yet how much of modern travel enables such deeper connections and understandings to emerge?

In some ways the swift, almost brutal discombobulating experience of flight that whisks you from the cool, grey urbanity of London's Heathrow to hot, steamy, frenzied Chhatrapathi Shivaji airport in Mumbai actually serves to reinforce perceived barriers and divides, confronting us joltingly and jarringly with our differences. But flightless travel eases us more smoothly across and through those elements that might separate us, from topography to the way we talk. Its grounded gradualism reveals far more about what connects us and what we all share in common, celebrates our unity, not our relatively petty differences.

Mahatma Gandhi once advised that 'there is more to life than increasing its speed'. The ongoing human obsession with moving ever faster raises questions about our experience of travel. I've always loved the notion that flying you see almost nothing, driving you see something, cycling most things, and walking everything. This speaks to me personally of the purpose of speed and how it changes our relationship with the world around us.-

We have witnessed around two centuries of unimpeded acceleration since Stephenson's pioneering railway engine 'Rocket' first took to the tracks in 1829. Almost constant innovation ever since, from coal to diesel to high-octane aviation fuel, through steam, combustion and jet engines, brought us to the pinnacle of supersonic passenger travel: Concorde. However, following its retirement in 2003 we experienced a moment unheard of in over 170 years: human travel just got slower.

Is this the end of progress? Well hardly. In so many areas of bustling modern life the desire to slow down just a little is not only increasingly attractive but also rewarding. Take food, for example. The supposedly inexorable trajectory of fast food should find us all shovelling convenience fuel frantically into our faces, a functional, efficient and effective way of cramming other more important things into our day. Yet we know this is not the case: there is something special about a lovingly sourced and prepared home-cooked meal to be savoured in every sense of the word.

Travel is no different, and there is something inherently satisfying about a sedate, sinuous and scenic train journey. Time is all we have in life. Paradoxically our response is to go at life harder and faster in the belief that this will mean we get more out of it. To some extent this might be true. But as Abraham Lincoln famously put it, 'It is not the years in your life that count, it's the life in your years'. In the travel sense, it is not about where we journey, but rather about how we do it.

I'd long had a desire and hunger to see the world in all its down-and-dirty glory, without contributing to the very forces such as climate change that threaten it so irrecoverably in the process. There seemed to me something wilfully perverse in the notion of a 'last-chance-to-see' approach to the world. The climate-stewing slew of carbon emissions that results from a long haul flight to the Maldives, for example, contributes to the sea level rise that threatens their very existence. There is a growing trend in this sort of tourism, a sort of travel 'realpolitik', with not-so-ironic articles and books suggesting '100 places to see before they disappear', even if the impact of the journey was in itself compounding the problem. I wanted no truck with the hypocrisy of that type of travel.

But equally I desired a metaphysical journey, a temporary escape from the relentless hustle of London and the hectic life of the business, Futerra, that I had co-founded back in 2001. I wasn't living life at the right speed. I was ungrateful, disconnected from the fact that I was unbelievably fortunate to have been brought up in the relative safety, security and comfort of 20th-century Britain. More worryingly, my sense of hope, of the possibility of a better future, was becoming dangerously compromised. I was becoming a glass half-empty pessimist, daunted and intimidated by the confluence of factors seemingly driving the world towards hell in an ironically slow handcart. Over-privileged, overworked and overstressed I needed a break, some fresh perspective, a chance to gather and contextualise my thoughts. To reflect, recharge and rediscover my sense of belief and my appetite for Futerra's longstanding mission 'To make sustainable development so desirable it becomes normal'.

I'd originally wanted to take inspiration from Phileas Fogg and attempt to go 'around the world in 80 *ways*'. However, once I'd started to list all the potential different modes of transport it swiftly became clear this would involve riding a lot of animals, not all of which would necessarily be available or indeed willing. Our trip was to be a reversion to a slower, more ruminative and reflective form of travel, the journey as a gentle seduction to be lingered over and appreciated, not the wham-bam-thank-you-ma'am of aviation and its relatively instant gratification. The trip of a lifetime: one in which we'd have the time of our lives.

Above all else, it was about adventure. As my friend Professor Jem Bendell of the Institute for Leadership and Sustainability puts it 'adventures in sustainability are coming...whether we like it or not'. So I wanted to embrace the prospect of the tempestuous turbulence to come. We are the generation that gets to surf this sustainability tsunami or be swamped by it. It was time to become a Big Wave rider.

At least my sea-legs were well honed by now, as the Eastern Atlantic swell began to build. Rascally squalls raced across the steely grey sea towards us. The *Horncap*'s round-bottomed hull rocked enthusiastically in the rolling waters, steering with all the handling grace of a block of flats. Bumping heavily into each 'pot-hole' between the waves sent a plume of white spray like a broad halo over the bow. The serene Sargasso this was not.

Up on the bridge Alexander, the ship's hangdog-expressioned second officer, gloomily shared his consistent meteorological pessimism. His outlook was invariably *Not good*, but his tendency to confuse the words 'better' and 'worse' didn't help matters. I pointed at the ship's roll gauge that was indicating a 15 degree angle from the vertical, noting that Dietlinde had experienced 39 degrees and that the gauge itself only went up to 40. *What happens after 40?* I asked nervously. *Lose vessel,* came

Alexander's humourless reply. *Is good ship. Is strong ship,* he added by way of reassurance. I experienced a flashback. It was almost exactly a year to the day that the captain of the ferry to Spain at the very start of our journey had said practically precisely the same thing.

Now, as the *Horncap* entered the busy shipping lanes of the Channel and we spotted Devon's Prawle Point, our first sight of home in 13 months, all this seemed a very long way, and time ago, behind us. The skies cleared, revealing a criss-cross of con-trails above, like some form of aviation jibe at our low-carbon efforts. The White Cliffs of Dover were soon to shine blindingly in the bright sunshine to welcome us home.

Rucksacks repacked for what must have been at least the hundredth time, we slipped down the gangway into the waiting arms of our families. Within minutes we were on the road back to London without a customs or passport check in sight. So much for UK border security! After 381 days on the road, we were home. It felt like we'd just stepped off a cross-Channel ferry.

But this book is not about destinations. Henry Miller wrote that *One's destination is never a place, but a new way of seeing things.* Our journey had changed us. Its reward was not our homecoming but a new perspective on our own lives. A fresh take on the collective challenge of billions of us living sustainably together on our one and only, lonely planet. A celebration of the people and places we'd encountered and explored in between.

# ALL AT SEA

*Being in a ship is being in a jail, with the chance of being drowned.*

— Samuel Johnson —

*I'd just like to reassure passengers that this is a good ship, a strong ship and there's nothing to be concerned about,* came the announcement, a future echo of Alexander's words on the bridge of the *Horncap* a year later, as another ferocious judder reverberated through the *Pride of Bilbao*. The captain seemed to be attempting to convince himself, as much as the rest of us, of his vessel's seaworthiness. We were doing what sailors call 'riding out the storm' outside Bilbao harbour. This had been closed because two ships had broken their moorings in the hurricane-force winds and were free-floating, hazardously, inside. We'd been doing this for 24 long, queasy hours.

'Riding out the storm' felt like a slight euphemism. What it actually entailed was turning the ship head to wind and riding bow-first into the incoming swell. It was less 'riding out' and more 'riding into', as we pitched and rolled. Despite the *Pride of Bilbao* weighing in at a cool 37,500 tonnes and being 580 feet long, we were tossing like the proverbial cork.

The ship would slowly crank up the face of each huge wave, lifting its prow high into the air. This thrust created the sensation either that we'd suddenly and dramatically increased in weight or that someone had turned the force of gravity up a couple of notches. Then, as the midsection of the ship passed over the crest of the wave, the bow would plunge down into the next trough. This caused our stomachs to climb up our throats and reminded me of the apparent weightlessness my brothers and I would feel as Mum drove us too fast over a particular humpback bridge on our way to our childhood summer holidays.

Occasionally, instead of riding from one wave to another, the ship would simply plough directly into the face of the next wall of water. An enormous crumping thud would then reverberate through the hull as several thousand tonnes of metal hit several thousand tonnes of cold Atlantic swell. Add to this a slewing movement from the buffeting of winds gusting at over 90mph, and we were most definitely experiencing the simultaneous 'six degrees of freedom' of a ship at sea: heaving, swaying, surging, pitching, yawing and, of course, rolling. It was a recipe for both violent seasickness and a feeling of creeping dread that we were actually going to die. The fact that it was also the 20th anniversary of the tragic Zeebrugge ferry disaster didn't help our sense of optimism.

Seeing us off at Waterloo station on the train to Portsmouth, where we'd catch the ferry, my sea-faring father had wished us well for our voyage through the Bay of Biscay. *I've had some horrendous crossings of those waters,* he'd recalled with a slight look of empathic trepidation in his eyes. In hindsight it appeared he'd inadvertently jinxed us, Jonah-style. Thanks, Dad.

This was hardly the most auspicious start to our trip. We had vast swathes of ocean to cross later in the journey, the small matters of the Pacific and Atlantic for instance, and here we were struggling to get to

*The Semmeringbahn, the world's first true mountain railway, Austria*

*The slow traveller's popular pastime of waiting for a train, this time in Slovenia*

Spain on a car ferry. It did not bode well, as we staggered around the ship clutching the handrails for dear life or just lay flat out in the cabin groaning softly, wishing it all to end. As any salty seadog knows there are two stages to seasickness: the first is when you're afraid you'll die, the second is when you're afraid you won't.

When we finally docked in Santander the following morning, our fate had become a local media event, as we were met by a gaggle of Spanish journalists. Clearly mistaking me for a Spaniard (probably something to do with my beard) they jabbed microphones and jabbered excited Spanish into my face. The following morning, in another strange future echo of the later *Horncliff* disaster, the headline in Bilbao's newspaper, *El Correo*, read 'I thought my time had come!' Thankfully, this wasn't a quote from the captain.

Armed with our stalwart student Inter-Rail tickets, we pored over the encyclopaedically-sized pan-European timetable. We had booked nothing for the trip except beds on the Trans-Siberian Express in a few weeks time. This was deliberate. We wanted the journey to unfold in front of us organically. We very vaguely knew the route we might take, which was largely defined by the timings of cargo ships that would take across the seas and oceans. Circumnavigating the world gives you a direction to head, in our case east, but it's also pretty much what you might call 'destination-neutral'. The uncertainty was liberating and exciting. It would give us the opportunity to explore whatever unusual, spontaneous travel suggestions the journey might throw at us, what cult American author Kurt Vonnegut describes as 'dancing lessons from God'.

That said, we planned to start with a ridiculous zig-zag route across the continent in order to visit friends and get into the rhythm of travelling. This was easier said than done. The frenzy of London life in which Fi and I snatched an evening or two together a week and maybe a few hours at the weekend was suddenly a 24/7 hot-house relationship. We simply weren't used to spending so much time in each other's company: it took a while to adjust. The control-freakery of work also crept in, with regular arguments about which of us was 'in charge' that day, a faintly ridiculous notion that we soon abandoned as we unwound from the pace of city living.

I was also haunted by the phantom vibrating of the mobile phone I'd left behind, imagining the cursed device in my pocket, or being seized by moments of panic in thinking I'd lost it. In retrospect this seems almost quaint, but it was an uplifting liberation to be freed from the usual constant electronic connectivity. Traversing Europe by train helped us slow down and relax. The tempo of rail travel and the stimulation of the ever-changing view settled us. Fi and I had plenty of time to talk, eat laid-back train picnics, watch as the European countryside rolled by outside the windows and become happy in each other's company. Becoming accustomed to life at this very different pace, we found ourselves on the sleeper train to Valencia. The train was due to arrive at 5.05am. We were a bit apprehensive about having to wander the streets for hours before anything opened. We needn't have worried.

Valencia station gave it away. It was throbbing, people everywhere; we soon realised why. We'd inadvertently blundered into the middle of Valencia's biggest festival, the Fallas de San José, celebrating the start of spring. The fiesta was still going strong. There were tens of thousands of party-goers out on the streets. Massive papier-mâché sculptures called *ninots* loomed over every intersection in town. They're satirical representations of politicians, celebrities and newsworthy events, and ranged from bare-breasted women to gurning cartoon and fantasy characters, human and bestial, leery and sinister, vulgar and crass, curious and weird. We'd never seen anything quite like it. On the last night of the Fallas all the sculptures, bar one that is saved by popular vote and placed in a local museum, are set alight and burnt in a fantastic frenzy of collective pyromania. Firefighters apparently stand by to hose down buildings adjacent to the burning *ninots* to avoid a conflagration. It was a health'n'safety nightmare, but all the more fun for it.

The narrow streets of the old town were still rammed with revellers, so we grabbed a breakfast beer – it was about six o'clock by now – and joined in. Dreadlocked crusties drummed, drunks lurched and people swaggered and staggered through the rubbish-filled plazas, the familiar festival carpet of cans, glass and plastic crunching underfoot. Every now and then the ambient atmosphere of pounding beats and raucous catcalls, laughter and chatter would be shattered by firecrackers, ranging in strength and volume from little snaps to great ear-drum shaking booms that left your head ringing.

As dawn approached we wove our way down from the main throng to the space-age architectural wonders of Santiago Calatrava's *Ciudad de las Artes y Ciencias* (City of Arts and Sciences). Watching the sun rise over the strange glass domes, intricate arches and interwoven web-like struts and buttresses of the buildings was as surreal as the bizarre sculptures we'd seen in town during the fiesta. Sitting in the warm early morning sunshine we could still hear firecrackers echoing across the city, giving the impression that, beyond the relative tranquillity of the *Ciudad*, the rest of the town was a war zone.

We soon came to realise that one of the special joys of overland travelling is the surprise of the unplanned, the accidental moments of brilliance you stumble upon when you least expect it. You go out into the world and 'stuff happens'. Gate-crashing Valencia's Fallas was a memorable example. Philosopher Julian Baggini refers to this as the difference between travel, in which the journey is a crucial part of the experience, and transit, a utilitarian emphasis on destination in which the journey is endured rather than enjoyed. The real joy (and sometimes pain) of travel often occurs in 'the interstices of the conventionally appealing'. Arriving in Valencia at the crack of dawn didn't feel like a great idea at the time, but led to what was one of the experiential highlights of the trip.

By reducing travel to transit we deny serendipity, because consumer culture trains us to expect and demand only what we want. We commodify simple joy into an expedient product. As a result, 'experiences are atomised into their component parts, the extraneous excised in an attempt to maximise the impact of the parts we prefer, with no thought to how their context changes them'. Planned plane travel from point to point typifies this, occluding the traveller's vision of the potential for inspiration or insightful inconvenience that fate, fortune or chance tend to conjure up when travelling on the ground. Overland travel is to embrace the impromptu and unforeseen, for there lies a fund of unanticipated knowledge. Trading the profoundly rewarding for ease, cost and convenience turns us all into 'airheads'.

The same 'spontaneity' principle applies to finding places to stay. These days, arranging accommodation when travelling is as simple as a quick Google search that invariably throws up hostel options and online booking systems galore. This means you can always be sure where you'll be staying in every destination before you arrive. But where's the fun in that? Far more entertaining is to go with the flow and see where you end up, usually in some pretty odd places. In Europe we found ourselves informally lodging in Salamanca in the spare room of a sweet little old lady's flat, in suburban Graz above a swingers club called 'Lady Sunshine', and with a lesbian couple in the coolest quarter of east Berlin.

On arrival at the Hlavni Nadrazi railway station in Prague we were approached by Tomáš, a rotund bundle of a man in a puffer jacket with a haphazardly shaved head. *Excuse me, excuse me,* he, literally, spat at us. Tomáš, we soon discovered, began practically every sentence with *Excuse me...* as if apologizing in advance for the fine mist of saliva he was about to veil you with. A swift, well-practiced monologue from Tomáš on the hideous expense of most Prague accommodation just persuaded us to view his nearby apartment.

He marched us onto the metro without tickets, *One stop is free!* Tomáš blatantly lied with a dismissive wave of his hand. His place was by the National Museum at the top of Wenceslas Square – where the activities taking place were more reminiscent of my home in Brixton than the famous Christmas carol might suggest. 'Good King Wenceslas looked out, on a sea of neon, where the dealers hung about, with tourists to prey on'. We then climbed a slight hill, which had Tomáš wheezing and sweating profusely. The room he offered us was basically half his apartment and scrupulously, bleachy clean. Perhaps uncharitably, this was more than could be said of Tomáš himself. We could still detect his 'presence' long after he'd left.

Inside, Tomáš became increasingly animated, proudly demonstrating the many features of the room. There was a half-eaten bar of chocolate on the table *Very good quality, very good brand,* he said, cramming several chunks into his mouth, projecting brown spittle onto Fi's sleeve, then apologizing, nervously wiping it off and handing us the remains of the bar. *I give you as present. —Thanks. — I learn English alone,* he continued, *no teacher, just with book, so I not proffy, my grammy not so good.* When we demurred that his grasp was far superior to our Czech vocabulary, let alone grammy, he retorted *Why should you learn Czech? Nobody speaks Czech!*

Tomáš seemed to be finding it hard to leave, repeatedly saying *I go now,* before finding another attribute of the room to demonstrate. He turned on the stereo, and a Beatles track sang out. *Very nice station, only 60s and 70s music, very romantisch,* enthused Tomáš wistfully and not a little lasciviously. For all the body odour, poor drool control and slightly scary physical appearance he was very warm and welcoming. Perhaps almost too welcoming and at ease with his guests as, on the next two occasions I spoke to him he was stark naked, poking his head around his front door furtively, answering my questions rather briskly.

That Friday night we drank plentiful amounts of Pilsner Urquell in a smoky Czech pub full of boisterous, raucous good cheer. It certainly helped me sleep soundly as I didn't notice the bed bugs nibbling that night in Tomáš's apartment: I woke the next day with a neat line of itchy red bites up my cheek and over my head as a souvenir of our stay. It looked like a route plan.

Continuing our unplanned exploration into the 'interstices of the conventionally appealing' after the festivities of Valencia's Fallas and Tomáš's flat in Prague, we were on the train to Warsaw, speeding happily through the Polish countryside after a couple of picturesque days in Krakow. The sun was setting over the ubiquitous birch forest. We were due to board the sleeper train to Moscow in an hour or two. Expecting to catch the Trans-Siberian in a couple of days time and head properly east to the wilds of Irkutsk, Mongolia and the linguistic, cultural and culinary delights of China, we were excited about venturing from the familiarity of Europe into the relatively unknown.

I was idly flicking through the guide book, my thoughts several thousand miles away somewhere on icy Lake Baikal, when I read a sentence which, despite my distracted state, made me stop instantly and re-read it in order to digest its implications. *What's wrong, you look shocked?* Fi said, as I looked up with my best poker face. *Er, I think we have a problem,* I muttered. Just occasionally when travelling in unfamiliar territory you get those moments of sudden, brutal clarity where a mood can swing from calm repose to deep, stomach-churning panic. This was one of them.

The sentence I'd just read was one of those wonderful guide book phrases which, when absorbed during trip preparation, is invaluable, but which when spotted en route is rather unsettling. It read 'To avoid the hassle of getting a Belarus transit visa consider taking the train from Vilnius'. So, in about two hours time we were due to get a sleeper train from Warsaw to Moscow that would take us through a country with a notoriously difficult border policy. With no transit visas. A key aspect of overland travel is that you actually have to cross a lot of borders which in a plane you simply soar right over. Whilst you wouldn't necessarily describe this as part of the fun, it certainly keeps you on your toes. This wasn't to be our last bit of visa- or customs-related fun by any means.

Our chances of getting a Belarusian visa in Warsaw on a Friday night seemed so slender they would make Kate Moss look morbidly obese. Poles are resourceful people but I doubted we could identify and locate the necessary contacts to obtain a Belarus transit visa, especially given our 45-minute window of opportunity between trains, and total lack of ability with the Polish language.

We vaguely contemplated getting on the train regardless, pleading ignorance/foolishness/sheer stupidity, maybe trying to win over the Belarusian border police by 'paying a fine' (i.e. a bribe). This idea was almost immediately relegated to the chocolate-teapot file, especially when we recalled the stroppy armed border police we'd encountered through the rest of central Europe. Like the folk who man airport baggage scanners, they're not renowned for their sense of humour. So the prospect of playing a quick game of 'Where's the visa?' with gun-toting guards near a Polish border village in the small hours of the morning didn't really appeal. Nor did being hurled off the train into the aforesaid Polish border village at that time of the night.

We managed to remain cool, calm and collected, despite the complexity and apparent desperation of the situation. We suspected we hadn't the chance of a rat in a bag of cats of getting from Warsaw to Moscow in time to catch the Trans-Siberian, as we wouldn't be able to get a Belarus transit visa till Monday at the earliest. The train then wouldn't arrive in Moscow before Tuesday night, when our train east would already have been...heading east.

This was a real, proper travel challenge. Inter-railing in Europe had been a cinch: all you needed was your passport and your ticket, and away you went. Suddenly we were running into our first glitches of the trip and, whilst worrying and annoying, it was also fun in a weird masochistic way. It certainly became more amusing in hindsight, once we'd overcome the problem. But there was also a sense this was what overland adventure is all about, even though our travails were largely self-induced due to my sketchy geo-political knowledge of the region.

We had by now established a good rapport, in the absence of a common language, with the fantastically helpful woman behind the ticket counter. She had also intimated to us animatedly, that getting on the train without a visa was a Very Bad Idea. We collectively pored over a map of Europe, attempting to identify a route to Moscow that didn't involve going through Belarus. Annoyingly Belarus is a hoofing great country and was somewhat in the way.

In the end it was the legendary Man in Seat Sixty One who came to our rescue. I found myself hurriedly consulting his extraordinary website in the insalubrious internet café next to the station. A passionate advocate of rail and ferry travel globally, his site is one of the most invaluable and comprehensive information resources online. Sure enough, within minutes of rummaging around, I'd found a route around Belarus, complete with bus times. Silently saluting our saviour Mark Smith, who sits in the eponymous seat, I leapt into action.

We swiftly cancelled our now useless Warsaw-Moscow sleeper tickets, getting a 90 percent refund despite the fact that the train left in ten minutes time. Try asking for that in the United Kingdom: you'd be told exactly where you could stick your request. We then booked a ten-hour night bus to Vilnius, Lithuania on which the heating was broken and the radio, which blared all night, was set to a 1980s station. This led to semicomatose dreams as we drove through the dark birch forests, played out to a haunting soundtrack of Charles and Eddy's 'Would I Lie to You?', Murray Head's 'One Night in Bangkok' and Rick Astley's 'Never Gonna Give You Up'.

The only respite from this audio backdrop was the half-awake panic generated by the driver's overtaking strategy. He liked to see if he could overtake a fifth truck before the headlights of oncoming vehicles, which had been visible for what seemed like many minutes, ploughed right into us on the seemingly-endlessly straight roads. This concern was justified once dawn had broken, as outside Vilnius we passed a burnt-out coach collision being tended by no fewer than four fire engines. Not nice. It would have been a truly ignominious end to go out by being genuinely, literally, 'Rickrolled'.

In Vilnius we caught another five-hour bus to Riga, where a guy we'd asked for directions to the train station said *Why are you in Latvia?* Very good question, we acknowledged, explaining our accidental visit and visa shenanigans. *Do many English people come to Latvia?* we asked. *Yes, but they are usually drunk,* came the astutely observed and resigned reply.

From Riga we took an 18-hour overnight train to Moscow, luxuriating in a cosy, curtained, carpeted and wood-panelled two-bed cabin. The carriage was kept ferociously hot by an old coal-stoked boiler as yet more birch forest rolled past the window. Tea on tap from a steaming samovar made everything so much more civilised. Ironically we arrived in Moscow only 12 hours after we had originally planned, after a few hundred extra last-minute miles, a sleepless night on a freezing bus and a vast detour through two additional countries. I think it's safe to say we put this down to insightful inconvenience rather than inspiration, but it had been quite an experience. We'd now been on the road for a little over five weeks. We were leaving the relative comfort zone of Europe for our big overland push across the biggest country in the world: Russia.

# THE BIG MELT

*In Russia, drunks are our kindest people. Our
kindest people are also the most drunk.*

— Fyodor Dostoevsky —

*We used to have internationalism under the Soviet system, and it was
more than just a word, it had real meaning with people from diverse
nations and cultures living together,* explained Marina sadly. *Now this
has changed,* she sighed.

Marina was a friendly if world-weary matron of a woman who worked
for the political football of Anglo-Russian relations that is the British
Council in Moscow. Their Russian offices had been shut down and
reopened repeatedly in recent years in a diplomatic tit-for-tat between
London and Moscow over lurid accusations of espionage and worse.
From fake 'listening rocks' placed for covert surveillance in a Moscow

park, to failed extraditions of exiled oligarchs and the insidious charges of state-sponsored murder via the unlikely mechanism of tea poisoned with radioactive polonium, trust between the two governments had sunk to a Cold-War-level low.

I'd met Marina through my company's work in Russia, training journalists how to communicate climate change. While we were in town, she'd invited us to attend the formal opening of the newly-extended State Darwin Museum of Natural History. After a minor panic about what to wear – our backpack wardrobes were somewhat limited as we hadn't anticipated being invited to many formal functions along the way – we dug out our (relative) gladrags and agreed.

It was an authentically Russian affair. The inaugural exhibition was all about hunting; a cat, symbol of good fortune in Russian folklore, was the slightly surreal host of the ceremony. We were sensitively discussing how Russia was changing, how the collapse of the Soviet Union had given rise to a resurgent nationalism, and the yawning wealth gap: *It is a big problem but in Russia no-one does anything, we know the problem exists, but no-one will tackle it. Most of the people with money are politicans' relatives or girlfriends.*

The event was awash with booze. I met Dr Dmitiri Ivanov, a molluscan taxonomist, as he attempted to top up my glass from a bottle of neat Cinzano. An oriental-looking Russian, his grey ponytail and the long goatee that he habitually grasped in his fist and tugged animatedly while talking gave him a conspiratorially Confucian bent. I had originally trained and worked as a marine biologist; we soon established we had academic friends in common. So, after some slightly tipsy bonding, Dmitri insisted we visit him at the Moscow University's Zoological Museum the following day.

Housing one of the 12 biggest collections of zoological specimens in the world, the museum had closed its doors to the public in 1991 to become a research institute. We were buzzed through the aged grandeur of the main entrance into a dusty vestibule of faded, oil-painted panels depicting woolly mammoths frolicking in pre-ice age Siberia. As we signed a venerable yellow and dog-eared visitors book, Dmitri arrived, grinning broadly, to show us around.

Founded in 1791, this is one of Russia's oldest museums, with much of the content dating back to the pre-revolutionary era. A giant salamander from Japan neatly curled into a huge bell-jar, as if sleeping, immediately caught my eye. Many exhibits were a little moth-eaten, but most were impressively holding it together; some of the shell collection was even smoke-blackened from the fires in 1812 when Napoleon had disastrously invaded and the city was burned.

In his artfully-cluttered office among teetering towers of books, journals and piles of mollusc shells, Dmitri proffered black coffee and cigarettes, both bitter and fiercely strong, and produced a bottle of 'White Stag' Scotch whisky. *You know this brand?* he asked hopefully, before lamenting the dearth of funding support for the science of systemic classification, expressing his frustration at the 'faddism' of trendy topics 'like climate change' sucking up large amounts of research time and money.

*We have only one hundred years of good data,* he opined, *this is very small.* Well, from the perspective of an evolutionary taxonomist it certainly is. *I am not an expert,* he voluntarily confessed, *but nor am I concerned,* he added with a contented flourish, topping up our whiskies and lighting another fag. It was barely eleven in the morning.

Dmitri's welcome had been warm, his company generous and funny, but his scientific scepticism on climate change was worrying. The consensus on climate change is anything but a done deal in Russia. as corroborated by the climate change team at the British Embassy. *The mysterious nature of the Russian soul means we are all pessimists,* laughed Liya, a slender Azeri with a mind as quick as her humour was sharp. *You must use fear and scare people about climate change, connect it to their health and immediate concerns.* I disagreed with the former, the evidence showing that scare tactics just switch people off or into denial, but agreed with the latter about making the challenge directly, personally relevant to people.

*We have already seen climate change,* Liya continued, *there was no snow in Moscow till January this year ,and apparently the bears couldn't sleep during the winter as it was too mild.* The scientific debate on climate change in Russia continues to rage, a situation not uncommon in ostensibly more progressive but comparably resource-rich nations. Norway's North Sea oil and gas and Canada's tar sands have both opened rifts around domestic climate-change policies on renewable energy and energy efficiency, and the inevitable conflicts with their own large-scale fossil fuel exports. Russia has far fewer qualms: it is perhaps more honest in its climate-change attitudes and international gas trade. *Lowering expectations on climate-change action in Russia might bring pleasant surprises,* Liya advised. *Expect nothing. That way if you get something you'll be happy,* she chuckled before noting that in Russia our trip would likely be perceived as *a little bold, a little crazy.*

Life seems rather nasty, brutish and short for those Russians excluded from the robbery of the state economy, mafia-controlled commerce or political gerrymandering and corruption. Outrageous, ostentatious wealth sits alongside dire, abject poverty. Novelist John Updike notes, 'You don't go to Moscow to get fat'. As a result, Muscovites do a good line in dark, sarcastic humour and prodigious vodka consumption. Lord knows, they need both to cope with their gritty city.

Like many capital cities, to the unwary Moscow can be ludicrously expensive. There are many poor bedraggled baboushkas begging on the street, the communist-era cast-offs of the new Russian cut-throat capitalism. Destitute old ladies (the men don't get old, they just die; Russian male life expectancy is not much more than 60) and inebriated men, drinking to escape the cruel realities of Moscow life, huddle on the pavements. Alcoholism is visibly rife, in the same way that rice might be perceived to be popular in China. Beer is informally classified as a soft drink and considered a good way to start the day.

For us Russia was all about homestays, living with real Russians in their homes. In Moscow we stayed in a flat near the spectacular space-age looking Elektrozavodskaya metro station; its curved ceiling with hundreds of inset lamps is reminiscent of a futuristic set from Kubrick's film *2001: A Space Odyssey.* This is all the more remarkable given that it was designed and built in the 1940s. We'd found the apartment through online legend 'Uncle Pasha'. His fabulously grumpy and curmudgeonly website offers unique, only half-joking 'Misery Tours' and other delights such as 'Suicidal Airport Transfers' and 'Trips Down the Volga River in a Leaking Wooden Boat'. It also acts as an informal accommodation agency with a list of classified ads that Pasha gleefully comments on if the offer is, in his opinion, 'crap' or uses lazy, meaningless adjectives like 'beautiful' or 'nice'. Apparently confident the advertisers on his site won't be able to understand his criticisms of them or their homes Pasha described one landlord as 'the most boring man on the planet. You'll want to axe him or yourself before long' and the offer of a 'bed' on a leather sofa in the living room of another apartment as 'laughably substandard and frankly risible'. An outpouring of honesty so refreshing you could practically shower under it.

Anya, our willowy, bookish hostess, spoke good English. She was also sardonically funny. Her spacious apartment was in an apparently nameless, numberless block that we'd managed to locate more by luck than design, having negotiated a long-since retired intercom system, cigarette-littered and urine-scented stairwell and a fearsome metal cage lift. She welcomed us with piping hot black tea and a little bowl of blackcurrant jam. We waited patiently and hungrily for some bread on which to spread the tasty looking preserve. It never arrived. We learnt only later Russians put the jam in their tea to sweeten it.

I mentioned to Anya we'd noticed that the Intourist hotel I'd stayed at on a previous visit to Moscow in 2000 had been demolished. As it was a huge grey slab of concrete blotting the skyline adjacent to Red Square, full of prostitutes and decorated in Soviet 1970s chic, this was no great loss to architecture, interior design or tourist facilities. Like Uncle Pasha, Anya was particularly fond of the word 'crap', which came in useful for her observations on her home city. *That hotel was very crap but not the crappiest,* noted Anya, *There is still another one nearby which is also very crappy.* I mentioned our climate change discussions with other Russians; Anya revealed she was a passionate environmentalist. *I feel it in my heart.* On learning of our travel plans she suspected that there was also a secret deal between the Russian Railways and various tourist agencies, as she couldn't understand the appeal of the Trans-Siberian Express. *I think one day of birch trees is enough.*

She memorably described Moscow police as 'dirty bastards', which was certainly true from our experience. There were major anti-Putin demonstrations the day before we arrived. These had been violently broken up by baton-swinging paramilitaries and snatch squads that – according to the *Moscow Times* – simply bundled groups of people, including curious onlookers, into police trucks for interrogation and detention. The police presence across the city was not so much heavy-handed as wearing concrete mittens – as opposed to the neat line in cement footwear the mafia provide for paddling in the depths of the Volga river. Gangs of mean, sour-faced cops loitered on every street corner, idly harassing the passing public, including us, checking papers and soliciting fines – a handy supplement to their meagre wages. Luckily we'd been forewarned of this tactic, so we carried only a photocopy of our passports, which is sufficient to show the police, so were spared the casual extortion that some unwary tourists fall victim to by having their documents seized.

Our stay in Russia's capital was relatively brief, but we could not wait to leave. In *Star Wars* Obi-Wan Kenobi describes the Tatooine spaceport Mos Eisley as a 'wretched hive of scum and villainy', an apt description that could equally be applied to Moscow's Yaroslavsky Station. It was with a great sense of relief that we successfully navigated the drunks, beggars and belligerent police both outside and in this enormous rail terminus and boarded the Trans-Siberian Express to Irkutsk. The key to making the most of this marathon journey is meeting fellow travellers, befriending your carriage's attendant, watching the world roll past your window and sampling the various culinary titbits available for sale from wizened baboushkas on the platforms.

It was almost midnight as our huge train grumbled slowly out of Moscow into the surrounding darkness. In the compartment next door were two 60-year-old Finnish men, Seppi and Peppi. *What do you call it in English when you don't work and still get paid?* asked Seppi. *Retired?* I offered. *Yes! We are retired from Finlanda, Fine Land!* was his standard introduction to all and sundry. They'd been tucking into a large bottle of cognac, which they'd already heavily dented before boarding. This revelry had attracted the attentions of the Moscow police, six of whom had interrogated them for half an hour, searching their bags and checking papers before finally letting them onto the train. To celebrate Seppi then produced a bottle of the sweet, fizzy white wine that the Russians ambitiously refer to as champagne. The cork was refusing to budge so he handed it to me for assistance, only for it to explode open in a plume of froth. We were wet, winey and sticky, and we'd only been on the train for 15 minutes.

Armed with only his Russian-Finnish phrasebook, an eclectic but effective grasp of schoolboy English (he'd never even been to the United Kingdom and had learnt English 40 years previously) and enough Dutch courage to give a small pachyderm the shakes, Seppi was on a one-man mission to rehabilitate Finno-Russo relations. These have historically been tense since some particularly bloody battles during the Second World War. Finland's supposedly meek kowtowing to its superpower neighbour during the subsequent Cold War led some Western commentators to coin the term 'Finlandisation' for when small countries feel obliged to comply with the foreign policies of a larger, dominant neighbour, an art described by one Finnish political cartoonist as 'bowing to the East, without mooning at the West'. Seppi was continuing this tradition with some literally rather spirited diplomatic bridge-building.

Peppi, though, spoke no English or Russian; he just smiled benignly through a cognac haze for the whole trip. Their charm offensive peaked when the two surly train policemen, Mihail and Rafik joined us for drinks in the Finns' compartment a couple of nights later. Mihail, the younger, more junior officer, revealed a large black scorpion tattoo on his shoulder from his stint in the army in Chechnya, the epicentre of Russia's bloody Caucasus conflict. Disarmed, at ease and joking with us that night, by day the police were armed, cold, dispassionate authority incarnate. *They are serious, but they are good guys,* said Seppi.

En route we'd planned to eat Russian-style by buying food from the station vendors we'd expected to be prowling the platforms. Worryingly, at the first stop in Vyatka the sellers were mainly touting huge polythene sacks of luridly-coloured cuddly toys, handy as presents for distant relatives, not so good for dinner. Things improved at Balyezino where

*Walking the tracks and tunnels of the Circum-Baikal railway, Baranchiki, Siberia*

we skipped across the railway tracks to a small kiosk to buy bread buns stuffed with cheese and sweet cabbage. This can be a risky manoeuvre in itself as if another train pulls in you're forced to duck underneath it to get back onto your own. Later in Perm, the most easterly city in Europe, best known for its munitions factories and gulag labour camps, we stocked up on Baltika beer to share with the Finns. We bought several bottles from a solitary, mobbed baboushka who cannily upped her prices to match her captive market position.

Beyond Perm, the sheer scale of the Siberian landscape was awesome. There were literally thousands of miles of scrubby birch forest and land that was bleak, brown and heavily waterlogged with stagnant pools from the spring melt. Ramshackle wooden houses clustered in tiny, wildly remote communities gave a sense of a post-apocalyptic vision, of people struggling to overcome some huge disaster in a back to basics lifestyle of log cabins, open fires and subsistence farming. The broken brick remains of what could have been previous civilisations were still evident amongst the rickety huts and shacks. The bullishness of the former Soviet authorities during the Cold War and their apparent fearlessness of nuclear Armageddon may be because in Siberia it looks as if the apocalypse has already happened.

As Anya in Moscow had warned us, you'd have to be a pretty hard-core tree lover not to be sated by the sight of the endless birch trees we saw from the train. These create a disturbing sense of circular time, continual *déjà vu* and utter disbelief as to the scale and similarity of such vast tracts of Russia. It makes Britain look positively perverse in terms of the diversity of landscape jammed into one small island. The variety and range of our hills, plains, crags, valleys, moors, dales, cliffs and beaches reveals the waywardness of our topography. Especially in contrast to the monotonous consistency of birch, birch, birch in Siberia. If Henry Ford had done landscapes, his Siberian model would have been available in 'any colour you like so long as it's brown'.

Great gouges of industrial desecration occasionally ripped into the boggy, tundral scrub and relentless birch. Concentric rings of grey concrete blocks of flats surrounded priapic chimneys, mine heads, power stations and all manner of extractive and smelting activities, hell-bent on exploiting the vast mineral wealth of the region. Weirdly, these man-made monstrosities were almost comforting reassurances that the train was not simply going to roll off the end of the line into some abyss of swampy grassland and scraggy trees, but did in fact have a destination. They were also a powerful visual reminder of the fact that Russia is still primarily a natural-resource economy, hauling everything from coal, oil and gas to gold from beneath the ground, and chopping down the trees above. With such riches, and with more to become potentially accessible as the Arctic ice cap retreats, it's little wonder that, , despite the perverse irony, the Russian nation is less than convinced by climate change – as we'd found through our discussions in Moscow.

*It's like an investment,* mused Seppi when hearing of our plans for the trip. *Instead of putting money in the bank, you are putting memories in here,* he said tapping a finger sagely against his temple. Soviet dissident writer Alexander Solzhenitsyn, who spent many years imprisoned in Siberia, recommended something similar when he advocated letting 'your memory be your travel bag'. The sentiment was later echoed by the elderly rakish white-haired Danish widower Niels, from the next carriage along. When he and I stood together on the tracks one night taking the frosty air between the dark steaming bulks of two locomotives, he'd told me how riding the Trans-Siberian had always been a dream. *I feel young…but I am not so young,* he laughed, *so I must do this now*, clearly appreciating the value of this adventure over a little extra money in the savings account. Time felt precious, experiences priceless.

Peppi, meanwhile, was showing us pictures on his mobile phone of some of the one hundred or more reindeer he'd shot, including some monstrous half-ton specimens. Following our train diet of 'emergency' Chinese instant noodles, these were starting to look extremely appetising. Not to be outdone, Seppi whipped out a photo of his aged cat. *Cats know love,* he announced solemnly and unsolicited, explaining how the cat likes to lie on his chest in bed each morning. *Sometimes the love of an old cat is better than the love of an old woman,* he mused a little dreamily, before concluding *but an 18-year-old woman on your chest is better than an 18-year-old cat!*

After four days on the train we'd settled into an odd routine. The constant rocking motion of the carriage as we made our way eastwards was strangely soporific, and we slept heavily. We'd passed along the busiest stretch of freight railway in the world, through Barabinsk, where coal is taken to the Urals' fuel-hungry industries. Just beyond Zaozernaya a branch line snaked north towards Krasnoyarsk-45, a closed town that didn't officially exist or appear on maps until 1992 due to its role in enriching uranium for the Soviet nuclear programme. We were in Russia's secretive but productive 'outback' and felt like slightly covert, clandestine observers as we trundled through.

Meals revolved more around station stops rather than traditional timings. The food offered by the baboushkas got better and cheaper the further east we went. Our final supper on the train was a veritable feast of roast chicken legs, fried piroshki dumplings stuffed with egg, cheese and spring onion, boiled meat dumplings, smoked fish, cabbage and even a couple of hot potatoes plucked from a towel-wrapped bag in the smiling baboushka's wicker basket. I read Boris Pasternak's *Doctor Zhivago* as Russia unfurled itself to us, imagining Yuri's epic journey through this arduous landscape as the vicious battles of the revolution raged around him. The hours thus passed surprisingly quickly, punctuated by the bodies of comatose men sprawled next to the tracks. We became acutely chronologically confused by the Russian railways' adherence to Moscow time, despite the five time zones we had crossed on the way to Irkutsk. As a result, on arrival we felt jetlagged, an unusual sensation without having been anywhere near a plane. Plus, at barely 8p a mile, our £250 first class tickets meant the Trans-Siberian was probably the cheapest mode of transport we took all year. Compare this to what must be the most expensive public transport journey in the world, the 260 yard jaunt on the London Underground from Leicester Square to Covent Garden. That comes in at a cool £4.50 for the unsuspecting tourist, or £28 a mile. The Trans-Siberian is then over 300 times cheaper!

So, after more than 3,000 miles, we'd arrived in the town of Irkutsk, allegedly the 'Paris of Siberia' – but then the competition is slightly less than intense. Europe, family and the friends we missed suddenly felt a very long way away indeed. We had a real sense of that distance, as we'd bounced, laughed and jiggled our way slowly over every inch of it. A mere half-million people strong, Irkutsk had the feel of a large frontier town after the daunting intimidation of Moscow; laid-back, friendly and manageable, if a little down at heel. You could stroll across the centre in less than 20 minutes, admire the *de rigeur* statue of Lenin and take in most of the 'sights'.

We learnt about these from our lovely host Svetlana, a fiery red-headed Buryat woman, and her son Denis with whom we were 'home-staying'. The Buryats are the most northerly of the Mongol tribes, the indigenous people of the region. Svetlana showed us a fantastic set of Soviet era postcards of Irkutsk from 1986. These glorious hand-tinted pieces of Technicolor propaganda depicted the local tourist attractions: the shopping complex (big grey metal box), the government-owned Hotel Angara (big grey metal and glass box), the new housing developments (series of big grey metal, concrete and glass boxes) and the bridge over the Angara River (big grey concrete thing). They reminded me of the 1970s postcards of the United Kingdom that celebrated our equivalent achievements, such as the brilliant urban design of inner Slough.

Denis had met us off the train and walked us to the bus stop through clouds of choking exhaust fumes from the poorly-conditioned engines of the traffic. The air had a distinctly sulphurous, metallic flavour as we struggled with our backpacks, trying not to breathe too deeply. We hopped on one bus only for it to break down a few hundred yards up the road. We then crammed ourselves into an already-jammed minibus for the bumpy 20-minute commute out to his mum's place, Apartment 10 in the quaintly named Building 55. It was in a proper Soviet-style satellite suburb of slab-like blocks interspersed by rubbish-strewn bare earth squares in a landscape of dusty brown monotony.

Being in people's homes embodies the travellers' oft-sought but frequently misconstrued notion of 'authenticity'. Sharing meals, wine and the occasional cigarette with Svetlana in her sparsely furnished but cosy flat was fantastic. Russian homestays are infinitely preferable to the formal hotel accommodation on offer. It felt good to press some rubles directly into her hands and supplement her meagre state pension. We enjoyed evenings of laughter, drawing and gesticulation together, the almost-complete lack of common language compelling us to be more creative in our communication. I recall those nights now as full of wonderful warmth, though in hindsight how those happy hours passed and exactly what we 'talked' about is a mystery. Not that this matters, as the feelings of friendship remain, Svetlana gifting us a small Buryat figurine and a copy of a Shakespeare play in Russian as mementoes of our stay. As adventure travel writer Tim Cahill says, 'a journey is best measured in friends, rather than miles'.

This notion of people triumphing over places as the most powerful and poignant memories of our trip was to become more profoundly true as we progressed. Vistas and landscapes, panoramas and seascapes or wonderful wildlife all left indelible impressions on us. But it was experiencing first-hand the old saw of strangers being 'friends we just hadn't met yet' that really left its mark and marked our passage. The extension of hospitality, kindness and generosity was continuously faith-restoring. It polished off the tarnish of cynical suspicion to leave us shinier, more trusting, more open to the world. The process was unsurprisingly self-reinforcing: the brighter and warmer we felt, the more we encountered this reciprocally in those we met and befriended along the way.

We were expecting to freeze our extremities off in Siberia but, even though it was only early April, it was nearly 20°C and almost worryingly warm. This created some sartorial challenges as we rummaged through our rucksack clothing options in search of something suitably summery to wear. French writer Antoine de St. Exupery says 'He who would travel happily must travel light'. I would have to agree. The more I travel, the less I tend to take. Especially when having to lug it everywhere. This is one of many reasons why I have a slightly irrational hatred of 'wheelie' suitcases. Besides the incredibly irritating way they trail behind as trip hazards to everyone else, they also encourage us all to overpack. As a result, we take more than we would ever do if we actually had to carry our luggage. Lord knows the carbon implications of the additional unnecessary weight being transported around the world as a consequence of this. But I suspect they are massive.

In order to minimise the burden of our own baggage, we really only had clothing that we thought would be appropriate to the climate in which we'd find ourselves at any one time. This obviously changed a lot. Our Siberian woollies would later be discarded for more seasonal attire in sweltering South-East Asia, for example. The upshot was that very few items made it all the way round the world with us. If nothing else had changed mentally, emotionally and physically by the time we got home again, at least our outfits had.

In anticipation of the harsh and challenging Siberian weather that ultimately failed to materialise, I'd been mentally preparing myself by reading Apsley Cherry-Garrard's harrowing memoir of the ill-fated, tragic Scott Antarctic expedition, *The Worst Journey in the World*, and *South*, Ernest Shackleton's equally gruelling but positively heroic account of his mission's arduous escape from the Pole's icy clutches. Their stories of frozen teeth shattered by uncontrollably chattering jaws, and subsistence diets of sooty seal fat, endured stoically by men from an altogether different era and character, were inspiring, haunting and humbling. In contrast our journey was ludicrously straightforward and laughably easy. Instead of shivering we found ourselves in T-shirts soaking up the first sizzling sunshine of the season.

As temperatures drop to -30°C in winter, you could see why apparently every young woman we saw was making the most of the first joys of spring. Knee-high leather boots, micro-minis and necklines that plunged lower than a Soviet apparatchik's popularity ratings were the order of the day. You could understand why Russians are at best ambivalent about climate change, perversely enjoying the potential prospect of milder weather even if this could unleash terrifying amounts of carbon from the melting permafrost of the north. But if the weather continues the female sartorial trends outlined above, I fear that we're almost certainly fighting a losing battle to control the carbon emissions of the Russian male. It won't just be the mercury that rises.

The Russian relationship with winter is instructive in this climate-change context. The mounting evidence of Arctic melting is the canary in the coalmine, the early warning system of global warming. Images of floundering polar bears swimming the expanding distances between fragmented ice floes are symbolic of the planetary shift we have unleashed upon ourselves and the rest of the earth's biodiversity. Part of the problem is perhaps that, as humans, we are historically inclined to associate ice-melt with positive implications: the end of the harsh season of constraint, the promise of spring and fertile plenty to come. You even see this in the naming of revolutionary uprisings such as 'the Arab Spring', suggesting the possibility of new birth, new systems, new potential. We are hard-wired to look forward to the coming of spring. Maybe this is why, despite our best intentions, we find it difficult to grasp the disappearing ice cap as a bad thing.

Of course the terrible irony of all ironies is that, as the Arctic ice melts, the open water left behind allows another phase of exploration to take place, a resource grab from the waters and seabed previously protected by the now-thinning and retreating ice. As climate change increases human access to the Arctic, so we prospect for more oil and gas, thereby driving further climate change. The negative feedback loop is tight, and is a damning indictment of our collective short-termism. The potential for conflict over hydrocarbons, minerals, fisheries and the control of new shipping routes is also considerable. Russia has already provocatively planted its flag in the seabed beneath the North Polar ice in a territorial claim straight out of the Middle Ages.

If we needed compelling evidence of the impact of climate change on our ice caps, this gearing up of Arctic activity by oil giants like Shell for the twisted feast to come should be proof enough. It is not just avarice, commercial short-sightedness or lack of creative vision that takes them there, although all no doubt contribute to the collective failure of 'Big Oil' to transition to 'Big Energy' and , of course, renewable sources like solar, wind, wave and tide. Their problem is that they are fundamentally asking the wrong question – 'How can we defend and justify what we currently do and that we make large amounts of money from for the next few decades?' and *not* 'How can we secure a clean, safe energy future for all?'

If climate change is difficult to visualise in the public consciousness and is something that happens to 'someone else, somewhere else, tomorrow', then similarly Arctic oil and gas exploration is starting up under the radar. Campaigners like Greenpeace intend to change this, to make the global risks that Shell and others are taking in the far north transparent. If we think the damage wrought by the world's biggest man-made environmental disaster, the *Deepwater Horizon* explosion and subsequent oil spill in the Gulf of Mexico, was serious, imagine the impact of an oil well spewing crude into the relatively pristine Arctic environment. Winter ice formation could prevent such a leak being capped for at least six months. The consequences are potentially devastating. Disconcertingly, Shell has already suffered the running aground of a tender vessel and a test rig in Arctic storms in the first season of exploratory drilling. The outlook is bleak, and the groundwork for one of the most cynical moves of a generation goes on.

In addition we are now seeing films like *Chasing Ice*, photographer James Balog's attempt to creatively document glacial collapse through compelling visual time-lapse footage of our warming world. We are used both to magnificent still images of melting Arctic ice and to film footage of disparate extreme weather events like Superstorm Sandy, which devastated Haiti and the United States' east coast. Yet somehow these fail to make the case for climate change. Stills can be dismissed as static, remote, isolated; the disaster footage as 'bad luck', a one-off event with only a correlative not a causal relationship with climate change. There is something different about watching the ruthless, relentless, spectacular progressive collapse of a massive glacier in the same place, year on year, unfolding before your very eyes. *Chasing Ice* is brutally compelling and has the potential to shift even consciously confirmed climate sceptics. It enables us to visualise climate change in our mind's eye. Never again will we be able to claim that we didn't know.

After a couple of days in Irkutsk, Denis and his girlfriend Marina joined us on our trip to experience the vastness of nearby Lake Baikal. It's astounding in scale. A powerful source of shamanic power and significance for the Buryat people, Baikal is also the world's oldest, deepest lake, having been in existence for 25 million years; it holds one fifth of all the freshwater on the planet. A vast, polluting paper pulping plant squats incongruously on its southern shore.

*Denis and Marina tuck into tasty smoked 'omul' fish on the train to Port Baikal, Siberia*

Perhaps fortunately, the Baikal paper mill is currently in receivership; its future is uncertain, after almost half a century of pumping chlorine-contaminated water from its bleaching processes into the relatively pristine waters. A closed water system introduced to the plant by order of then-prime minister Putin in 2008 ended its worst polluting excesses, but its closure would also mean challenges for the 15,000 workers whose livelihoods directly or indirectly depend on it. It's a classic trade-off dilemma of environmental versus economic risks and benefits.

This is significant, as Baikal is home to many rare and wonderful endemic species including the *nerpa*, one of the world's few freshwater seals. Quite how a normally marine mammal came to make the lake its home, given the vast distance from seawater, is uncertain; most probably a historical connection to the ocean at some point in the last couple of million years. It would seem both prudent and appropriate for the lake and its unique denizens to be liberated from the yoke of industrialisation.

We took our slow-travel mantra to the extreme with a six-hour, 60-mile train journey on the remains of the Circum-Baikal railway. It was previously part of the original Trans-Siberian route but, beleaguered by the natural processes of rock-falls and mudslides precipitated by audacious cliff-side engineering, a replacement line was built. What had been known as 'the golden buckle on the steel belt of Russia' is now a fragment of its former self. Nevertheless the railway passed through 33 tunnels and across 248 bridges and viaducts as it wound its way above the icy plain of the still-frozen lake below. Chugging languidly along the lakeside, our dinky two-carriage train was airless, crowded and broiling as the potent spring sun poured in through the windows. *I didn't expect to be too hot in Siberia,* I joked, to the amusement of Denis, as we frantically fanned ourselves. He asked the guard if we could open the windows to stave off heatstroke. *We only open the windows in summer,* came the positively Soviet reply.

We tucked into smoked *omul* fish, a species only found in the lake, and cold, boiled sausage, while below us Baikal basked in all its frozen glory. Denis taught us the Russian for 'tasty sausage', *kusna sassiski,* as we munched, an expression which swiftly became our standard Russian phrase. Marina meanwhile demonstrated an extremely healthy appetite, devouring the fragrant fish, sucking the bones and licking the smoky grease from her fingers with relish.

The train afforded views over 30 miles of sheer ice to the craggy, snow-capped peaks of the Kamar Daban mountains on the far eastern shore. Two of the fierce forest fires that blight the region in summer were already billowing clouds of thick smoke into the blue skies above. Baikal is as big as a sea, but the ice deadens all sound, so there's no lapping of waves, only an eerily-hushed calm. This was strange for us islanders, as I explained to Denis who was born and bred in seriously land-locked Irkutsk. The fact that nowhere in the kwhole of the British Isles is more than 70 miles from the sea astonished him. Maybe Leicester, the furthest city from the coast in Britain, would astonish him too.

We got off the train at Baranchiki, a village that time had apparently not only forgotten but then subsequently denied it had ever known. This is a pretty, higgledy-piggledy collection of wooden houses hunched in a small U-shaped valley, where we were met by a rag-tag gaggle of curious, grubby-faced kids on rusty bikes. Huge half-wolf huskies howled and barked, lunging ferociously on chains outside each house as we nervously searched through the hot and dusty lanes for Anastasia's homestay, where we hoped to spend the night. Thankfully her yard was protected not by some Cerberus-like canine but by a tiny, grey, yipping puppy so small it couldn't even climb the stone step into the house.

Anastasia's greeting was as warm and bright as the reddish-orange tinge of her thick curly hair. The house was as chaotically cluttered and arranged as her impressive teeth. She spoke three words of English, making even our paltry 25 or so Russian words feel relatively fluent. *Milk?* was her favourite, as she generously offered us still-warm freshly squeezed cow-juice from the large brown heifer stood sedately in the front yard. Seeing we were sweaty from our steamy train-ride she fired up her *banya* and we enjoyed our first Russian sauna.

A weighty iron stove made the small dark wooden shed fiercely hot, and ladles of icy Baikal melt-water provided the steam. There was no running water in the village, as the bitter winter weather would swiftly

*Preparing to board the 'padoushka' (hovercraft) at Cajka, Lake Baikal, Siberia*

freeze any pipes, so the *banya* is the only way to wash. Fi and I thrashed each other a little half-heartedly with the birch twigs provided, gasping and squeaking as the freezing water on our hot pink skin snatched our breath away. We stood glowing outside afterwards, the silence almost oppressive, dark cliffs dropping steeply in shadow to the ice below, which was almost luminescent under the brilliant white moon and night sky's dusting of stars. Only the occasional mutter of conversation from one of the snug, hunkered-down houses or a lone bark broke the serenity. We sucked in the frosty air, and drank in the atmospheric scenery of the wonderfully simple but brutally hard place.

After a breakfast of semolina with berries and a cup of udder-fresh milk, we spent the next day walking the track of the railway as the lake ice creaked and groaned in the sunshine. We explored the tunnels and the rusting hulks of long-since abandoned freighter ships that languished in the frozen harbour at neighbouring Port Baikal, and then said our farewells to Anastasia. This gave her a chance to use her other two words of English *Good luck!* We paid a scowling, whiskery woman on the ferry to take us across the mouth of the Angara river to Listvyanka, tossing the traditional donation of a ruble into the chilly waters for a safe passage as two hardened men took what looked to be a painfully refreshing dip in the lake.

The following morning we awoke to find the ice on this southern part of the lake had vanished overnight. Yesterday's frozen peace was now wind-whipped white horses. The familiar sounds of choppy waters had returned, this time accompanied by the gentle musical tinkling of millions of floating ice crystals. Our thirst for Baikal's beauty still unquenched, we made plans to head 150 miles north to Olkhon Island, a four hour journey in a cosily crammed, juddering *marshrutka* minibus. Haggard cattle lingered dangerously on the road as our Buryat driver overtook heavily plodding trucks in desperate surges of acceleration. The road narrowed and became intermittently unpaved as stupas and shamanic totems draped in coloured cloth, ribbons and prayer flagsappeared on either side , the driver reverentially removing his cap as we passed each one.

At Cajka, on the lakeshore further north, the lake ice was still intact. We were bundled along with about a dozen others and all their associated

*Shaman Rock, near Khuzhir, Olkhon Island, Lake Baikal, Siberia*

bags and chattels into an eight-seater *padoushka* or hovercraft – the word *padoushka* means 'cushion' in Russian. The skirt inflated under the overloaded craft, and then we were skimming unnervingly but exhilaratingly over the ice towards the low hills of Olkhon, Baikal's largest island. As we crossed, we passed groups of fishermen and a lone pair of walkers in the middle of the sound, black dots in the blinding whiteness and hazy light. They seemed confident that the frosting was thick enough to avoid a disastrous dunking.

The ice is deceptive, however, especially at that time of year. During the numb winter months people happily drive 20-ton trucks across the surface on established ice roads. Come the spring melt it's a different story. The ice softens unevenly: while it is safe in some areas, in others it becomes treacherously thin and downright dangerous. We later learned that 11 vehicles had been lost that winter and nine people drowned in the deep, dark, icy waters when the apparently reliable ice had suddenly given way beneath them. Worse still, it's often impossible to find where vehicles have disappeared. Rather than crashing through the icy crust and leaving a tell-tale hole, what tends to happen is that plates of ice tip up, sliding the vehicle into the water below, before returning to the same position. There is usually no trace left behind of the doomed driver's fate.

With this grisly demise in mind we were thankful for the *padoushka*, safe in the knowledge that if the ice cracked we weren't going through and into the depths below. And what depths! Baikal is 5,400 feet deep at its most abyssal point. As a result, the water remains startlingly cold, even in midsummer. It's also terrifyingly clear, with visibility as much as 120 feet down, resulting in some swimmers suffering from vertigo.

A motley selection of vehicles awaited us on the Olkhon shore: a jeep, a couple of grey vans and a car so rusty and dilapidated that l thought it was abandoned until someone drove off in it. Our driver was Anatoly, a Russian Tom Selleck in his *Magnum P.I.* days, all fat 'tache, gold teeth, wily grin and wry sparkling eyes. He spoke no English, so we quickly endeared ourselves to him with our stock-in-trade ice-breaker, *kussna sassiski,* before he drove us at breakneck speed along a 20-mile dirt track scramble to Khuzhir on the island's western shore.

The main street of Khuzhir resembled the set of a spaghetti Western, hugely broad, uneven and dusty. You half expected a couple of bow-legged cowboys to start taking potshots at each other at any moment. Then there were the dogs. Everyone in Siberia seems to have a hound. They ranged from the huge, savage wolf-like beasts like those we'd seen in Baranchiki, thankfully usually chained up, lunging frantically to the fullest extent of their tethers in a fury of teeth, slaver and frustrated snarling, down to the smallest, dinkiest, meekest beasties imaginable. It can't be fun being a small dog in Siberia.

We stayed at Nikita's homestead, owned by a retired Russian table-tennis champion. It consists of a collection of wooden buildings and log cabins with intricately carved window frames, arranged informally in a large stockaded compound. Around the interior lay an intriguing confusion of corroding saws, milk churns, lifebelts and even an old type-writer and an accordion. More or less every time we went out for a walk we were accompanied by the homestead dogs, a huge black thing called Orsic (like the French for bear, rather appropriately) and a ratty little mutt we christened Fleabag in the apparent absence of any more formal name for the poor creature. Throughout town their presence prompted stand-offs with other canines. Most of these were simple teeth-baring, growling challenges, all-mouth-but-no-trousers threats – like a suburban pub on a Saturday night in Britain. Occasionally, however, they spilled over into real, nasty violence and venom. This leaves you, as the 'dog-walker', in a dilemma: do you intervene in the furry blur of fangs and claws, or leave them to it? We invariably adopted the insouciant 'Whose dogs are they?' approach and walked calmly on.

We were almost the first tourists of the season at Nikita's, being beaten to this honour by a German couple who'd arrived only the day before. We later met them naked in the *banya*, thus making friends perhaps more quickly and intimately than we might have anticipated. The *banya* itself was a fearsome device that consisted of a section of heavy metal pipe set into the wall and heated by an intense wood fire from beneath. You created the *banya* atmosphere by hurling mugfuls of water into the pipe's super-heated interior, where they instantly vaporised, sending a plume of

*Trees near a sacred spring decorated with traditional Buryat cloth strips, Arshan, Siberia*

angry steam out at crotch height, threatening to parboil your essentials if you were standing in the wrong position.

Being almost the only guests at the homestead, we were treated like slightly weird, if welcome, oddities. That night Nikola the caretaker – *Because I take care of things* – serenaded us with Englebert Humperdinck numbers on his accordion. This was a distinct improvement on the Russian disco track we'd heard on the radio in Irkutsk, which had ambitiously managed to rhyme 'tequila' with 'Venezuela'. Nikola expressed incredulity when we told him how lucky we thought he was living on wild and nostalgic Olkhon. *Lucky? We are Siberians! This is normal for us!* It was like being part of a small family, a world away from the summer hordes that descend on Olkhon in high season.

*Don't go on the ice,* Nikola advised. *People think they know where it is safe, but they don't,* he warned, recounting to us yet another tale of a traumatic demise. *Don't trust the stuff. It owes you nothing.* Anatoly was returning the next morning to take us ice-fishing. *Would this be OK?* I nervously asked Nikola. *Anatoly,* Nikola echoed, *is no problem. He is specialist,* he assured.

*Kusna sassiski,* shouted Anatoly in greeting us the following day as we clambered into the back of the 4x4 that he affectionately referred to as the 'Russian Rollercoaster'. After a tentative walk out across the fickle but fortunately-firm crust we dangled our lines through holes like glistening tubes in the foot-thick frozen lake surface. Open fissures and the guttural rumble of ice sheets grinding together reminded us of the sinister abyss beneath our feet as we hauled shimmering silver omul, harius and little golden bullheaded fish from the lake. When we made our first catch Anatoly, as the self-styled 'fishing priest', stepped up gleefully to baptise us. This consisted of being beaten repeatedly about the face with the tail of the freshly-caught fish. And to think we were paying him for this privilege!

An off-road tour of the north of the island followed; actually there are no 'roads' as such on Olkhon, just rutted dirt tracks. This was a prelude to our explorations to come in Mongolia. Anatoly had a worrying penchant for driving recklessly close to cliff edges and other precipitous drops en route whilst casually chatting over his shoulder or looking the other way, blasé and seemingly oblivious to our terrified faces. We later found he did this deliberately, as he thought tourists enjoyed the adrenaline rush.

Our route took us through steppe-like brown meadows over which marmots scampered, with incredible views over the cracked patchwork of ice on the lake. We paused for lunch among the pine trees above a frozen bay, Anatoly laughing at my long unpracticed fish-gutting technique as I prepared our catch. I should never have mentioned I was a marine biologist! After washing the bloodied fillets in a hole in the ice, a finger-numbing ordeal in itself, we grilled them with garlic on a small fire Anatoly had lit, and ate the freshest imaginable lake fish, accompanied by hard brown bread and cheese and hot, herb-infused tea. I don't know whether it was the drama of the wild, frozen scenery, the huge lungfuls of pure fresh air or the elegant simplicity of the food that stoked our appetites, but it was one of the most wonderful meals I have ever eaten.

One depressing aspect of Olkhon's environment was the rubbish. On one of our walks around Khuzhir we'd stumbled upon, or rather into, the town dump, a foetid sprawl of bottles, rags, plastic and junk strewn over several acres of ground beneath the pine trees that flanked the outskirts. The nature of remote island life meant that goods only arrived in, rubbish never left and, in the absence of any formal recycling, inevitably accumulated. Plans for an incinerator had been vetoed by local environmentalists because of the risk of toxic dioxins entering the lake and, despite efforts by concerned staff at Nikita's to educate about littering and to collect some plastics for recycling in Irkutsk, the battle to preserve Olkhon's environment was clearly being lost. I couldn't help but feel that the combination of living in a place with such a vast sense of wild space, coupled with the lack of easy solutions, meant that this wasteful behaviour seemed somehow acceptable. Certainly the visible scale of the dump offered the 'social proof' that it was. Like the climate sceptics who challenge the idea that humans might be fundamentally changing the skies, I feared Khuzhir was similarly in denial about its own impacts.

By the time we left Olkhon after almost a week of brilliant isolation, Nikola had started referring to us as 'the aboriginals' as we'd been there so long. Our destination-less travel and loose, almost infinitely flexible, itinerary meant it was sometimes hard to galvanise ourselves into moving on. What was the urgency? Why didn't we just stay another day? There was an understandable appeal to lingering in wonderful places. Why not? The lulls were lovely, connections with landscapes and, more importantly, people, deepened. The stillness was beautiful. Yet we also yearned for more of Vonnegut's 'dancing lessons with God'. As always we needed both stillness and dancing.

It was thus with heavy hearts that we re-boarded the *padoushka* for our return journey to the mainland across the now rapidly melting ice. The hovercraft lurched and rolled disturbingly as it skimmed from shelves of ice onto open water and vice versa. It was time to re-board the train and take the Trans-Mongolian railway round the bottom of the lake, through the Buryat city of Ulan-Ude, into the kingdom of Chinghis Khan.

Russian attitudes to climate change had surprised me, from Dmitri's scientific data scepticism, through Liya's slight cynicism, to the state's determination to forge ahead with a fossil fuel future in both exports and exploration in the melting Arctic. It felt like climate change was yet another transformational challenge being thrown at an already harassed nation.

As in all too many countries in the world, the last hundred years have not been smooth for Russia – from Tsarist feudalism, through civil war and revolution, the gruesome carnage of the Second World War, Stalinist purges, the collapse of communism and empire, to the final cruel indignity of asset-stripping, robber-baron capitalism. Out of this upheaval emerges a collective character that is part resignation, part resilience. The 'dark brooding Russian soul' that both Denis in Irkutsk and Liya in Moscow had referred to, and that is so celebrated – if that's the right word – in the great literature of Tolstoy, Dostoevsky, Pasternak and (my personal favourite) Bulgakov's *The Master and Margarita*, has undoubtedly been shaped by the hardships its people have faced.

And yet the Russians whose homes we had shared or whom we'd met along the way had shown us a generosity of spirit and hospitality that was disarming and heart-warming. They demonstrated a sense of the better collective, communitarian aspects of the legacy of communism that still survives, and that felt refreshing from our rather more relatively individualistic and perhaps slightly more selfish Western perspectives. I couldn't help thinking these values might yet prove invaluable as the impacts of climate change really begin to bite, and we realise we really are all in this together.

Russia continues to change but, as Nikola on Olkhon put it, *Being Russian is not a nationality, it is a state of mind.* Tackling climate change successfully will be about not countries, but mindsets. In the words of Shakespeare's Henry V, the play that Svetlana had given me a copy of in Irkutsk, 'All things are ready, if our minds be so'.

# OFF THE ROAD

*The air is sweet in Mongolia,*
*the wind is scented.*

— Enkhamgalan ('Eric') —

Though the train journey across the beautiful steppes from Ulan Ude in Russia to the Mongolian capital Ulaanbaatar is only 270 miles, it takes almost 24 hours. Rather than a demonstration exercise in slow travel, this average speed of about 11 miles an hour is due to the interminable customs procedures that bestride the border.

Earlier, in the waiting room at Ulan Ude station, I'd had a moment of acute cultural disorientation when the familiar theme tune from *Top Gear* blared from the television in the corner. Sure enough, my environmental nemesis Jeremy Clarkson appeared onscreen, weirdly dubbed into Russian. A deep Slavonic accent lent a suitable Bond-villain air to Clarkson's characteristic petrol-headed rantings. Whilst Jeremy

but hopelessly unsubtle smuggling operation, let down only by the fact that some exuberant traders had blatantly been drinking half the night to celebrate the successful run. Their vodka breath alone, when cornered in conversation in the corridor – *Where you from?* – was enough to make you squiffy.

'Man of the millennium', Chingis Khan, as Genghis is locally known, is still – seven centuries on – rather popular in Mongolia. You can buy Chingis branded beer or vodka, there's a nightclub named after him, numerous restaurants and cafés and an enormous memorial statue in Sükhbaatar – Axe Hero – Square. The original macho hard man, he was initially named Temujin, meaning 'Of Iron', but his later *nom-de-guerre*, Chingis, is thought to mean 'Limitless as the Sea', implying his superlative power and reflecting the scale of his empire. The personality cult of the Great Khan is going strong. In fact, rather like a Muslim's pilgrimage to Mecca, it's customary for every Mongolian to have their photo taken with the big man at least once in their life. Strange in some ways, when you consider he was a fairly violent sort of chap, whose armies often slaughtered every man, woman and child living in the path of their advance. Even Europe quaked before the threat of the savage barbarians from the east under Chingis' son Ögedei Khan, who sacked Krakow and Pest (half of modern day Budapest) and even threatened Vienna. Historians speculate it was only his untimely death that halted Mongolian conquest 'all the way to the Great Sea', the Atlantic. We were let off the hook.

In this sense, Mongolians are some of history's very greatest overland travellers, creating the biggest contiguous land empire in human history. The *Pax Mongolica* of the 13th and 14th centuries stretched over 6,000 miles from the Pacific to the Caspian Sea. This enabled the establishment of the trade links that created the Silk Road. In the process the Mongols developed a communications system, called the Yam, with relays of horse riders that could carry a message from one end of the empire to the other in less than six weeks. They also changed the ethnic and political profile of much of Eurasia before the empire fragmented in a perhaps inevitable series of brutal succession battles and disputes. A tribute to Chinghis' popularity is the more recent revelation that around 8 percent of all men in Asia (or 0.5 percent of all men in the world) carry a Y-chromosome that appears to have originated in Mongolia around 1,000 years ago. The pace and scale of the spread of this gene sequence is probably only possible through clan and social selection, the suspicion being it is Chinghis' male heirs who have passed it on. There is therefore a little bit of the Great Khan in rather many of us.

Ulaanbaatar itself is a quixotic mix of old Soviet-style concrete blocks and huge suburbs of ghetto-like encampments of *gers*, the traditional round tents of Mongolian nomads often referred to by their Russian name, yurts, arranged along narrow, muddy lanes flanked by sheet zinc and wooden fences. A central grid of streets seems almost permanently locked with traffic, drivers leaning wearily on their horns or harassing already-harried pedestrians as a distraction to the chronic congestion. Traffic flow is controlled only by the cacophony of shrill whistling and manic arm- and baton-waving of put-upon traffic police, who stand choking amid the fumes and chaos.

You could see why the traffic was so densely concentrated as soon as you left the city that many affectionately refer to as UB. The roads ended. We were attempting to escape the thrusting hubbub of the city by embarking on an overland expedition into the Gobi Desert for a few days. We were in an indestructible Russian built UAZ ('Wuzz') truck, driven by our indefatigable Mongolian drivers Mishka and Nema. We'd not even left Ulaanbaatar when, at a busy traffic junction, our van ground into the car adjacent to us. Our rugged Wuzz was unscathed, but the car's wing and headlight were well and truly 'dunched', as one of our travelling companions, a Geordie, reliably informed us. Four hours of interminable Mongolian police bureaucracy later and we were again edging through a solid jam out of the city. Next to us, in a grisly pick-up truck full of bloodied animal bones, the young guy in the cab was delicately applying lip-gloss.

On the outskirts of town we paused at a garage to stock up on fuel and food. There we met Menghis, a Mongolian sushi salesman. *Where do you get your fish?* I asked innocently, thinking of the spectacular distance of his business from the sea. He just laughed. As we left and he handed us

*Venerable yurt or 'ger', Gobi Desert, Mongolia*

*The only puncture we sustained in almost three weeks of road-less travel in Mongolia*

a gift of a lunchtime sushi box, I understood why. Mongolian sushi isn't made with fish, it's made with spam (canned pork offcuts). I could almost visualise the marketing slogan; 'Do you want sushi, but don't like fish? Then you'll love spamushi!'-

Mongolian 'roads' are little more than dusty tracks, often consisting of numerous loosely-aligned lanes. Occasionally one of these veers off into the wilderness to a destination unknown. They also lack any notion of straightness. Unlike the Romans, the Mongols never marched armies in straight lines between cities, they simply hopped on a horse and galloped there, along with a few thousand heavily armed mates. This lack of need, or indeed respect, for roads seems equally evident today. Even over enormous plains devoid of obstacles, tracks wend, weave and swerve in completely arbitrary, inebriated squiggles.

At one point we hit the surreal sight of a freshly-laid, smooth tarmac road, so brand, spanking new it was still under construction. Highway building of this type is still a fairly recent phenomenon in largely road-free Mongolia, as workers idled down the middle of the highway insouciantly painting white lines amidst the traffic. We passed a steam-roller being loaded onto a low truck by two entrepreneurial Indian guys. We assumed they hadn't actually driven it here overland.

*Mongolia is a good place to be a road builder,* someone quipped and, as we drove over the brow of the next hill, you could still see the cryptic, swirling calligraphic scrawl of informal tracks scribbled across the valley floor, now replaced by the bold Times New Roman of linear tarmac trunk road. It was debatable which caused more damage to the landscape, the tracks scything a vast swathe of countryside or the compact modern road, though it was unarguable which was the quicker and more comfortable. I couldn't help mourning the loss of freedom that the archaic tracks seemed to offer in comparison with the restriction of the new road. The highway constrained possibilities; it didn't liberate them. It brought a sense of permanence to what was previously transitory. Then again, I didn't have to drive along this valley every day either.

We were accompanied by a motley crew of Europeans, including a physiotherapist, a town planner, a couple of postgraduate physicists working respectively on space telescopes and nuclear fusion, an engineer, a geologist and a medical student. With this mix of skills we felt able to tackle anything. Especially Ralf, the Swiss town planner, who felt his skills might be put to good use in a nomadic country where the whole notion of even semi-permanent settlement is somewhat alien. Put it this way, he had plenty of space to work with.

Needless to say, this fantastic array of talents proved utterly useless the first time we encountered a broken-down vehicle. The unwritten rules of the hostile Gobi oblige you to provide whatever help you can to the unfortunate. A sort of 'wilderness solidarity', as you might find yourself in a similar position. Stopping to assist, Mishka and Nema were quick to offer useful, practical advice to the stricken driver. Meanwhile the mechanically-incompetent rest of us stood around looking slightly foolish like the proverbial useless, superfluous lemons.

You can see for vast distances over the huge open spaces of the arid Gobi plateau. Our van would chase the dark shadows of clouds passing overhead, keeping pace with the speeding gloom, before a major rut would force us to slow. Then the darkness would fly on ahead, immersing us once more in the hot desert sunshine. From rolling, green, misty grassland, we passed through red mud to immeasurable dusty plains, jagged black mountain crags ripping up from the sand below. Bewildering rock formations grit-blasted by desert winds and carved by seasonal rainfall made for striking landmarks in the otherwise often featureless scenery. However, the very simplicity of the Mongolian landscape is often its power. The stripped-down palette of dry but delicately green steppe beneath a sky of almost implausibly vivid blue, in which puffy white clouds sail serenely by, makes the need for a wider spectrum of colour seem ridiculously indulgent.

On our first night we had the honour of staying in a family *ger*. We slaughtered the Mongolian language and hung it out to dry in much the same way as they'd probably prepared the meat for our dinner... the previous year. Although the mutton broth was delicious and cubes of tender fat melted in the mouth, dried shreds of flesh wedged themselves into gaps in our teeth we didn't even know existed. Every meal we ate in the Gobi also included grit as a key ingredient, almost inevitable in a windy desert, reminiscent of sandy sandwiches eaten on the beach during childhood summer holidays back home.

We made several inadvertent cultural faux-pas that evening, including an attempt to sit on the family dinner table, and yet another linguistic error with the phrasebook. When explaining to the family where we were from I misinterpreted 'Ikh Britani' as 'I am British' (in fact it means just 'Great Britain') leading to our Swiss companions saying they were from 'Great Switzerland' and our French friend being from 'Great France'. The family looked at us like we were all crazy, arrogant, foreign boasters. *Ikh Mongoli* [Great Mongolia], said the mother, pointing to herself with a knowing smile.

Later, our enquiries as to the location of the toilet were met by a vague sweep of the arm over the surrounding sand outside. This huge choice of location in a landscape often startlingly flat and bereft of cover definitely confuses European sensibilities, not least by creating uncertainty as to what precisely constitutes a polite distance.

Nomadic Mongolian life revolves around animals. The flocks of sheep and goats, herds of cows and camels and semi-wild horses sustain the population on their milk and meat diet. This is not a country for vegans. There was something brilliantly circular and sustainable about this pastoral Mongolian lifestyle that appealed to my environmental sensibilities. It has also left the vast majority of the country's natural space more or less unchanged by man. Perhaps I am romanticizing this, but the interdependence of people, livestock and landscape first-hand is impressive, each roving family almost entirely reliant on their animals for food, fuel and shelter. The long-evolved and close adaptation of Mongolians to their environment left me with a sense of attunement, of existence expertly eked out in intimate alignment with the grain of nature. The lifestyle felt timeless, pragmatic and smart in the simplicity of its solutions to the question of survival in such challenging terrain.

We later came across land in which farmers were apparently embarking on Mongolia's new green revolution. Fume-belching tractors struggled to plough the hard soil into ridged 'fields', the roughly regular patches on the surface of the immense Mongolian landscape. These first attempts at conventional agriculture seemed incongruous in a nation of itinerant herders, whose lifestyle and culture are so tightly entwined with their animals and the seasons. Mongolians migrate with the growth of the pastures and, to avoid the extremes of the winter weather, subsist on the meat and the milk the animals produce from grazing, and cook and heat their *gers* with the dung, a wonderfully tight, almost closed-loop system. You couldn't help but wonder which practice might be more sustainable, the pastoral livestock system or the new intensive agricultural methods. Unless you're vegetarian, in which case it's probably a little more clear-cut.

Mongolians make alcohol from fermented mare's milk, which is a testament to human ingenuity in facilitating fermentation from even the most limited of available resources, and in milking a lactating horse in the first place. The resulting drink, *airag*, I heard memorably described as like 'sour milk that has had cockles kept in it'. That's one of the more favourable accounts.

Then there are the dogs, which made the Siberian canines we had encountered look like docile puppies. One day two monstrous, snarling beasts hurtled after the van, attempting to chew the wheels off as our driver Nema nonchalantly dangled his hand out of the window as bait. They pursued us at high speed for a couple of miles. *I don't fancy my chances of outrunning them,* noted one of our fellow travellers wryly. Dogs are not pets, they're for protection, and a typical Mongolian greeting on approaching a *ger* is *Nokhoi Khori*, 'Hold your dogs'. These were not the type of pooch you keep in your handbag.

Even Mongolians, isolated as they are from much of the modern world, and though not responsible for much in the way of carbon emissions, are already suffering dramatically from the impacts of climate change. Having experienced 2°C of rising average temperatures in just the last 70 years, many researchers are referring to Mongolia as a global 'climate change laboratory', a barometer of what might happen elsewhere as the world warms. The prognosis isn't promising. Droughts are drying up rivers, pastures are less productive, grazing is harder for animals and the resulting leaner livestock and therefore less fuel means that surviving the tough and periodically extreme winters is getting considerably harder for rural Mongolians. It is the terrible winters, or *zuds*, that are really doing the damage. Whilst these conditions are not unambiguously attributable to climate change, the ability of herders and their weakened animals to endure them is most certainly affected. When underfed livestock perish as a result, the whole fragile web unravels: a way of life intact and largely unchanged for hundreds, possibly thousands, of years becomes untenable. Mongolians not only feel the effects of climate change, they see that others are largely to blame. They are understandably unhappy.

Three *zuds* in a row at the turn of the century killed millions of animals and perhaps tipped the balance of the Mongolian economy and culture forever: thousands of destitute nomads descended on UB, creating the shanty towns of *gers* surrounding the city. As a consequence, one of the recurring motifs of any hinterland Mongolian journey is the skull – sun-bleached, dusty, symbolic of death. Goat, horse and camel bones dot the open countryside as visible reminders of the temporary and sometimes tenuous nature of life. At one point in the empty vastness we came across a very young abandoned foal, alone and vulnerable. At our insistence, Nema reluctantly stopped the van so we could give it some milk from our supplies. After several minutes of pathetic, unsuccessful bowl-proffering by us, Nema unceremoniously grabbed the foal, held it between his legs, prised open its jaw with his fingers and poured the milk roughly down its throat. His robust Mongolian disposition was obviously unimpressed by our weak sentimentality. As we set off again, the clearly-condemned beast gave hopeless chase to our moving van. It was a poignant moment.

Despite the harsh, inhospitable environment the Gobi also has a wealth of wildlife. Eagles soared overhead, squat vultures hung around in gangs near the bloated carcass of a horse or camel lying nearby, lizards scampered over the hot sand, antelope skipped across the track ahead and haughty two-humped Bactrian camels regarded us dismissively. The camels were predominantly brown, but every now and then we'd spot a blonde one. It was hard to tell whether they were having more fun or not. The camels often had their hindquarters shaved, the equivalent of a

*The doomed image of a lost foal in the middle of nowhere, Gobi Desert, Mongolia*

*Becoming camel cargo on a tick-ridden ship-of-the-desert, Khongoryn Els, Mongolia*

'back, sack and crack' wax, presumably to prevent parasites. I'm guessing it's hard to dip a camel in a desert, but even the creative depilation wasn't enough to prevent grotesque, bloated, thumb-sized ticks clinging vampire-like to the camels' undersides.

Ticks became a recurrent theme. Trousers were tucked into socks to prevent invasion, so we resembled itinerant scoutmasters who'd lost their troop. One rocky pinnacle we scaled was like a tick launching pad, prompting swift retreat and diligent mutual body checks later. Not the most salubrious task after several hot days without a shower, as popular tick hang-outs include the armpits, groin and other moist bodily crevices. I later read a news story about an entomological taxonomist who found a tick, which turned out to be a species previously unknown to science, up his nose after a field trip to Uganda. All the tick chat reminded me of a preacher I once heard on a bus in Jamaica who proclaimed *there are many ticks that suck the blood, but the tick that sucks the most blood is the poli-tic.*

Our Gobi days were spent exploring the incredible landscape, from the sedimented, stripy cliffs of the former sea-bed at Ulaan Suvraga, now thousands of miles from the nearest ocean, to the rugged rocky canyons of the Yolyn Am ice valleys south of Dalanzadgad, where frozen rivers lay petrified along the gorge floor, and solid waterfalls hung in silent stillness from the cliffs down which they tumbled. We rode recalcitrant camels to, and climbed the steep slopes of, the giant dunes at Khongoryn Els, where a fat tongue of Gobi sand hundreds of yards high probed for miles into a stony valley between the surrounding mountains. We fossicked amongst the burnt orange crevices of the Flaming Cliffs, where the first fossil dinosaur eggs had been found. Everywhere we went, we were left breathless with excitement at the spectacular scenery around us, or through the sheer exertion of hiking over, scrambling around or scaling up it.

Nights found us huddled in a *ger*, sat on the mercilessly hard woven-metal and thin-mattressed beds that were like poorly disguised chain-mail, or perched on the small milking-style stools that served for furniture, space being at a premium when you live, cook and sleep in one modestly

*Cattle grazing in Yolyn Am ice valley, Dalanzadgad, Mongolia*

sized round room. The night chill of the desert was kept at bay by a fragrant dung fire roaring in the stove, the only sounds the murmur of low conversation, the bleating of the livestock or the occasional gruff dog bark. Outside, the cool night air and magnificent cloud-free skies created a personal planetarium of star-studded wonder. So many pinpricks of light peppered the heavens it was hard to distinguish the haze of the Milky Way against the twinkling celestial background. I regretted the urban skyglow of the United Kingdom that has effectively stolen from us this fundamental connection with the universe above and beyond.

One night we enjoyed a personal concert from a wizened old musician called Baska. Resplendent in a dark blue traditional Mongolian tunic with red and gold trim, and rather camp knee-high white leather boots, Baska treated us to a selection of Mongolian classics on an almost exclusively equine theme. *This is a song about a fast horse... This one is about a horse race... This is a melody about a man's love for his horse.* The Mongolian wilderness can be a very lonely place. He mixed it up a bit with a *tune about a baby camel* and topped his set off with some incredible 'Khoomi' or throat-singing. This is a wonderfully bizarre vocal feat that simultaneously generates a resonant grumble and a high pitched wheezy whistle from a doubtless over-worked larynx. Oddly ethereal, weirdly beautiful and strangely moving, it still made a small philistine part of you want to shout *Just cough man, for heaven's sake!*

We lunched the next day by the craggy chasm of Chuulyut Canyon, a deep, steep boulder-sided scar of river valley where curious hawks circled above. Just when you think the Mongolian scenery has blown your mind as much as it can, it pulls another spectacle out of the bag and once again you are agog at the rare, rugged beauty of it all. In this case it was the Great White Lake – Terkhiin Tsagaan Nuur – and the huge hollow crater of the long extinct Khorgo Uul volcano. Beneath the typically hyperbolic Mongolian skies, all puffed-up cumulus cloud and weather fronts, we stood on the edge of the precipitous volcanic cone surveying the wrinkled black lava flows below. In the distance, the partially frozen lake surface shone brilliantly in its own personal patch of sunshine while we watched a dark threatening blizzard drawing in. The combination of mountain and meteorology was magical.

We roused ourselves at 4am the following morning for a freezing scramble up the crag above our *ger* to watch sunrise over the lake. Our wheezing efforts were amply rewarded as the beauty of the dawn took our breath away again. The still waters of the lake turned from deep dark to iridescent silver, the breaking day edging the still-murderous looking clouds above with an incongruously delicate shade of pink. Back at camp I made coffee, then went to gaze contemplatively over the dawn-lit waters. *Do you speak English?* came a voice from behind. *I think I should be asking you that*, I thought. I turned to greet a beaming Mongolian who introduced himself as Enkhamgalan. I tried, ineffectively, to repeat this a couple of times. After he'd stopped laughing at my attempts, he said *Call me Eric*. He'd learnt English at Shepherd's Bush College, was returning to Mongolia to run a travel tour company. He had strong views on the tension between nomadic Mongolian life and the urbanisation of Ulaanbaatar: *In the country you battle with nature; in the city you battle each other.* From the number of impromptu punch-ups we'd witnessed in Ulaanbaatar, I could well agree with him.

*We are naturally aggressive people,* he continued. *When the Russians came, they freed Mongolian men from the Buddhist monasteries that the Chinese Manchu Dynasty had introduced to pacify Mongolia.* He had taught English in Guangzhou in China for several years and, like many Mongolians we met, was extremely wary of his southern neighbours, former hosts and pupils. *They asked me in Guangzhou why I didn't speak Chinese. Because I am Mongolian! In fact, China is a part of Mongolia!* he added, with some degree of historical accuracy – Chinghis Khan having defeated the northern Chinese Jin Dynasty in the 13th century and effectively occupied much of what is now modern China.

*The Chinese stole Inner Mongolia,* Eric claimed, *by offering Chinese slaves to lazy Mongolians. Now those slaves run the country.* I suspected I was on the receiving end of an ever-so-slightly xenophobic rant at this stage. *Chinese are slow learners. I know this from teaching there; only the educated English-speaking Chinese really understand the challenges they face; they think they can just control everything. Chinese would look at the shape of that mountain over there and decide to change it,* he

*Terkhiin Tsagaan Nuur - The Great White Lake, from crater of Khorgo volcano, Mongolia*

*Being an object of curiosity, Gobi Desert, Mongolia*

grinned. *When I first came to this lake five or six years ago the water level was much higher; there were no islands. Mining is also destroying our country: the river here used to be big, now it is just a trickle. Two years ago the Chinese came and caught all the fish.* I started to interject but he was warming to his international relations theme now. *We are stuck between two superpowers who now give us nothing. We have no port. All our trade must go through Russia or China. Mongolia's answer is for our third neighbour to be the English language. We must educate and understand this and lift ourselves up. China kept Mongolia's population low so we would not be a threat.* He didn't elaborate on how the Chinese did this but, after Chingis' historical escapades, you can understand why they might have been keen.

Eric described the challenges faced by the country since its democratic revolution following the dissolution of the Soviet Union. *Before 1990 work was guaranteed, but after that for young people it was very hard. Many drank, family units and social networks broke down leading to crime, prostitution and abandoned street children. Prostitution is still very bad, for $1,000 you can buy any woman. It doesn't matter if she is professional or even married. Everyone has their price.*

Eric's words by the Great White Lake – *Mining is destroying our country* – resounded days later as we passed through Mongolia's second largest city Erdenet. It's home to one of the world's biggest copper mines, which consumes a large proportion of Mongolia's electricity and whose mountainous piles of mining tailings dominate the skyline. Some have dubbed the country 'Mine-golia' because of its enormous mineral wealth of copper, coal, gold and the increasingly resource-hungry digital industries' favourite metal - lithium. This glut, in such close proximity to China, could be a blessing: it has already led to economic growth rates similar to those of its rapidly growing neighbour. Equally it could lead to what some commentators call the 'resource curse' in which developing nations cope poorly in the face of sudden material wealth due to a swift influx of money, lifestyle changes, divisive economic disparity and corruption. The jury's still out for Mongolia as more mines open up, but some tensions already exist with many Mongolians, like Eric, looking with suspicion on Chinese

*Horse skull, Khorgo volcano, Mongolia*

investments, intentions and motivations. This is perhaps understandable when you consider the densely-populated and resource-poor Chinese sitting adjacent to the under-populated and resource-rich Mongolians.

The mine outside Erdenet generates a huge amount of heavy truck traffic, which was even more intimidating to us given our recent off-road isolation. So it was with relief that shortly afterwards we turned off towards the monastery at Amarbayasgalant, where we were to spend our last night out of town. That night, in a *ger* next to the monastery, we ate another typical Mongolian dinner, a spicy variation on the hot greasy mutton/goat/camel meat broth that had sustained us throughout our trip. At lunchtimes we'd cooked for ourselves, parking the van up in some suitable beauty spot, of which there was scant shortage, stewing some vegetables on a little gas stove. This was important, as we had been warned before departure that the western gut doesn't tend to cope well with a solely meat and dairy diet, leading to inevitable 'blockages'. In the morning we were tucking into an equally representative, colon-clogging breakfast of dry sour-milk biscuits, a Mongolian staple made more palatable by dipping them into jam or chocolate spread, when there was a knock on the door and George Clooney stuck his head inside.

*Good morning! Would you like to try some cheese?* he said with a grin that complemented the tasty-looking wares on his plate, a selection of cheeses from a firm, holey yellow cheese to a creamy white ricotta. OK, so it wasn't actually George Clooney, but an uncanny look-alike Swiss called Ueli who it turned out to be an international Buddhist cheese-making guru. Based in Karnataka, India, he was visiting the monastery to teach the monks how to make cheese as a generator of revenue.

*I'm teaching them how to use rennet,* he explained. *Anyone can make sour cheese; milk does that by itself if you leave it long enough.* We knew that much from the rather rancid sour cheese breakfast biscuits we'd been eating across Mongolia for the last month. He'd just finished his first lot of cheeses; we were to be his guinea pigs. The cheeses were really very good. Ueli had also been making yoghurt from a culture he'd had sent in by DHL. *It was very expensive,* he bemoaned, though this was perhaps unsurprising given the monastery's somewhat isolated location in rural

Mongolia. However, the monks were so taken by his first batch that they'd literally licked the bowl clean, meaning he'd no culture left to start another! Ueli rolled his eyes as he explained that thankfully our hostess, whom he'd also been training in the dark arts of dairy manipulation, had some yoghurt left, so he didn't have to courier in another seed culture.

Leaving Ueli and his cheese-making monks, we experienced a fairly abrupt transition from 'wild' Mongolia back into the relatively civilised realm of UB, although the difference in temperament of the people is less pronounced than the change in the road surface. One minute you're bouncing along on rough grit in a rugged wilderness; the next, you're jammed onto a generally smooth-paved but pot-holed surface and back in amongst the horrendous traffic of UB rush hour.

I'd arranged to see a man about a *ger*. Struck by the elegance of the structures, the design of which has remained more or less unchanged in a millennium, the beauty of the hand-painted roof struts and the sense of spiritual space inside, my inner-hippy was curious to see how hard it would be to buy one in Mongolia and ship it back to the United Kingdom. Not that difficult as it turned out, largely down to one man, the veritable Mr Fixit of UB.

Sebastien is a big, barrel-chested Frenchman full of boisterous bluster and in possession of an unambiguously firm handshake and a booming, throaty, Lucky-Strike-enhanced voice. We met in his bookshop, Libraire Papillon. After years working in what he euphemistically described as 'international security', including a stint spent protecting Chinese businesses during the Indonesian riots in the late 1990s, he'd married a Mongolian woman. Having settled in UB, he'd begun building a business empire which now included the bookshop, a restaurant next door, Bistro Français – *naturellement* – a printing company, a fire safety company, a security company with over 500 employees and various other enterprises of which his *ger* export business was but one small part. The UB economy would clearly have been somewhat impoverished without him.

Smoking and wise-cracking furiously, Sebastien had arranged for a car to take us to his *ger* workshop on the outskirts of UB to survey his wares. *The advantage of being fat is you always get to sit in the front,* he explained as I and a French couple buying *gers* for the school they were teaching at in Mongolia jammed ourselves intimately into the back seat. As the driver wrestled through the urban throng, Sebastien pointed out the homes of various politicians and foreign embassies along the way. *We make tourism, so it is not a complete waste of your time,* he roared. *This is School Number 5, all places in UB are numbered. No names, so no-one gets upset!*

The workshop was in a dusty walled compound at the foot of a steep hill Sebastien dubbed 'Snake Mountain'. Inside, a series of pristine *gers* were being constructed and photographed before being packed and shipped to their Canadian buyer, alongside a very old, dirty, ragged clearly 'lived-in' one. Sebastien snapped the wretched looking *ger* on his mobile phone *I send this to my Canadian contact and tell him it is my new design,* he chuckled. He then expertly took us through the *ger*'s attributes, the hand-cut wooden poles, the camel-skin bindings, the horse-hair ropes and the thick felt insulation, all produced in different parts of Mongolia and then traded between communities. He outlined the special modifications he'd made for the European and North American markets, such as the water-proofed canvas covers and rain-catching 'lip' on the rim of the central roof hub. *We made 2 million euros last year on gers,* Sebastien announced proudly as his polished sales patter drew to an end. Well I was certainly sold on the idea and, many months later, once safely back home, I became the proud owner of one of Sebastien's beautiful yurts.

On the way back to UB, Sebastien asked what I did for a living, so I explained my work on climate change and our no-fly trip. *Ah, we are very pro-climate-change in Mongolia,* he laughed. *We have very cold winters and I am buying Gobi sand to make a beach when the sea finally reaches us.* He also said he was stockpiling good Scotch whisky and so wasn't worried about potential water supply issues due to climate change. *I will be 100 years old and won't need to wash!* he exclaimed. *It is best to be in UB and be drunk on whisky if the rest of the world is going to shit.* Possibly he had a point.

On our last night in Mongolia, being British and after endless meaty broths, we had a hankering for only one thing. Curry. Fortunately we'd found the Taj Mahal Indian restaurant, so headed there for our final meal. The owner, Babu, a wiry Indian from the southern state of Kerala, with a bristly toothbrush moustache 'to balance my face', joined us after we'd feasted on a fine array of feisty, spicy dishes. *Seggie!* he'd shout repeatedly to his poor Mongolian wife, *More apple juice!,* and she'd bring yet another glass of whisky to appease him.

*I am a machine gun,* Babu announced, when we commented on the rapid pace of his scotch-fuelled delivery. On discovering they'd run out of vodka he insisted that we have a tequila so he wasn't drinking alone. This was probably the last thing our stomachs required on top of a substantial curry. *Mongolians must do things in odd numbers,* said Babu. *You cannot have two drinks, you must have one or three,* as we forced down our third hefty measure from salt-rimmed glasses with only one small chunk of lemon between eight of us. *Lemon is very expensive in Mongolia,* rued Babu. I mentally noted the obvious lack of citrus groves.

I was curious as to how he'd arrived in UB. *Fate!* Babu shouted with a flourish, *I have now been here nine years. In the summer we get fat and in the winter we live off that fat!* he said patting the little pot belly that sat oddly on his thin frame. Babu moonlighted as a lecturer in tourism and restaurant management. *Mongolians are useless! They are all animals!* he cried, *They don't want to work. The Chinese? They work like ants!* As we were thanking him and leaving, Babu asked us how the meal had been and why we'd chosen to come. *We missed good curry,* I told him. *Then you are still missing good curry,* he grinned back.

# APPETITE

*For my part, I travel not to go anywhere,*
*but to go. I travel for travel's sake.*
*The great affair is to move.*

— Robert Louis Stevenson —

Rolling through Inner Mongolia on the train, everything was going swimmingly, though the chances of a quick plunge in the relentless, flat yellow sandscape were remote unless you fancied a dust bath. We were sharing our compartment with a young Chinese guy and a twinkly-eyed older Japanese man named Mirosawa. *Me 61*, he said. *After ten years…*, and he gestured a slow decline with his hand, indicating a gentle deterioration of mind, body and spirit. But he wasn't quitting travel just yet, with trips to Cape Town and Lhasa already planned. He'd caught the travel bug in his early 20s while washing dishes and teaching judo on a cruise ship sailing between Japan and San Francisco via Hawaii. Like me, he was also planning to take the ferry from China to Japan *I like ship!* he said gleefully with a broad smile, and was also tickled by our no-flying approach to travel. *Ship, ship, ship. You love ship!* We had a lot in common.

It all started to go a little pear-shaped at the Mongolian-Chinese border in Erlian, just after midnight. Crossing borders is all part of the drama of overland travel, as we'd already found, having to bypass Belarus, and during the protracted entry into Mongolia a month earlier. Our train was stopped in a huge shed: the railway gauge is different in Mongolia and China, so the massive, heavy wheel bogeys have to be changed, and there were customs checks and visa controls. Examining our passports, the squad of Chinese border police pointed out our visas had expired three days previously, the Chinese Embassy in London having issued them for ninety days from the date of application, not the later date we'd requested. *And now for formalities,* announced the ever so sweet, smiling female official politely, as we were hauled off the train by armed guards. They marched us through the shed on a walk of shame, as all the other passengers watched us curiously with their faces pressed against the windows.

Thankfully our expired visas were put down to foreign incompetence as opposed to anything more nefarious. After a short van ride through dark, dusty streets, we had an hour hanging around nervously like naughty schoolchildren, in the office of an official who alternately made phone calls and made repeated, valiant attempts to clear his throat. We were then fined, given 'special permits to enter' and were able to re-board the train as a Mandarin version of Rod Stewart's 'Sailing' blared from the station tannoy.

After a swift visit to the ominous-sounding People's Security Bureau on arrival in Beijing, our visas were being sorted. While we waited for the wheels of bureaucracy to turn we stayed at a gorgeous *hutong*-style hostel: single-storey, with little rooms facing through windowed doors and heavy red curtains onto a paved courtyard. Lacquered furniture,

Chinese lanterns, a cage full of live birds, a koi fishpond traversed by a wee wooden bridge and even a life-size replica of a terracotta warrior in the corner – to make any deceased visiting Emperors feel at home, or at least comfortable with security arrangements – created a relaxing scene in which to regather ourselves. After a month of Mongolian yurt-dwelling it seemed like the height of indulgent luxury. It was lovely and, at a few pounds a night and big bottles of cold Tsingtao beer for a few pennies, it became lovelier with every passing moment.

And we did need to acclimatise a little. Air quality in Beijing and much of urban China is an oxymoron. Heavy industrial activity and sandstorms that whip in from the Gobi cover the city in fine brown dust, like cocoa on a giant chocolate cake. The sun is a rare and elusive celestial body glimpsed only occasionally through the metropolitan fug. After weeks in the wild open spaces and fresh clean air of Mongolia, populous, pulsating China – Beijing in particular – was intense. There are more than 20 million Beijingers, more than seven times the entire population of its northern neighbour (which itself is the area of western Europe). The sheer volume of people on the thronging city streets was almost overwhelming. It's a striking reminder that approaching a quarter of all humanity is here. An alien spinning past our planet and assessing life below might surmise, 'Mainly Indian and Chinese'.

I am an unapologetic Sinophile and find the experience of being immersed in such a sea of people a suitable antidote to the solipsistic tendencies of travel: that sense of self-importance, the centrality and significance of your own perspective, the notion of the world as your own show, with you as the brightest, most shiny star at the heart of it all. It is so easy to define yourself as somehow 'other', as separate, apart from and –in the worst moments of cultural arrogance – superior to the society in which you find yourself. To mock, disparage or demean what is different, alien or unusual. Or as writer Robert Louis Stevenson describes it 'there are no foreign lands, it is only the traveller who is foreign'. However, despite the obvious physical distinctions of being a westerner in Asia, and the linguistic gulf between English and Mandarin (a veritable Grand Canyon in its depth and breadth compared to the relatively narrow, shallow cracks that separate Latin or Roman tongues), in China I always feel part of something much bigger than myself.

I belong to that larger humanity that transcends race, colour, creed or nationalism. In many ways this is a cliché, the Brotherhood of Man. Or better, but perhaps cheesier still, the Human Family (which at least liberates us from historical notions of male supremacy and patriarchy). This is such a truism it might not seem worth mentioning, but the late American writer David Foster Wallace tells a lovely story about the importance of such apparently platitudinous statements: 'There are these two young fish swimming along, and they happen to meet an older fish swimming the other way, who nods at them and says, 'Morning, boys, how's the water?' And the two young fish swim on for a bit, and then eventually one of them looks over at the other and goes, 'What the hell is water?'

Wallace was referring to the choices we make on a daily basis on what we believe, and specifically how we perceive, interact and behave in relationship to the personal, peopled and physical world around us. Are we to enjoy 'the freedom to be lords of our own tiny skull-sized kingdoms, alone at the centre of all creation' or aspire to think and be something better? China takes me out of my own tiny skull-sized kingdom, reminding me vividly and visibly of my connection to this much, much bigger 'we'. I've heard other travellers say the same thing about India. When I worked in Jamaica as a volunteer teacher I loved their national motto 'Out of many, one people', uniting the diverse mix of European Caucasian, Black African, Indian and (a dash of) Chinese races that blend together in a genuine melting pot. Or, as it's more directly stated, 'One blood'. It can be trite to say these things, as they are so palpably true. As Wallace puts it: 'It is about simple awareness – awareness of what is so real and essential, so hidden in plain sight all around us, that we have to keep reminding ourselves, over and over: This is water, this is water.'

We are of course 'all one', and this comprehension becomes ever more crucial in the context of collective, global challenges such as climate change. We must make our 21st century stand together, or divided we shall fall. We must remember the water. For me this unity, empathy and reason is encompassed within my own messy belief in a loosely defined 'humanism' – a conviction that shares much common ground with ancient Chinese Taoism.

One of the key inspirations for our slow travel trip had been the Taoist proverb 'the journey is the reward', so we seized the opportunity to visit the Dongyue Taoist Temple in Chaoyang in Beijing. Dating back to the 14th century, the temple is arranged around three tranquil courtyards, overhung by shady trees and filled with pagodas and large standing stone tablets engraved with the stories of great Taoists' lives. Around the edge of the central courtyard dozens of smaller rooms full of life-size plaster figures represent the different 'epartments' of the Taoist supernatural world.

These Departments all had fantastic titles. There were 'career' departments including the Department for Bestowing Happiness (with respect to reasonable material profits), the Department of Accumulating Justifiable Wealth (with respect to fortune and happiness), the Department of Suppressing Schemes (against underhand plotting), the Department for Upholding Integrity, the Department of Official Morality (officials shall be honest, fair, without corruption or snobbishness) and the Hall of Wealth where Bi Gan (the God of Civil Wealth) and Zhao Gongmi (the God of Military Wealth) come together to 'make profits on a fair and competitive basis in any commercial transaction'. No concerns about the military-industrial complex in the Taoist world then.

There were 'healthy living' departments: the Department of Jaundice (for smokers, drinkers and those leading a 'loose life'), the Department of Opposing Obscene Acts (to 'give up filthy lust and desire'), the Department for Promotion of 15 Types of Decent Lifestyle, and the aptly-named Toxicant Department (mainly about booze, fags and opium). Many of the statues in the different Departments were also highly disturbing. The Department for Halting Destruction of Living Beings featured aggressive figures brandishing bloodied knives, the Department for Controlling Evil Spirits was fronted by a multiple-breasted black being with a pig's head, while the Department of Rain Gods housed a rather froggy and fishy-looking crew. The Punishment Department contained figures having their tongues cut out, being eviscerated and other delights, and the Department of Petty Officials, whose stated aim was to ensure they are 'selfless, kind, benevolent, careful and discreet in words and deeds' consisted of big scary green guys with large spiked maces! Were these supposed to represent the petty officials themselves or the enforcers sent to keep them in line?

What was amazing was the attention to detail in the Taoist world view. There was a department for everything. The environmental activist in me obviously approved of the Department for Preservation of Wilderness and it was nice to see a Department of Controlling Bullying and Cheating, as well as an Urging Department to encourage more good deeds. The Department for Upholding Loyalty and Filial Piety seemed suitably high-minded too. Others felt awkward in a modern Chinese context, like the Department for Judging Intention, which sounded like it was about thought crime. Or the Hall of Descendants, whose role was to 'bestow many children on people', which seemed to jar with China's 'One Child' policy.

There were even departments for the little things in life, such as the Signature Department that 'controls immortal world bureaucracy'. Is it good to know that even the supernatural after-life needs bean-counters and red tape? My personal favourites, however, had to be the Department for Reducing Longevity, where you might lose 100 days of life for a minor fault or 300 days for a major one, the Department for Demons and Monsters that 'forbids them to wander and bewilder people' and, lastly, the Department for Implementing 15 Kinds of Violent Death. This ultimate one even listed what these might be for the more darkly curious among us; starvation, clubbing, revengeful murder (except apparently with a club?), killing in battle, death caused by fierce animals or snakes, burning in fire, drowning in flood, poisoning, tricks of evil person or ghost, incurable disease, suicide, an outbreak of madness and finally – a challenging and probably unlikely one for a boy from the flatlands of Norfolk like me – falling into an abyss.

Suffice to say we wandered around the temple goggle-eyed, with our minds boggling at the whole 'points mean prizes' approach to Taoist life. I loved the philosophy of compassion, moderation and humility that underpinned Taoist beliefs and the notions of interdependence, connectedness or 'one-ness', whcih seemed to link or at least resonate with my own compromised and complicated, hippy, vaguely pagan, atheistic Humanism. It was all about simply 'doing the right thing', living a good life in the moment, where success is measured by good deeds accomplished, self-awareness, responsibility and determination are to be celebrated, and personal reinvention is always possible. That is where the real freedom from our own self-centred, skull-sized kingdoms comes from. Or as David Foster Wallace concludes: 'The really important kind of freedom involves attention, and awareness, and discipline, and effort, and being able truly to care about other people and to sacrifice for them, over and over, in myriad petty little unsexy ways, every day.'

Focusing on these lingering life lessons and the journey as reward, we took a pointless but symbolic trip to Shanhaiguan where the Great Wall of China meets the sea. We could complete our marathon crossing of Eurasia by dabbling our toes in the warm waters of the Bohai Sea, check out the Wall and enjoy the historic city itself. I love Chinese trains, having criss-crossed the country on them several times during the development of a major climate-change communications campaign for China we'd created a few years previously. At any one time, it is speculated, there are around ten million Chinese people on trains, so it is also a brilliant way of getting in among the people.

We decided to travel in authentic Chinese style by going for the cheapest 'hard seats' on the train. There were six of us sitting on facing wooden benches. Opposite us, a fat man, shirt open to his waist, was displaying the full handsome and fleshy expanse of his imposing belly. There was a wiry, weathered-faced guy with curly hair and sunglasses, like a Chinese Lou Reed. Jammed between Lou and the rotund gentleman was a thin, cheery man with an immaculately trimmed David Niven-style pencil moustache. In the absence of language, we all greeted each other with generous amounts of smiling and nods of respective acknowledgement. The elderly woman next to Fi was feeling the thickness of Fi's upper arm and apparently clucking something about her needing 'feeding up', whilst my journal-writing was attracting a curious crowd of rubber-neckers. This included a middle-aged lady who was hanging over the back of my seat to get a better look. At one point she entirely unselfconsciously belched long, loud and unrestrainedly three times, just next to my right ear. Across the aisle a young couple were smooching romantically and nibbling on chicken feet. It was great to be back in China again.

Shanhaiguan wasn't quite what we'd anticipated. Instead of the bustling main street of food vendors and historic traditional architecture of this classic walled city, we walked straight into one huge building site. The entire high street had been demolished; the centre of the town was now a tangled mass of scaffolding and trucks pouring concrete foundations. Why restore when you can rebuild better? This seems to be the Chinese way. Revolution, change, upheaval and a recorded history that goes back millennia have made China much less sentimental about heritage than the United Kingdom, where even an objectively-dispiriting concrete monstrosity from the 1970s can be preserved for historical, architectural value, something the Chinese would probably find hilarious too.

The ground-up 'renovations' in Shanhaiguan had displaced the usual array of handy street food we'd been hoping for; eating became more of an adventure. With terrible famines and mass starvation in living memory, the Chinese relish and appreciate every mouthful of their extraordinarily diverse and delicious cuisines. From the fiery chilli-laden dishes of Hunan, to the peppery zing of Sichuan, or the more familiar Cantonese-style delicacies of Guangdong and Uyghur-influenced kebabs, there is a profusion of choice. I also appreciate the ruthless efficiency in which nothing is wasted if it can possibly be stewed, broiled or turned into fragrant stock, part of the enormous challenge of sating 1.4 billion hungry people. It puts us to shame in the West, where almost a fifth of edible food is thrown away. In the face of such feasting, the food-as-fuel memories of Mongolia's mutton- and milk-based morsels were swiftly banished. However, actually ordering food in China, or even understanding what's on offer, is a different kettle of fish altogether – which, incidentally, is just what you might end up being served.

That first night, at a shadowy, unlit stall outside the city walls, we ate a strange cold dish of thick, ribbon-like noodles, greenery and something spongy and unidentified that could have been bean curd or perhaps tripe. Or cold bits of wet sponge, for all we could tell by the taste and texture in the semi-darkness. Following this with grape ice cream from a wooden barrel, washed down with a delicious icy beer, we enjoyed the curious looks and 'Hello's' from passers-by.

Struggling to find sustenance the next morning, we chanced upon a steaming cauldron of broth on a gas hob outside what looked like a garage. As soon as I'd sniffed curiously at the bubbling pot, a trio of amused women emerged from the garage-kitchen where they'd been making neat little *gyoza* dumplings and beckoned us into the grubby room next door which served as a diner of sorts. Much excited but mutually incomprehensible chattering later, we tucked into a huge pile of hot, freshly fried pork *gyoza*, gingko beans and celery, tangy brown pickles and a bowl of cool, grainy porridge. All served with a big bottle of breakfast beer. It was brilliant.

Thus fortified, we headed to the coast where we gazed out over a steamy, murky bay, the gantries and cranes of the port visible to the north, a huge junk at anchor just offshore and the Great Wall itself snaking round behind us before ending in a dragon-headed watchtower above the sea. It's 5,162 miles from London to Shanhaiguan as the crow flies, but our highly indirect and wandering route had encompassed over 11,500 miles by my reckoning. As Seppi on the Trans-Siberian Express had anticipated, I had a burgeoning bank of continuous mental images and memories of the entire trip in my head, an incredible, invaluable resource that I was already enjoying accessing and playing back to myself in idle moments. This is how the writer Pat Conroy describes the experience of travel: 'the voyage never ends, but is played out over and over again in the quietest chambers'. *The mind can never break off from the journey.* We ceremoniously paddled in the stony shallows to mark our first transcontinental crossing. Around us, people were foraging for unappetizing-looking shellfish in the cloudy waters. Sneaking for a quick surreptitious pee next to the massive stone edifice of the Wall, we realised we were surrounded by small marijuana plants growing rather successfully, like the weeds they are. Fi took photos of me grinning amongst the ganja, something that I was to regret a few days later.

Sometimes we ordered food by scanning the plates of other diners and gesturing to suggest we'd quite like what they're having, please. This evening, though, we needed to develop a new food ordering technique, finding ourselves in a street café where copying others' food was unlikely to work as we were the only customers. Having declined their offer of a plate of the questionable shellfish we'd seen folk collecting earlier on the beach, and encountering the usual linguistic barriers when presented with the menu, the waitress handed me her pad and gestured for me to draw what we wanted to eat. I sketched a handsome looking chicken and a bloke eating noodles. She reappeared holding a piece of chicken in one hand and an egg in the other with a facial expression that clearly said *Which would you like?* Either that, or she was trying to engage us in a timeless philosophical and evolutionary debate as to which came first.

We pointed at the meat and 20 minutes later a huge bowl of steaming chicken noodle soup arrived. It was delicious, with big, fat ,juicy mushrooms bobbing happily in the rich stock and classic morsels of Chinese chicken in the usual cleavered chunks of bone-splinters and flesh. Fi delved a little more deeply with her chopsticks and the hen's head rolled ghoulishly up to the surface to confront us accusingly. I should probably have drawn a headless chicken.

Back in Beijing a day or so later, we went for dinner with Harry and Lee and their partners Lin and Julia, two Chinese couples we'd met whilst travelling in Siberia. They took us for a traditional Beijing hotpot in a restaurant where we had a private room, which is popular in China but I always feel undermines the whole point of going out for a meal. Perhaps they wanted to be circumspect as, not long into the meal, Lee pointed out it was the 18th anniversary of Tiananmen Square, that fateful juncture in modern Chinese history in 1989 when swelling student-led demonstrations were ruthlessly and brutally suppressed by the hardline authorities.

Lee revealed that both he and Harry had been students at the time and were actively involved in the demonstrations. He'd been 'in charge

*Tanggu, Port of Tianjin, China*

of one of the underpasses' coordinating student movements in and out of the square. *I only saw two dead bodies – both shot,* he admitted when I pressed him on casualties. No-one has ever been able to put an official figure on fatalities that night. Somehow Lee had evaded arrest in the subsequent military action. Harry, however, had been rounded up and identified as a ring-leader. *They showed me a film of me in the square and demanded 'Is this you?'* he explained. *I had to say yes!* he laughed. He spent six months in prison, which seemed relatively lenient under the circumstances.

We talked about the iconic image of the lone student confronting the tank, and the international profile of this picture versus its utter invisibility in censored China. But generally, the conversation was strangely jovial as the banter between Lee and Harry seemed to suggest the demonstrations had been part of some naive, youthful folly. They were now both embarking on careers as copper traders and brokers, very much part of the thrusting, internationally-educated and money-making emergent urban elite. Fi asked Lee if the events of that night felt distant. *No, it still feels close,* pondered Lee, *but China is a very different country now.*

Stepping onto the China Express Line ferry in Tanggu involved some degree of trepidation. For the first time in three months of travel I was alone, Fi having opted to stay in China while I took a ferry to Japan to visit an old friend since I was 'in the region'. We were to reconvene in Shanghai in ten days or so, but the shift from constant companionship, shared experience and teamwork to solitude, solipsism and going solo was abrupt. I was also, perhaps irrationally and unnecessarily, a little concerned for her travelling on her own. Initially I found myself frequently looking around for her or turning to share a thought or observation, only to find a Fi-shaped hole next to me where she would normally have been. The loneliness of unaccompanied travel after so long together kicked in quickly. I was left ruminating reflectively and introspectively in my own head now the expansive banter with my spirited soulmate and sounding board was gone.

This sense of isolation and separation wasn't helped by the fact that our last ferry journey, on the *Pride of Bilbao,* had been the voyage from hell;

72 hours of Force 10 winds and 25-foot waves. I didn't fancy enduring that again alone. I was also reading Kazuo Ishiguro's bleak dystopian organ-harvesting novel *Never Let Me Go* which scarcely improved my mood. Onboard the *Yanjing* in my 16-bed shared cabin, a message from the captain outlined the safety procedures: *In case of emergency the urgency signals will be given by whistle or ringing bell. Kindly follow our instruction carefully and don't get excited.* In the event of disaster I hoped to be able to contain myself.

My fears were unfounded, however, as the Bohai Sea was as calm as the surface of a thickly cold martini. Beautifully bright weather blessed our 48-hour passage, once we'd cleared the dense smog that hugged the Chinese shore. This was initially an unnerving experience, as huge container ships would suddenly loom out of the gloom without warning, passing us at a proximity I'd consider to be an invasion of personal space in any other situation, certainly a hazard to maritime safety. Once fully at sea, though, we chugged languidly through glassy, smooth water with an almost oily iridescence to it and past a succession of verdant rocky island archipelagos off the coastline of Korea.

During the journey I sang karaoke with the Captain of the ship for some 'cultural adjustment' therapy. This invitation had been pitched to me as an honour by one of the crew who spoke a few words of English from his merchant navy days. Which was amazing, as he'd only ever been to Glasgow, not a place renowned for its crisp, clear enunciation. *Very cold there,* was his assessment in an accent that combined Japanese with an authentic Glaswegian patter. In the karaoke lounge the Captain sang a couple of – to my untrained ears – slightly squawky Chinese ballads. I insulted the memory of Frank Sinatra with my renditions of 'The Lady is a Tramp' and 'Somewhere Beyond the Sea'. The captain then shook my hand and left and, seeing as we had been the only two people in there, I got up to leave too, only for the barmaid to insist that I pay for my two songs! Ambush karaoke fees? I was distinctly unimpressed.

The next day I got talking on deck to a retired Japanese battery engineer called Miura. *I'm into lead: acid,* he deadpanned. He'd been consulting in China, *Why travel by boat?* I asked. *Killing time,* came the reply. Clearly Japanese longevity and the prospect of a long retirement is not all it's cracked up to be. *China's biggest challenge is energy,* he told me, something that any climate change activist will tell you, usually while trotting out the terrifying statistic that on average China constructs a new coal-fired carbon-spewing power station every week. Actually it's more like one a fortnight. But that's still terrifying.

*We're lucky with this calm weather,* Miura commented, and I could only concur gratefully. Beyond the window a flotilla of squid-fishing boats bobbed on the East China Sea. Vessels dotted the horizon by day and illuminated the dark depths by night with their brilliant white calamari-catching lights. These beamed deep into the water, irresistibly luring the wide-eyed cephalopods from the abyss below. Miura was concerned about the new Chinese taste for seafood. *They want everything; they don't care. There is a big debate in Japan about who taught the Chinese to eat fish,* he grumbled. The Japanese already devour 10 percent of the world's total fish catch, so they're clearly concerned about the potential appetite of their hungry neighbours.

Later on in the trip I corroborated his concerns whilst visiting Xiamen in south-west China. It is probably Miura's worst nightmare, famous for its fresh, live fish and shellfish. A trip to a restaurant is a grisly experience. You wield awesome power as you make arbitrary decisions on which beasts to devour. You point your terrible finger of death at a gang of cowering prawns or a sullen, resigned-looking fish. Only the clams look oblivious to their fate. The waitress then goes into action with her net, the chef does his bit with the wok, and it's bubbling aquarium-to-plate in literally seconds. Seafood doesn't come much fresher than this, and you probably wouldn't want it to. The Chinese were wolfing it down. But so, rather shamefacedly, were we.

I made a Chinese friend on the boat too. Despite the absence of any common linguistic ground, we established a reasonable rapport. Our 'chat' consisted of him writing out reams of Chinese characters in my journal in the vain hope that eventually the penny would drop. Sadly and unsurprisingly it didn't. My spidery scribblings were similarly inexplicable to him. He eventually showed me his official ID badge which indicated he was studying fisheries, and we made a connection. Lots of sketching of various sea-life and fishing techniques followed, including those used by the boats alongside, and a non-verbal bond was forged between fellow marine biologists. Later he presented me with an odd gift, a small, glittery heart-shaped cushion on a string. It was very kind but I was starting to question where all this was going. My initial unease was vindicated when he reappeared, just as I was getting into bed that night, with more presents; a ridged, knobbly cucumber and a large pink sausage. I thanked him rather sheepishly, drew the curtain on my bunk and considered the rather worrying Freudian symbolism of it all.

On the final morning as we slid up through the main channel between Japan's southern islands of Shikoku and Chugoku, I passed the time of the day with the ship's doctor. *Normally no patients, so very quiet,* he sighed wearily. Meanwhile Miura was wrestling with the bank of hi-tech Japanese vending machines. *So complicated I can't work out what to do!* he said in exasperation. At least you can read the instructions, I thought, having spent the last 48 hours playing my own version of Japanese roulette with them. My Glaswegian friend then asked me to help him choose the best pictures of the crew to use on the display board at reception. It really was time to get off the ship.

As the only westerner on the ferry, the Japanese Port of Kobe customs officers had a field day with me, relishing the opportunity to practice their English. I was immediately hauled off, and they gleefully picked through my dirty laundry bag, strewing the grubby contents of my rucksack around the small interrogation room. On discovering a packet of dodgy-looking Vietnamese tobacco and some crude Chinese rolling papers, one turned to me and said *Marijuana?* Despite my protestations to the contrary, he flamboyantly produced a drug-testing kit. *If it turns purple, it's marijuana,* he informed me. *I wish it was,* I stopped myself saying, being by now well-acquainted with the humourlessness that's an essential character trait of customs officers everywhere.

Having disappointedly established that the tobacco was just that, they turned their attention to my digital camera. As they flicked through recent images, the photo we'd taken the previous week by the Great Wall of China in Shanhaiguan popped up. It was the snap of me gurning in the ganja patch at the Wall's base. The officer pointed excitedly at the apparently incriminating pic, *Marijuana!* he repeated. My cockiness was now eroding swiftly.

Despite the certainty of my innocence, I was succumbing to the guilt you experience when circumstantial evidence starts to stack up against you. My righteous mind kicked in and I was mentally preparing my legitimate defences. I was trying not to get frustrated with their probing, for fear that my ire might tempt them to subject me to a probing of a far less comfortable nature. I drew a map of China to explain where the picture was taken, but then the grilling continued. *You smoke marijuana?* barked one of them. *Er...yes,* I said in a moment of misplaced, risky honesty. *When you last smoke marijuana?* he demanded. *Er...three months ago,* I guessed. *Where you smoke marijuana?* he pressed. *Amsterdam,* I revealed, at which point, in unison, they nodded and echoed knowingly *Ahhhh, Amsterdam,* as if to suggest that if they were in Amsterdam they too would be smoking marijuana. In the end they settled on confiscating all my fruit, including the cucumber and sausage 'gift' combo, and it was a relief only to be relieved of my recent acquisitions.

Arriving in Japan is a strange experience for a Brit because everything is clean, new and shiny, and it works. As I navigated across Kobe by light railway and underground metro, plasma screens flashed greetings; polished, brightly-lit vending machines offered tantalising titbits and drinks; the interchanges were seamless and synchronised. All the while, a gentle symphony of electronic beeps, bilingual announcements and jingles, a paean to Japan's modernity in the machine age, chimed along musically in the background.

My techno-love affair with Japan continued as I caught a Shinkansen Bullet train to Tokyo, a ride so smooth I could have safely performed delicate neuro-surgery during the journey. We tore through the countryside, then raced on raised tracks over the Tokyo rooftops. It certainly wasn't slow travel but it was definitely slick, sexy and exhilarating. Some might argue that in the context of a slow-travel mission, high-speed rail journeys are hypocritical. That there is more to slow travel than just simply not flying, and a Shinkansen is practically 'flying on the ground', so disconnected are you from the landscape and people you're swiftly scything past. I agree. To a point. But this 'slowlier than thou' criticism doesn't take into account the fact it is still very much low-carbon travel, generating around 25 percent of the carbon of an equivalent flight. Hopefully and very occasionally even a committed slow traveller like me can be forgiven for succumbing to the thrill of and the 'need for speed'.

Following my fishy discussions with Miura on the ferry, while in Tokyo my inner marine biologist was determined to visit the world's biggest fish market, where 1,600 stalls flog over 450 different species from the world's oceans. In order to catch the tuna auction that is the highlight of the show, you need to be there by 6am. Up at five, I managed to navigate the Tokyo metro, silently praising the fantastic efficiency and accessibility of the Japanese system. I emerged from Tsukiji station blinking in the bright sunlight, into total commercial bedlam. A seething sea of trucks, wagons, handcarts and weird motorised trolleys surged in and out of the vast warehouse complex of the market. I tiptoed tentatively inside.

Deep within the many dark arcades, a large brick building contained serried ranks of fin-less, gill-less frozen tuna carcasses, lying in neat rows like icy, white-frosted torpedoes. The beautiful fish stripped down to a base commodity. A plump auctioneer perched on a stool was calling the prices, ululating his voice, flapping his arms with his belly wobbling in synchrony, as the value of each lot rose. Around him stood a gaggle of poker-faced bidders eyeing up the sashimi-to-be.

Critically endangered bluefin tuna are truly magnificent giants that can weigh in at over half a ton. Their sleek forms reach swimming speeds of up to 40 miles per hour and fetch insane prices on the market, going for thousands of pounds per kilo. At the time of writing a bluefin just sold for one million pounds at Tsukiji. These are seriously spectacular fish, whose blood pumps hotly round their smooth, muscular bodies thanks to a counter-current heat exchange system. In his book *Four Fish: The Future of the Last Wild Food*, Paul Greenberg describes the bluefin as a *machina ex deo* – a machine from God. This is because of their propulsive power and the stunning but ephemeral iridescent pulsing patterns of their skin. The warm blood allows them to prey deep into cold sub-Arctic waters. The mysterious third-eye on their foreheads is thought to act as a sextant and enable them to navigate vast distances across the oceans. These fish, the super-heroes of the sea, were gathered here in some icy marine Valhalla, having met an ignominious end.

Scientists estimate there's been a catastrophic 96 percent decline in bluefin tuna stocks, the last individuals being landed are now too young to breed, but each one is valuable enough to make an entire fishing boat crew rich. So we are fishing the last generation of bluefin into extinction with grim determination: the triumph of humanity's baser, physical urges over its higher moral purpose. It's a world that values the brief but exquisite, destructive pleasure of consumption, over the inspirational delight of knowing that these incredible, ancient *machinae ex deo* would grace our oceans forever. Soon the only bluefin in the world will be frozen bodies held as 'investments' in icy high-security warehouses. This priceless flesh will be the last chance to eat a once iconic species. It was enough to make you weep.

Once the tuna were sold, market workers, armed with vicious looking hooked metal spikes, dragged the frosty fish off for dismemberment and distribution. I wove my way dejectedly through this chaos, trying not to get in the way, slip on the wet cobblestone floor, trip on a tuna, get run over by a trolley or become impaled on some violent tool. In the end, I took the safest option and just stood with my back to the wall to survey the scene.

Guys with circular saws removed the heads from the rock-solid bodies; a sort of fishy carpentry was taking place with both frozen and defrosted tuna. Stallholders armed with huge samurai-type swords were performing the delicate, detailed tasks of dissection, artistically slicing away at the soft pink tuna flesh in an almost loving, but surgically-precise fashion. Another vendor was proudly displaying his rare wares, fat chunks of bloody, ragged looking steak. Whale meat. Just what your average environmentalist wants to see before breakfast. There were octopuses, live eels, chunky clams, myriad fish mouthing desperately in bubbling tanks, spider crabs, shiny pink roes and a plethora of shapeless gelatinous beasts from salps to sea cucumbers that you never see on a Western plate but which are highly-prized treats to the voracious Japanese palate.

The cornucopia left me with a false sense of unlimited maritime bounty. This belied the facts of chronic global over-fishing that I knew to be reality. Ninety percent of global commercial fisheries are under threat, an argument brilliantly brought to a wider public audience by Charles Clover's book *The End of the Line* and the subsequently successful, hard-hitting and moving film of the same name. As he says; 'We are fighting a war against fish. And we're winning'. Technology and sheer scale of fishing effort allows us to hit declining fish stocks ever harder. Or destructive practices like beam trawls and dredging trash the entire seabed ecology repeatedly, relentlessly and ruthlessly multiple times a year. We will need this potential protein to feed our burgeoning population. Yet fisheries are a woeful example of politicking, pitiless pragmatism and piracy.

Like climate change, over-fishing is a nightmare scenario that is well documented, evidenced and almost entirely predictable. Yet action to tackle it is similarly hobbled by short-term economic concerns and vested interests. Our common marine heritage, which could in principle be a bountiful, sustainably managed resource in perpetuity, is being devoured at an incredible rate. Many of the effects are irreversible. For example, the removal of key species such as cod from the once hugely productive Canadian Grand Banks, and sharks, often viciously 'finned' for soup and thrown back alive, shifts ecosystems into different but stable ecologies of inedible invertebrates and choking swarms of jellyfish. These systems don't recover once fishing collapses: they have found a new 'normal' equilibrium. In much the same way, climate change may shift global temperature regimes in non-linear fashion into steady, stifling states that would take millennia to reverse.

Our children will ask where all the fish have gone. Our answer, as Charles Clover suggests, will be 'We have eaten them'. I felt this viscerally and personally. It was my own frustration as a fisheries scientist that I could spend my entire career repeating the mantra 'If you don't stop catching all the fish, there won't be any fish', to no avail, that led me to co-found Futerra and get into communications and behaviour change.

*Whale meat for sale, Tsukiji fish market, Tokyo, Japan*

As a nation, Japan is probably eating around five times its fair share of marine species, but we are all responsible. The solution is quite simply to fish differently and eat less and different types of seafood, hence Miura's concern about the relatively recent revolution in China's appetite for marine fish and shellfish.

That afternoon, another Shinkansen Bullet train whisked me to Kyoto, where the famous Climate Change Protocol was agreed in 1997. It was essential that my slow travel mission include a brief pilgrimage to this historic city, if only to pay homage to the only binding international agreement on climate change the world has ever delivered. It's possibly the only one there'll ever be, if the dismal failure of recent summits in Copenhagen, Cancun, Durban and Doha – to name but a few - is anything to go by. The UN manages to continually resuscitate its own interminable negotiation process, whilst its members repeatedly fail to reach agreement on any strategy that might actually tackle climate change. This just reinforces my suspicions that the very real scientific urgency of our challenge will not make us change in time. What just might work is if we believe we might achieve better, the power of a positively-uplifting vision of the future, rather than living the energy-draining terror of a nightmare. A narrative that opens up possibilities and inspires creativity, opportunity and action, without condemning, constraining or blaming people into denial. That is my personal hope, my faith.

Like all good pilgrims, I sought out a spartan night of zen simplicity, staying in a traditional Japanese *ryokan* guesthouse. My *tatami*-floored room had an austere feel to it and made me understand the inspiration for modern minimalist design. It looked like the previous occupant had stolen all the bedroom furniture. Nicking hotel bathrobes is one thing, but the entire suite?

It was a completely blank room with nothing but a low table and two small cushions to sit on. I felt very alone as I sat and ate my multi-course *kaiseki* meal, which turned food presentation into an art form of intricately prepared and arranged delicacies. Dainty pickles, a tiny sweet fish accompanied by a pair of scallops and a fragile sliver of radish, soft sashimi and pungent wasabi, followed by a plate of stewed aubergines

'Torpedoes' of frozen tuna, Tsukiji fish market, Tokyo, Japan

with a cube of moist white fish, and finally another whole leaf-wrapped fish, to finish. All was beautifully presented on a range of brightly coloured ceramic dishes of various shapes and sizes. I was unsure whether to photograph it or eat it. So I did both. However, my visit to the Tsukiji market had somewhat tainted my ability to eat such seafood without more than just a little pang of guilt.

After dinner, the maid produced my futon mat bed from the hidden wardrobe with a revelatory illusionist's flourish. I lay on the floor drawing up mental plans to destroy all my obviously superfluous furniture at home, as the *tatami* space was so wonderfully relaxing: the kind of room you walk into and instantly feel an exquisite sense of calm. Once the anxiousness about who's made off with all the furniture has receded, of course. But I was also gripped by melancholy, a lonely sadness induced by the quiet contemplation of the room, the usually uplifting but unremitting effort of constant travel, and being apart from Fi. It was a rare experience of *ennui* but a significant one.

It seemed, in this contemplative moment, that the trip was simply compounding my concerns about the issues I cared most about. The carnage of Tsukiji almost broke my heart and its long love affair with the sea. Equally, the threat of mining and its impact on the people and pristine panoramas of Mongolia had depressed me, as had Russian scepticism and cynicism about climate change. Always the eternal optimist, I was finding scant succour for my usual idealism. If the world wasn't quite yet actually going to hell in a handcart, it certainly appeared to be picking up speed in roughly the right direction.

Though I had enjoyed the ritualised deference, order and respect of Japanese culture, it had also been a rather claustrophobic experience. I was looking forward to plunging back into the relative chaos of China, which probably says more about me than it does about either place. But, despite my affectionate Sinophilia, the prospect of returning to China's chronic, ubiquitous reminders of unsustainability was exhausting me just thinking about it.

In the morning, I caught the ferry from Osaka back to Shanghai. Onboard I met James, a Californian who'd been teaching English in

Thailand for the last three years. He was wearing a Thai Church of God T-shirt and an earnest expression, so it wasn't a shock to discover he was rather devout. Wary of being stuck in his company for the next two days on board, I broached the 'God' topic gently with some subtle, incisive question along the lines of *So, are you quite religious then?*

James, it turned out, was a philosophy major and actually quite sceptical about

organised churches. *I guess I'm still searching,* he said, preferring to *go to the Bible direct* for spiritual inspiration. He later revealed he'd been brought up in the Worldwide Church of God, an odd, cult-like offshoot of evangelical Christianity founded by an ex-advertising executive in the United States. So his disdain for formal institutions was perhaps understandable. Being the heathen that I am, we engaged in a lengthy debate on the nature of God and biblical prophecy. *I do question my faith,* James confessed, *and whether God exists to allow all the suffering in the world. But we have brought it upon ourselves. We have free will,* he pontificated. What about the 'accident of birth' issue I asked, where those suffering the effects of climate change for example, are usually those least responsible for it as in Mongolia? *But if they were born into the position of the oppressor, they would do the same,* he responded, betraying a rather fundamental cynicism toward human nature. *We will ultimately fail because of our self-centredness, because our hearts don't love in the right way. We may pull together when our backs are against the wall,* he observed when I suggested climate change might be a great, powerful inspiration and unifier for collective, global action, *but even if we succeed we will then fight each other once again.*

I asked James how likely it was I might also be saved after the resurrection. *It depends on whether you will join the path,* James told me. *Unity is the key.* My concern was whether my responsible intentions and actions, lazy pseudo-Christian principles such as 'do to others as I would be done by', would count in my favour even if I'd failed to actively practice the faith? James thought for a moment. *You'll burn for all eternity in the Lake of Fire,* he concluded, entirely straight-faced. He later, jokingly, referred to me as an infidel. This wasn't going too well from my perspective. Having consigned me to the eternal BBQ and seeing the somewhat-concerned look on my face, James then hastened to reassure me. *Don't get me wrong, I don't think you're rotten to the core.* Gee thanks. It was a long, slow boat journey back to China.

The ferry made its way up the Huangpu River right into the heart of Shanghai. I felt like a star-struck immigrant amid the built environmental splendour. What I could see of it, that is, the city being shrouded in the usual perpetual miasma of smog and sub-tropical steaminess. Shanghai is one of the biggest engines of the speeding Chinese economic juggernaut. The government struggles to keep this vehicle from careering off the narrow road of controlled growth; gripping the steering wheel with white knuckles, holding a straight line, eyes closed and hoping for the best.

In optimistic mood you would have to say the Communist Party of China has been responsible for the single biggest uplifting of people from poverty in history, as hundreds of millions of Chinese lives have been transformed. This is no mean feat and is easily forgotten. However, in a pessimistic frame of mind you have to ask 'but at what cost?' The awakening of the slumbering Chinese Dragon, as prophesised, has 'shaken the world' and massively stressed China's own environment and the planet's in the process. The very same uplifted middle class now want an environmental quality of life to match their material one. As media mogul Ted Turner famously said, 'It's no fun being rich in a dying world'. The Chinese are beginning to think the same way.

Fi and I were reunited not long after I docked, independently and unknowingly checking into the same hostel – great minds think alike – and then bumping into each other in the street entirely randomly on the edge of Renmin Square. She was armed with a fist-full of 'things on sticks', one of our favourite mystery street foods. My heart leapt when I saw her again.

Later that evening, we strolled beside the historic colonial architecture of the riverside Bund, opposite the futuristic, whimsical buildings of Pudong, all brash surreal space-age globes, probes and spires. It's clear in Shanghai that part of the burgeoning commercial success of the new China is based on counterfeit goods, gizmos and gimmicks. Plus a mind-numbing array of what might uncharitably be described as 'plastic crap'. All along the Bund, street vendors proffered us entirely useless products: irritating 'stones' emitting screeching electrical crackling noises when thrown into the air; glowing red devil horns, which gave the night-time waterfront a strangely Satanic feeling. James, my God-fearing friend from the ferry, would hate this, I thought. Stuffed mice on strings that scampered convincingly when tugged. And this season's 'must have': illuminated, flashing disco skates you strap to your shoes, enabling you to break your own neck in true *Saturday Night Fever* style. Given the explosion of 'enterprise' rocking modern China, it seems weird that the Chinese people's inimitable mercantile spirit could ever have been suppressed by communism. Now it was bouncing back with a vengeance.

If the quality of the goods wasn't enough to tempt you, the sales pitches of the vendors just might. What they lacked in observation skills they made up for in polite persistence. I swear you could walk down the neon-lit lunacy of one of Shanghai's major shopping streets wearing a massive imitation Rolex watch, swinging a giant fake leather Gucci bag full to bursting with pirate DVDs and still be constantly asked: *Watch? Bag? DVD?* The bustling hordes of people hustled along to a soundtrack of distinctly odd tunes emanating from the shops piled high with fake designer goods. At one point the Benny Hill Show theme tune rang out, cutting through the background of incessant chatter and mobile ring-tones, which seemed to favour electronic versions of Christmas carols and (my personal favourite) an appropriate cultural choice, 'Chopsticks'.

As always, the more interesting life was on the back streets, where people wandered in their pyjamas, played cards or mahjong on small wooden tables, smoking, hawking and spitting. Where cluttered stalls sold pancakes, dumplings and noodles hot and fresh from the pot, wok or hotplate, releasing a tantalizing suite of bewitching aromas. Where vendors sold small, woven wicker baskets containing live crickets for singing or fighting competitions. Where pet shops might also be grocers – the fate of a small piebald piglet and aquaria full of fish by no means certain

*Temple of the 10,000 Buddhas, Hong Kong*

and possibly more attuned to customers' stomachs than their hearts. But sadly these traditional streets were in retreat, pushed back a few more blocks from the centre than on my previous visit a couple of years earlier, and likely to be shoved further in the future as the redevelopment bulldozer rumbled on.

Leaving Shanghai didn't mean we entirely escaped its pervasive entrepreneurial influence. Even the train guards were in on the act. One appeared with a basket of 'indestructo' socks, delivering a highly-polished sales pitch. With a real 'I'm robbing myself here Guv'nor' tone he gave a lively practical demonstration of the socks' rugged resilience. He raked the hideous, shiny synthetic material with a wire brush, ran a lighter flame over it, then held the ends of one sock and swung his whole body-weight on it from the luggage rack above. All were crucial factors to be considered in any sock-purchasing decision. The socks just screamed 'sweaty foot hell' even if they would last forever, which they probably will, only to be unearthed by future archaeologists who'll marvel at the durability of early-21st-century Chinese foot insulation technology.

This all felt like *déjà vu*. A similar, equally improbable scene had played out in my hotel room in Beijing in 2000. I'd answered a knock at the door one evening to be confronted by two attractive young girls. *Hello, we are selling socks!* they chorused. Given the reputation at that time for unsolicited hotel room visits to Westerners from attentive Chinese women, I thought I'd misheard. *I'm sorry?* I blabbed. *Socks!* they repeated, smiling winningly and proceeding to give me the now familiar indestructo-sock demonstration.

If anything, the entrepreneurialism intensified in Hong Kong. There is no skyline quite like it anywhere on earth. A multitude of skyscrapers jammed onto a thin coastal strip, fertile green mountains above and ferries plying the harbour below. At night, it transforms into a neon- and laser-lit fantasy land, as a million twinkling lights illuminate the city. We enjoyed a few days reconnecting with friends and family, but Hong Kong is not a good place for the psyche of the slow traveller, relentless as the pace of life is there – the three-minute bowl of noodles, the tailored suit stitched overnight and the 24/7 shop-till-you-drop mentality. Materialism is shoved down your throat at every opportunity in ever-more creative ways. We even saw one shopping centre designed to look exactly like a cruise ship rammed between the surrounding buildings by a careless captain.

This was precisely what we were trying to escape from on the trip. But whereas the ubiquitous advertising in China had been mainly impenetrable to us, as it was in Mandarin, in partly-anglicised Hong Kong we were re-subjected to its ministrations. The insidious, subliminal absorption of commercial messaging that seeds insecurity and sows temptation, that nurtures wants into needs and causes nascent consumers to bloom under its anything-but-benign and benevolent beams was back in our lives. As it beat down on us, it became unbearable, the return of a sort of mental 'white noise', as suddenly the hundreds of corporate messages we're typically exposed to in normal London life returned. Our ebbing appetite for consumption was involuntarily stirred. After months of freedom, Hong Kong had jolted us back into the reality of the 21st century, not just through its architecture and frenetic nature, but in the way its moneymaking soul penetrated your psyche in sinister and underhand ways.

As if to ram this point home, back in mainland China we'd got stranded in Guangzhou, a city that does the most convincing impression of the opening sequence of the film *Bladerunner* I've ever seen, as we were lashed by drenching downpours of torrential rain. The municipal authorities appeared to have adopted a philosophy of 'more is more' on neon lighting, as buildings flash, glow, ripple or screen adverts on enormous LED panels. Even the boats and ferries that cruise the grey waters of the Pearl River are illuminated to a multi-coloured extent that is gaudy even by Chinese standards. They also have a love affair with complex road flyovers – the higher, more convoluted, more complicated to navigate, and the more ᵗ tenth-storey apartment windows you can look into from a passing bus, the better.

Beneath the tagliatelle-like ribbons of roads and pulsating neon towers old Guangzhou lives on. We revisited familiar haunts such as the legendary Qingping market with its diverse culinary delights. To the western eye, it's like a sort of unlikely cross between a zoo and a restaurant. This was the first market in China to be deregulated by Deng Xiaoping as part of his capitalist experimentation in the late 1970s. As the saying goes, the Cantonese 'eat everything with legs except the table, and everything with wings except an aeroplane'. This doesn't rule out much, and most of it is on display: dogs, cats, turtles, scorpions and various body parts, tendons and sinews, fresh and dried, from a bewildering variety of unidentifiable beasts and birds. Another Chinese joke is that the first question a Cantonese asks himself on seeing a new species is 'Steam or fry?' We sidestepped the opportunity for a domestic animal-based dinner. Instead we prowled the damp, durian-scented streets and found an Uyghur restaurant where we devoured chargrilled lamb skewers, hot flat breads and pak choi in sesame oil. It was a reminder of China's easily forgotten ethnic diversity as we munched along to an Arabic pop music TV channel.

We'd been stuck in Guangzhou as we'd been unable to buy train tickets onwards to Nanning. Queuing repeatedly in the melée that typifies Chinese railway station ticket offices, I'd handed over my carefully-written ticket request in my best Chinese characters, only to be inexplicably declined each time. Finally, after a combination of luck and sheer dogged persistence we managed to secure hard sleeper seats out of town. After three sweaty days in the humidity of the Pearl River Delta, we were on the move again, putting the world's most populous nation behind us and heading towards Pingxiang on the Vietnamese border and the popular backpacker circuit of South-East Asia.

# LIGHT AND DARKNESS

*If an ass goes travelling, he'll not come home*
*a horse.*

— Thomas Fuller —

Borders are propaganda opportunities; the Chinese border with Vietnam at Pinxiang was no exception. We'd first noticed this phenomenon back in March, crossing the Guadiana River from Portugal into Spain. In Vila Real de Santo António, a hot, dry and dusty border town on the Portuguese side, we'd walked through the seedy streets of a run-down industrial estate, walls crumbling, road surface pocked and pitted like some spotty adolescent's face. Rheumy-eyed dogs stared at us from the shade, giving the impression that they'd happily have given us a good savaging if it wasn't quite so unforgivingly hot. A small car ferry had then taken us

*Ngoc Son Temple, Hoan Kiem Lake, Hanoi, Vietnam*

to Ayamonte, where it seemed the Spaniards were deliberately trying to make a comparative point between the two countries, as Ayamonte was as pleasant, clean and well laid out as Vila Real was dilapidated, dirty and fragmented.

The Sino-Vietnamese Freedom Pass was very similar, a point made starker by the fact that relations between the two countries had been frosty, if that's possible in such sutropical climes, since China invaded Vietnam in 1979. A brief but bloody month-long war had followed, in which each side suffered 10,000 or so casualties and both claimed victory. Tensions had remained high, with the occasional skirmish occurring, until a new border pact was signed in 1999. The Freedom Pass was all immaculate order and brisk Chinese efficiency on the Sino side. Neat marble stone steps patrolled by the People's Liberation Army descended from China into the rolling jungle that straddled the divide between the two countries. It was a little different on the Vietnamese side. In a battered red-brick building we jostled with several Chinese tour groups at the border guards' counter. There, you had to stuff your passport through the crush onto a chaotic pile the other side of the glass. Three uninterested staff then made their way erratically through the heap, clearly mortified by the prospect of employing any kind of logical system by which to do this. It was a blunt reminder of the often showy, rigid autocratic bureaucracy of China compared with the slightly more carefree nature of its far more informal and laid-back neighbour.

Twon, a smooth-talking Vietnamese guy whose impressively taloned fingers looked as if he'd just stepped out of a south London nail salon, sidled up to offer assistance. Long finger nails denote wealth and status in many Asian cultures, implying that the owner does not have to resort to manual labour to earn a living. Clicking his claws together, Twon escorted us in a taxi to Lan Song to catch a 'very nice bus', as he persuaded us of the wisdom of our decision not to take the train. *Train takes seven hours, very hot and busy, bus takes three, own seat, air-con and straight to Old Quarter in Hanoi,* he oozed. *And good music?* I enquired sarcastically, recalling our overnight bus ride through the Baltic States. *Of course! Good sound system!* he replied. It wasn't the speakers I was worried about.

Half an hour later, we all sat cheek-to-moist-cheek as we'd filled the bus with more bums than seats. Ben, a big, hairy, wise-cracking and witty Kiwi guy we'd met on the train from China was now perching with one buttock on and one buttock off the end of his now-overcrowded bench. *I want half my money back*, he grumbled good-naturedly, recalling Twon's earlier sales pitch promising an altogether more favourable gluteus-seat ratio. We drove to Hanoi in what we were now becoming familiar with as the favoured style of bus drivers the world over, to a backing track of shrill Asian power-pop. Travelling three vehicles abreast regardless of oncoming traffic, our driver executed reckless overtaking manoeuvres and last-second swerves to avoid melding the bus with the front of approaching trucks. We attempted to distract ourselves by admiring the passing scenery of steep, humpy limestone karsts. It was as if the earth had risen and blistered like some over-baked loaf, with glimpses of coarse rock and dark cave mouths visible through the broken skin of verdant greenery that enveloped anything that didn't move.

Things didn't exactly calm down when we hit Hanoi. Thankfully we hadn't hit anything else on the way, one apparently suicidal motorcyclist spared only by an impressively instinctive jab on the brakes by our driver. Due to the vast import taxes on cars in Vietnam, everyone has a motorbike. There are only 1.2 million cars in a country with a population of 85 million, or one for every seventy people, compared with the United Kingdom where it's one between two. The motorbike is thus truly the 'people's choice', probably because they have little option. Seventeen million of them zip around the country. Hanoi's six-and-a-half million people alone own three million 'wasp in a matchbox' machines, which surge relentlessly down the city's arterial routes in buzzing hordes and clouds of emissions. Parking is therefore at a premium, and at night the dark, narrow pavements are crowded with neat rows of tightly-packed bikes like brightly-coloured beetles.

As a consequence, crossing the street can be a hair-raising challenge, the liquid frenzy of coursing motorbikes creating an impenetrable stream of demented traffic. The only solution is to take a deep breath and walk slowly but steadily out into the middle of the two-stroke throng, making

*Junk dragon figurehead, Ha Long Bay, Vietnam*

*Junks moored up in Ha Long Bay, Vietnam*

no sudden moves or manoeuvres. This allows the speeding riders to navigate and swerve around you as you progress rather vulnerably amidst the seething flow. The effect is not dissimilar to Moses parting the Red Sea, although the Green Cross Code Man would probably be pretty unimpressed.

Hanoi's Old Quarter consists of tight streets arrayed beneath a cool canopy of trees that cast a welcome shade over the bustling pavements. These serve less as pedestrian thoroughfares, more as extensions to the shop-fronts of the joyfully-chaotic commerce that lines the roads. Vendors hawk paper kites and curios, crockery, wicker-ware and fresh produce from baskets stacked high with the palate-tingling mainstays of Vietnamese cuisine: onions, shallots, garlic, ginger, limes and chillies. A multitude of *pho* stalls dispense fragrantly-steaming bowls of hot noodles. Hungry customers slurp away, perched on the diminutive plastic chairs that simply exacerbate one's sense of being a fat, ungainly foreigner squatting with your knees next to your ears. Somehow, amongst this unruly congestion, conical-hatted women weave elegantly along, bearing yoked baskets of carefully arranged fruit and vegetables, treading a treacherous line between the crowded pavements and the motorcycle tempest beyond.

Sweating profusely in the sticky heat, we ate our first zingy Vietnamese meal on Cam Chi street, tucking into crispy fried tofu with chilli-laced fish sauce, garlicky spring rolls, salty crab vermicelli, mustard greens and peppered pork. Our taste buds exploded with the simple but potent flavours. We washed it all down and cooled off with cheap, icy *bia hoi*, fresh beer, the light, refreshing low-alcohol brew of choice in Vietnam, served in plastic flagons.

After dinner, we pottered in disorientated fashion through the by-now dark and empty streets, dramatically transformed from the commercial thrum of the day into a locked-down, shuttered world. The overhanging trees that had offered sanctuary from the sunshine now created a gloomy tunnel through the warm, quiet night air that was rich with the sickly-sweet smell of gently-composting rubbish. We strolled merrily back to the hotel, accompanied only by fat cockroaches scuttling audibly along the dirty pavements and the odd moped rider hissing *Marijuana?* at us in furtive tones.

Our arrival in Hanoi heralded a moment of mourning. We finally realised that Fi's 'pursuit of a politically preserved leader' was doomed to fail. We'd set off determined to glimpse at least one embalmed communist: Lenin's cadaver in Moscow, Mao's effigy in Beijing or Ho Chi Minh's lying in state in Hanoi. Alas, it was not to be. Long queues did for Vladimir Ilyitch in Red Square, Mao had been removed for a spot of cosmetic refurbishment in time for the 2008 Olympics, and Ho Chi Minh's mausoleum was inconveniently closed on our free day in Hanoi. It's hard to revere the remains of a former revolutionary these days.

One thing you quickly appreciate as a traveller in Vietnam is the deft way you're fielded onto a formal, organised tour. If you want to make a bus journey, it's a tourist bus you're pushed towards and independent travel be damned. Seizing the potential market with entrepreneurial glee, every Vietnamese seems to have a relative or buddy in the travel business, so enquiries into any destination usually lead to a recommendation for a particular tour company in the hope of some kind of kickback or benefit in kind. There's absolutely nothing wrong with this – the business acumen is admirable; it just makes it much more difficult to find out about public transport as folk are understandably reluctant to divulge information when there's a dollar or two to be made. We later coined a new word to describe the sort of packaged trips that proliferate as a result of this: 'tourpid' (from 'torpid': deprived of the power of motion or feeling; benumbed, lethargic, apathetic) meaning the loss of sensory feeling and independent motion you experience when part of a lobster-red tourist flock, digital cameras glued to faces, being herded by guides like panting sheepdogs from one photo opportunity to the next.

As an antidote to the tourpidity of many excursions, we invariably tried to do things a little more under own steam. From Cat Ba island, we hired kayaks and paddled out amongst the cluttered clusters of island peaks. *Stay close, very easy to get lost here,* our local guide Bang warned. We got a completely different perspective on the towering karst islets from sea level as Bang led us, limbo-style, under a low tunnel into an isolated,

'T' and a fine array of fresh produce for a cooking lesson, Hoi An, Vietnam

idyllic lagoon of limpid green waters. This untouched haven inside an effectively hollow island was surrounded by steep, roughly hewn walls – the peace broken only by the raucous drilling of cicadas, like a million manic, miniature carpenters.

Further south we hired bicycles for a 45-mile cycle ride from the hills of Dalat down to Mui Ne on the coast. A massive adrenaline rush, it was essentially a headlong plunge downhill along a road narrowed by wild vegetation into a green tunnel of fronds and foliage. We tore round blind corners as the gravity of the gradient persistently converted our potential energy into thrilling kinetic speed. Our fingers ached on the brakes and dry bamboo crunched under our wheels as we struggled to stay on the road. The soundtrack was the whoosh of wind through our helmets, whirr of tyres on tarmac, whip of long grasses as we sped by and, again, the constant background buzz of insects. When the road eventually levelled out we still had another 20 miles to travel, albeit on the flat. The pleasure of the descent swiftly evaporated as we ground our way wearily along the soft, fresh, black tarmac of a newly-laid road surface in the intense mid-afternoon heat.

As we passed through villages, every front yard seemed to disgorge a gaggle of kids screaming *Helloooooooo!* at the top of their tiny lungs, our *Sin Jao* reply collapsing them into fits of delighted giggling. The noise would alert the next house, and we'd glimpse little legs hurtling through the garden undergrowth towards the road to ensure their greeting was delivered to our faces not our retreating backsides. We scarcely had both hands on the handlebars for the last few miles as we were waving almost constantly. It meant we arrived in Mui Ne exhausted, puce in the face but exhilarated, with daft, broad grins on our faces.

It was trips like these that took us a little more off that cliché of 'the beaten track'. A debate has long raged that attempts to differentiate between the idea of travel and the practice of tourism. It continues to simmer in the backpacker hostels of Asia. There are smug and often snobbish semantics around the idea of 'tourists' versus 'travellers', though crudely speaking perhaps the most obvious distinction in the Taoist context might be one seeks 'destinations' the other 'journeys', one experiences 'transit' the other 'travel'. Suffice to say the endless hostel conversations that mentioned 'doing a country', as in 'Yeah, we did Laos' were a tad tedious. What does that even mean? Kissinger arguably 'did Laos' when he authorised secretly dropping three million tonnes of ordinance on it during the Vietnam war, but claiming to have 'done' a country after three weeks of hostel-hopping seems a bit rich, if lower impact.

By far the most irritating refrain was that of authenticity, the desperate attempts to see the 'real' Vietnam. Was everything else by implication therefore faked? As if in some selfish sense, the country can only be conjured up in one's comprehension via a deeply credible immersion in alternative, untouched travel adventures. This hunger for a more genuine experience is perhaps a reaction to the increasingly well-trodden tourist trail that winds down through the country. But it ignores the irony that the supposedly 'unreal' tourpidity is actually triggered by the recent dramatic influx of tourists (seven million in 2012, up by 50 percent in only two years, though still lagging well behind Thailand's 22 million). The tours are there because you are, not the other way round.

In Dalat we took a spin with the self-styled Easy Riders Motorcycle Club, a group of veteran guides on equally venerable machines. Each rider proudly bore a book of testimonials from satisfied tourists, full of hyperbolic ramblings by excitable backpackers repeatedly emphasising that this was the best way to see, you guessed it, the 'real' Vietnam. To escape the crowds, people wanted something different, and the Easy Riders offered a more personal touch. Precisely how bespoke was questionable, however, when they recited their range of pre-packaged offers. We went for the unselfconsciously-titled 'off the beaten track' option and joined a small convoy of other tourists and Easy Riders on what was blatantly a rather well-established circuit.

*They call me 'Little Man',* our grinning Easy Rider guide, Titti, informed us, *because I am small,* as if his vertically-challenged stature wasn't explanation enough. We rode recklessly helmetless through the coffee-covered mountain slopes, before getting caught behind a herd of ponderous cattle contentedly oblivious to the traffic obstruction they were causing. Whilst in India holy cows are the lords of the road, in

Vietnam they are more likely to be stir-fried than deified. They're not the only beasts on the menu though. Titti showed us the distillation vessel at a local rice wine maker, a massive metal drum heated hazardously by a naked fire of burning logs wedged beneath. We stood, fearing imminent explosion of inflammable spirit alcohol on one side, as three hot, grumpy, fire-baked dogs growled menacingly at us from the other. *People like to drink this when eating dog,* Titti explained, holding up a flagon of the potent liquor. I looked down knowingly at the hostile canines unaware of their fate. *Sounds delicious,* I murmured. The solid remains from the distillation process were, Titti continued with lip-smacking relish, *fed to the pig, pig gets drunk, sleeps, gets fat and when he wakes he is hungry again.*

As we rode, Titti told us how the agricultural boom had boosted the local economy. Dalat's fertile soils and temperate climate nurture bumper harvests of potatoes, carrots, cabbage and broccoli, though these were increasingly being displaced by cash crops of coffee and cut flowers. Driven by the need to earn foreign currency, aided by Dutch horticultural expertise, and visible in the proliferation of polytunnels and netted floral plantations, Dalat's economic success was something that Titti was both proud and wary of at the same time. Two dollars *for a bag of coffee is very good money... but we can't live on coffee,* he cautioned, concerned at the rate of land conversion away from traditional crops. *People here grow, work, live and sleep on coffee. 50 percent of people in Dalat work in agriculture, 30 percent for the Government and the rest live on fresh air and tourists,* he added with a wink. It was this sense of wry humour that often made quasi-tourpid excursions in Vietnam brilliant. The master of this art was Hai.

*My full name is Pham Van Hai, so my given name is Hai. This driver is Son, very good driver, and our mechanic Pung. In Vietnam it is very important to have a mechanic on the bus. Let's hope today he has nothing to do.* So we met Hai, our guide to the Cu Chi tunnels, the extensive underground complex that enabled the Viet Cong to keep a major base within striking distance of American-held Saigon during what the Vietnamese quite reasonably call 'The American War'. Resembling a

*Bac Ha market, Vietnam*

Vietnamese Ronnie Corbett, Hai had almost-perfect comedic timing. As we left Ho Chi Minh City he pointed out landmarks on the way. *To your right is the zoo. At night-time is very dark. Is good for flirting. Young people find dark place to be romantic. They do some sentimental talking. Sometimes the hands go somewhere.*

At the tunnels themselves we sat through a crackly black-and-white Viet Cong propaganda film about the heroes of Cu Chi that described American attacks in the area as by 'crazy, mad devils' for their indiscriminate bombing of schools, villages, hospitals and temples. Hai then leapt up and, grabbing a wooden pointer longer than he was tall, went into lecture mode. Using a diorama model cross-section of the subterranean complex he indicated narrower 'pinch points' in the tunnels that were usually only 30 inches high and 20 inches wide. *Viet Cong guerrillas not enough rice to eat so very skinny; American and Australian soldiers much fatter so get stuck.* The horrors of even attempting to fight in these tiny, claustrophobic passages weren't worth contemplating.

There were some waxwork arrangements in the jungle above the tunnels depicting scenes of guerrilla life, a woman combing her long hair, one man cleaning a rifle another writing a 'love letter' claimed Hai. *Sixteen thousand guerrillas in tunnels and only 100 women, so sometimes there is flirting and some women is not virgin. You know virgin? It is woman without husband who does not know how big the banana is.* Another scene showed a covert rice-wine making operation. Hai picked up a large plastic flask and warned us of the perils involved in a serious drinking session. *Very cheap, one bottle and you are drunk the whole day. Some drink wine and forget own name. Some write poem. Some karaoke. Some get too hot, take off clothes and walk around.*

A further installation was of brutal man-traps, involving vicious metal spikes designed to ensnare unwary GIs. It included the sardonically-nicknamed 'souvenir trap'. This consisted of a metal cage buried in a pit, with inward facing hooks that allow a foot to enter, but not to be removed. So called, as your only option is to dig it up and take it home with you.

As we walked through the jungle, we could hear raucous gunfire from the shooting range. An integral part of the Cu Chi experience is now the opportunity to fire off a few rounds from a menu of high calibre semi-automatic weapons. For $1.30 a bullet you can shoot an M16 into an elevated bank of earth-filled oil drums. There was no shortage of business as eager backpackers queued up to buy their live ammunition for the latest 'must-have' adrenaline experience on the merry-go-round, alongside bungy-jumping and white-water rafting. I found the desire to fire weapons specifically designed to kill people, especially in the context of Cu Chi, a little odd. I asked one guy why he'd been so keen to spend $40 for a few mere seconds of 'entertainment'. He was somewhat defensive: *I've never done it before, it's something new, you can't do it back home, I wanted to see what it was like. It's just boys and their toys isn't it?*

Maybe my personal experiences as a long-term Brixton resident familiar with gun crime and the glorification of firearms sways my opinion, but I found the apparent acceptability of middle-class backpackers spraying machine guns 'for a bit of fun' jarring uncomfortably with the vilification of south London street kids for similar aspirations. The sheepish responses from those I gently pressed a little further reinforced the notion of their actions as very much a 'guilty pleasure' and not something to be entirely proud of.

On the bus back to Ho Chi Minh City, Hai was angling for a tip in his own peerless fashion. *You buy bus ticket with my company, price is very cheap and service is almost OK. You pay more you get same trip, same bus, same propaganda film, but you get young tour guide, a little bit handsome. Not like me. I am a little bit ugly, but you get what you pay for.* We gave him a handsome tip.

If Hanoi had been hectic, then Ho Chi Minh City was manic. To escape the swarming streets, we sought comfort in a cold beer as the brooding sky threatened to unload a downpour of truly torrential proportions. A mobile food stall passed, a wheeled steel cabinet behind a bicycle, bearing strings of wrinkled dried squid that hung like laundry from a vertical display rack. We watched rapt as the Vietnamese guys we'd been talking to at the next table ordered a couple. The vendor grilled the squid over a burner in the top of the trailer then passed the hot, dry flesh through a mangle attached to the side before serving the crisped-up fish in a cardboard tray with chilli sauce. We couldn't resist. *Smells like cat food*, Fi said, but it tasted sensational, warm, chewy, salty and spicy. Hot mangled squid – our new favourite street food.

Most of the small, family-run hotels we'd stayed at across Vietnam shutter up their front doors ridiculously early, sometimes as prematurely as 10pm, forcing you to wake up the dozing night porter to get in. That night in Ho Chi Minh City, the heavens had followed through on their promise of a spectacular deluge and the word 'torrential' would be an understatement. Having arrived rather hastily and a little harassed, I hadn't really taken note of the name of our hotel, as we'd popped into a few along the same strip to check prices. Foolish, I know. Which is how, after Fi had returned to our hotel earlier and I'd gone to check email at a nearby internet café, I came to be standing soaked to the skin in a thunderous rainstorm outside a series of identically-shuttered and bolted hotel frontages.

*Hello, looking for lady?* lisped one or two decidedly damp and androgynous 'women' who'd pulled up on a motorbike. *No thanks,* I replied, unsure whether they would actually have been able to technically deliver on their offer even if I had been interested. Penniless and dripping wet, in the end I was forced to bang on the shutters one at a time, waking all the night porters to open up until I found a lobby I recognised. One rudely-awoken and understandably irate shopkeeper, a mouthful of justified abuse in Vietnamese and two drowsy night porters later, I made it in. *Where've you been?* asked Fi worriedly, *Don't ask,* I replied moistly.

The following day we visited the War Remnants Museum, which documents the American War from the Vietnamese perspective. It left us in a mix of anger and disgust. We're all familiar with Hollywood's treatment of the conflict, from *Apocalypse Now*, through *Platoon*, to *Full Metal Jacket*, scarcely a glorification of such a grinding, pitiless conflagration. The political torment of Vietnam's north-south schism was, of course, underplayed, and there was a slight propaganda-ish air about the overall exhibition.

But really the images spoke for themselves. American GI's floundering hopelessly in muddy jungle, pulverised into a quagmire by their own side's carpet-bombing. The young soldier with 'War is Hell' written across the front of his helmet. Skies filled with helicopters like swarming flies. The instantly-recognisable imagery from the self-immolating monk,

the Mai Lai massacre, the napalm attack aftermath with Kim Phuc naked and burnt running in agony towards the camera, the summary execution of Nguyen Van Lem. These were the lasting visual memories of the carnage and cruelty of the first 'media' war. For those of us brought up on video-game conflicts in the Gulf, featuring live nose-cone footage of supposedly-cool, clinical, disconnected 'smart' bombs flying down the chimneys of their targets, or remote drone warfare in Afghanistan, it is hard to appreciate the simple power of such imagery that fuelled anger and protest against the war in Vietnam around the world. The exhibition was also a tribute to the hundreds of journalists killed bravely bringing the story to people's attention, in an era before the military demanded they be 'embedded' amongst the troops, effectively suffocating true objectivity.

The war spanned the transition from black-and-white still photography to the full-colour movie newsreel, bringing the brutality of battle vividly into people's consciousness. The museum continued this idea of uncomfortable enlightenment by tracking the impacts and legacy of the systematic environmental degradation brought about by the American war plan. Frustrated by the wily elusiveness of an enemy fighting a brilliant guerrilla strategy, the US military effectively attacked the ecology of Vietnam. They sprayed a toxic cocktail of over 15 million gallons of herbicides and defoliants indiscriminately onto the countryside and its inhabitants in Operation Ranch Hand. This despicable tactic of destroying forest cover forced the depopulation of rural Vietnam. This pushed millions of innocent civilians into cities, decimating forests and biodiversity, and leaving a horrific legacy of poison for the land and its people.

Of these chemicals, Agent Orange is the most notorious. The museum documented the direct death toll of around 400,000 killed or maimed, and the insidious aftermath of cancers, hideous birth defects and other debilitating conditions that affected half a million more. Pictures of victims with malformed limbs, evidence of mental retardation and grotesque, almost abominable, disfigurements were living reminders that the hangover of a war that claimed the lives of over 50,000 US troops and three million Vietnamese still continues. On several occasions we encountered first-hand people bearing the scars of landmines, missing or mutilated hands and feet. There was one lad begging on a ferry across the Mekong who, instead of arms, had simply one solitary misshapen finger protruding from each armpit.

In a bitter twist of fate, the Commander of US Naval Forces in Vietnam, Admiral Elmo Zumwalt, who had himself ordered the use of Agent Orange, later lost his son, who fought in defoliated territory, to a rare form of cancer at the age of 42. His grandson was also born with congenital sensory dysfunction. Before he died Elmo Zumwalt Junior said *I am a lawyer and I don't think I could prove in court, by the weight of the existing scientific evidence, that Agent Orange is the cause of all the medical problems – nervous disorders, cancer and skin problems – reported by Vietnam veterans, or of their children's severe birth defects. But I am convinced that it is.* Some paltry compensation was eventually paid to exposed GIs by the manufacturers of Agent Orange, the environmentalists' old friends Dow Chemical Company and Monsanto, after the case was controversially settled out of court in the mid-1980s. A totally disabled veteran could expect $12,000 dollars in total, paid over ten years. Vietnamese claimants have received nothing. In the context of this first 'war on an environment' and its chilling, long term repercussions it was sobering to note that now in the so called War on Terror the US and its allies have decided to prosecute a campaign against not a nation, a people or even anything physical like the landscape, as it had done as a cruel proxy in Vietnam, but against an intangible idea.-

For me, the real testament to the courageous resilience of the Vietnamese people we met was their incredible ability to both forgive and look forward to the future, even whilst the trauma of the war lingers on. The Vietnam of today is an evolving triumph wrestled from adversity, a resurgent nation relatively uncowed and unbowed by the horrors it has experienced – a country able to acknowledge its violent recent past, but not be paralysed by it. I wondered how it must have felt to grow up in the aftermath of the war, amidst the devastation of physical landscape and infrastructure, the political divisions and schisms, the emotional heartache and grief. What reserves of energy, determination and positivity must they have had to summon up in order to rebuild the country, reconnect their relationships, mourn their losses, forgive their aggressors and focus once again on the elusive promise of a better tomorrow? It must have taken amazing vision, commitment and masses of serious hard graft. Just imagining these challenges was truly humbling. That the Vietnamese have somehow emerged smiling is almost miraculous.

The mindset and tenacious attitude of the people through this nightmare was therefore massively inspiring, perhaps an historical echo of what Brits refer to as 'the Blitz spirit'. If we are to overcome our struggle with global environmental phenomena such as climate change, and get through what my old friend Paul Gilding, a former head of Greenpeace International, calls The Great Disruption to a more sustainable, harmonious way of living and being, then we will need every ounce of this cohesive, collective and creative energy that we can muster.

In Graham Greene's novel *The Quiet American*, set during the 1950s war, this time with the Vietnamese battling the French in what was then Indochina, the central character Thomas Fowler is a world-weary British war journalist. 'They say you come to Vietnam and understand a lot in a few minutes. The rest has got to be lived. They say whatever it is you were looking for, you will find here', he reflects. I had found a *joie de vivre* in the face of hardship that made me grateful and appreciative of a solid, sometimes stolid life back home, but it also made me not a little envious of and excited by the raw energy of this amazing country. As Greene, through Fowler, himself described it: 'The smell; that's the first thing that hits you, promising everything in exchange for your soul. And the heat. Your shirt is straightaway a rag. You can hardly remember your name, or what you came to escape from.' After the incredible intensity of China, Vietnam had felt more open, less crowded, cleaner and more fertile, the people charming and full of laughter. Despite the occasional moments of tourpidity and the shock at the full horror of the war, the overall effect was incredibly uplifting and left me brimming with fond memories.

On our final evening in Vietnam we ensconced ourselves in a local *bia hoi* bar, where plastic jugs of refreshingly cheap cold beer were dispensed from a huge silver tank that took up half the shop. Next to us sat the appropriately named Mr Lung who, despite his slim stature, was sucking back beer by the litre and chain-smoking the local Bastos cigarettes (13p a pack). *I love foreigners!* announced Mr Lung loudly, shaking my hand firmly and grinning broadly to reveal an asymmetrical array of blackened, nicotine-stained teeth. *Vietnam! America! England! Number one!* added Mr Lung warming to his theme. He was a cyclo rider, a sort of Vietnamese rickshaw rider, which explained his wiry frame, kept lean by the effort of propelling hefty tourists around town. *I love Mr Bush, Tony Blair!* he continued rather more surprisingly, apparently thankful to them for helping to open up international support for and investment in Vietnam.

Over dinner we met Steve, a dour Scouser working as an English teacher who used to drive buses on one of our Brixton routes back home. *I was stoned on skunk the whole time I drove the bus,* he blithely informed us. *I had ten accidents in three years and was totally paranoid because I could have been busted at any moment.* He'd previously taught in Cambodia, *full of paedophiles and child molesters,* and had a distinct air of melancholy about him. The latest UK census revealed a 'missing cohort' of 600,000 young men, and Steve was clearly one of them. In the exciting, exotic context of Ho Chi Minh City on a Saturday night he was out for a curry by himself. I asked him how his Vietnamese was. *I didn't bother learning any as I knew I'd only be here eight or nine months or so,* came the reply. *I'm off to South America next, Chile I think,* he said. I wondered whether he'd find whatever it was he seemed to be looking for there. I doubted it. He appeared to be searching for something elusive in his own head that no change of scene would provide the answer to. Civil rights campaigner and author of *Strange Fruit*, the classic novel of the American Deep South, Lillian Smith suggests that 'no journey carries one far unless, as it extends into the world around us, it goes an equal distance into the world within'. Sometimes the journey is internal, and no amount of travel mileage or changes of scene will get you to your destination.

This is a point eloquently reaffirmed by Andrew X Pham in *Catfish and Mandala*, a beautiful travelogue that I had been devouring hungrily: a gripping and at times gruelling account of his experiences as a Vietnamese-American cycling through the country he'd left as a ten-year-old. His family, like hundreds of thousands of others, had taken to the sea as 'boat people' to flee the post-war Communist regime's 're-education' camps and the combat-ravaged landscape. It was a touching meditation on his cultural roots and origins, a personal search for meaning and context, and above all a deeply moving account of how the war affected one man and his extended family. In my own head and heart an important realisation was gently emerging of courage, tenacity and positivity. Pham's words would continue to resonate with me throughout the remainder of the trip: 'When it's all over, you'll realise that the answer is already within you.'

# SPECTRES AND SMILES

*Real adventure – self-determined, self-motivated, often risky
– forces you to have firsthand encounters with the world. The
world the way it is, not the way you imagine it. Your body will
collide with the earth and you will bear witness. In this way
you will be compelled to grapple with the limitless kindness and
bottomless cruelty of humankind – and perhaps realize that you
yourself are capable of both. This will change you. Nothing will
ever again be black-and-white.*

— Mark Jenkins —

When Jello Biafra of the Dead Kennedys wrote 'Holiday in Cambodia' it was intended as black humour, a joke on smug, white middle-American youth. Riven by civil war and a despotic regime, Cambodia was not exactly a prime leisure destination. Given the brutalisation of the country and its people in relatively recent history, it is unsurprising the country still carries a slightly troubled air, in stark contrast to the positive buoyancy of the Vietnamese, who somehow managed to draw a line under their own horrific experiences and to look resolutely to the future. The atrocities are not unconnected: the spill-over of the Vietnam War into Cambodia helped propel the Khmer Rouge to power in 1975, 'Year Zero'. Vietnam's subsequent invasion and occupation of Cambodia left the country isolated and impoverished. Unlike South Africa, where the harrowing but therapeutic Truth and Reconciliation Commission helped the nation to recover from past traumas, Cambodia has been denied the opportunity to heal the wounds of the past. Indeed, the deep physical and psychological lesions are arguably kept open and raw by the stalled legal proceedings against the perpetrators of the genocide.

The architects of the Year Zero programme largely escaped justice. The surviving members remain unpunished. Their warped plan to return Cambodia to an agrarian communist state relied on normalising extreme torture, casual violence and mass executions to bend the people to their will;an institutionalisation of terror that is all the more horrifying considering its almost medieval barbarity took place within living memory. The key sites of this system that remain and are preserved for visitors now offer a moving but terrifying and macabre insight into the darkness of the human soul. Most heart-rending and troubling are the atrocities seemingly ordinary people have apparently been able to perpetrate under the right – or rather very, very wrong – conditions.

S-21 (or *Tuol Sleng* - 'hill of the poisonous trees') was the central torture and interrogation centre for the Khmer Rouge in Phnom Penh. The carnage inflicted within its half square mile of grounds is made all the more awful by the site's former function as a school, going from the nurturing of one generation to the persecution and destruction of another. The basic concrete structures were eerily reminiscent of the

*Cell in 'S-21' detention centre, Phnom Penh, Cambodia*

school I'd taught at in Jamaica 17 years previously. I was mentally and emotionally racked by the competition of those happy memories with the grim evidence before me in such strangely familiar surroundings.

Classrooms became 'interview' rooms. They are now seen as they were when the Khmer Rouge regime finally collapsed. In each room, an iron bed frame with leg shackles stands in the centre of the otherwise-bare space. Instruments of torture, often as crude as a simple metal bar, lie casually on the floor. The terrible simplicity of the equipment is compounded by the massive image of the room's last victim on the wall, taken when S-21 was 'liberated'. Contorted, agonised bodies beaten to a bloody pulp lie twisted on the beds, their posture and pulverised features screaming of the contemptible violence and pain they endured.

Other rooms hold large display boards covered with black-and-white photos of the 12,000 or more prisoners 'processed' through the centre. Some held expressions of determination, proud and unbowed, others looked shocked, or tearfully fearful, a few smiled cockily, possibly unaware of their likely treatment or simply staunch in their defiance. The cumulative effect was extremely powerful and as my eyes met theirs the knowledge of their fate was a painful awareness that just intensified the empathy and misery.

Like child soldiers in Africa desensitised and traumatised by the violence they are encouraged to perpetrate, many of the staff at S-21 were children, some as young as ten years old. Given power and authority from such a tender, impressionable age, these youngsters often carried out the worst maltreatment and acts of sadistic cruelty on older prisoners. This grim corruption of innocence left us with a lingering sense of revulsion at the wickedness of which human beings are capable.

I've visited other infamous prisons, such as Robben Island off the coast near Cape Town in South Africa, where Nelson Mandela and many of the key anti-apartheid activists were incarcerated. But none left me with such a sick feeling, deep in the pit of my stomach, and a depressing deflation of what it means to be human. At least on Robben Island there was a notionally happier ending, with the liberation of the prisoners and the ultimate transition to inclusive democracy and majority rule. At S-21 the story remains incomplete, as the guilty remain largely unjudged and a whole country is therefore denied closure. Scots poet Robert Burns wrote that 'Man's inhumanity to man makes countless thousands mourn'. As we left we, too, were mourning, not just for those who met their ghastly, grisly end at S-21, but for Cambodia as a whole as it struggles to free itself from the ghosts of this haunting past.

A few days after we left Cambodia in July 2007, Khmer Rouge prison chief Comrade Duch was formally charged with war crimes and crimes against humanity. He was tried, convicted and sentenced to 35 years imprisonment by the UN-backed Extraordinary Chambers of the Cambodian Courts. In 2012 his appeal was rejected and his sentence extended to life imprisonment. He has no further chance to appeal. As I write, the trial of other indictees continues. I hope this long-overdue legal process may offer some catharsis for the Cambodian people.

The next day we cycled the ten miles out of town to Choeung Ek to see the villainous Killing Fields for ourselves. A towering *stupa* houses 9,000 skulls of disinterred victims from the 50 of about a 130 burial pits excavated so far. The largest of the pits contained 450 and it is estimated that over 17,000 people are buried on site. Whole families were executed, many by bludgeoning to save bullets. A loudspeaker system was used to drown out the sounds of the dying. Small children were simply beaten to death against a tree. There was not much to see bar a few shallow, grassy depressions in the ground, but the atmosphere of death was suffocating and claustrophobic.

*Take one of me here*, an Irish girl said to her camera-wielding boyfriend as she skipped into position above a mass grave. It seemed a rather awkward photo opportunity. I pictured her showing snaps to friends: *And here's me in the Killing Fields*. Later in Phnom Penh I spotted travel agency signs listing tour options: 'S-21, Killing Fields, Shooting Range'. It seemed a somewhat tasteless mix of experiences to cram into one day. I imagined the promotional text: 'Depressed at the darkness of human capabilities in the torture chambers of S-21? Shocked at the barbaric violence of Choeung Ek? You need to let loose a few rounds from a machine gun to exorcise your demons'. As at the Cu Chi Tunnel firing range in Vietnam, this type of activity didn't exactly endear my fellow travellers to me. By and large those we encountered in Cambodia weren't an especially endearing bunch.

A feature of the seasonal weather was the biblical rain, which seemed to reflect the dampening of our mood. The monsoonal downpours pinned us indoors, blowing in off the Boeung Kak lake, since filled-in by developers' bulldozers. Gusty winds flapped the blinds violently, and the noise of the rain drumming on the roof almost prevented any conversation. Almost. After Vietnam we'd become rapidly bored with backpacker boorishness – the constant, irritating bragging around getting 'local price' for goods and services and the eternal fear of 'being burnt'. It all seemed so perversely parochial as people sat, holed up in the guesthouse, stressing about the few pennies that might be saved here or there by screwing a local vendor through overly stubborn haggling. Especially when it was over amounts insignificant to even a backpacker budget but the margins of which were all too vital for the poor sod doing the selling.

One evening a wide-eyed, bespectacled and highly-agitated guy was attempting to round up a crowd from the hostel to attend a party at some exclusive mansion in town, with all the lurid promise of drugs and prostitution this would probably entail. His desperate, needy demeanour brought to mind chef Anthony Bourdain's description of Phnom Penh in his book 'A Chef's Tour' as being where 'the biggest loser, pervert, buttface can be king'.

Having had our fill of Phnom Penh's 'Heart of Darkness' and, after another long and dusty bus ride, we arrived in the city of Battambang, stumbling our way through dark, unlit streets. A rousing chorus of courting frogs reverberated from the inky blackness as we perused the invertebrate food stalls' grisly smorgasbord. Fried black beetles and roachy bugs sat in glistening, crispy piles alongside more appetising looking freshwater shrimps. We mused on the difference between eating crustaceans but not insects, deciding it's mainly because all the filthy things that prawns do in the sea are largely uncomprehended.

We'd come to Battambang to take the river route to Siem Reap, hometown of the temples of Angkor. Next morning we boarded our 'express' boat for the seven-hour journey. It was early and the riverbanks were just awakening, people bathing and fishermen throwing or setting their first nets of the day from either the steep muddy banks, on which trees clung with every last sinuous root, or the narrow wooden boats with 'all-seeing eyes' painted on the prow. Perhaps the boat painters were Illuminati or Freemasons? Along the way, smaller boats paddled out to add local passengers to our payload. Two guys running late attempted to scramble into a slim vessel to meet us. Then our wake hit them. In tragic-comic slow motion, their wildly rocking canoe filled with water and capsized, dumping the poor would-be passenger unceremoniously into the drink, to wriggle wet and muddy back up the riverbank for a change of clothes and to wait for the next boat.

Our boat's toilet was a stiflingly hot, diesel fume-filled cupboard next to the engine. The cistern lid was missing and from it a powerful jet of water hosed the ceiling, then drained down into the bilges. This probably explained the pronounced starboard tilt of the boat, not entirely attributable to the uneven distribution of passengers on the roof. The vessel rolled violently as the captain threw it into unfeasibly sharp turns on the winding, narrow watercourse. This was unnerving enough without unbalancing it further with ignorant tourist ballast and a few thousand litres of toilet water sloshing around inside the hull.

Pondering our stability or lack thereof I mentally prepared an Abandon-Ship plan, remembering from the ferry to Japan that the key thing was *'not to get excited'*. We were now travelling through extensive fields of ten-foot tall marijuana plants, not the worst place to be shipwrecked. The muddy channel was once again reminding me strangely of the Norfolk Broads back home. I kicked myself for making such lazy links. Going half-way round the world, experiencing incredible places and meeting amazing people only to fall back on 'it was a bit like Norfolk' by way of a description. The location equivalent of it 'tastes a bit like chicken'. Hardly the most insightful approach, but what's an East Anglian boy to do by way of a visual reference? The thing was, it really did look like the Broads.

Cambodian life is deeply connected to water. Too little rain, and rice crops fail; too much, and rising water levels make subsistence fishing much harder. We passed whole floating villages, including innovatively buoyant basketball courts, pr Strangler fig, Angkor Wat, Cambodia Strangler fig, Angkor Wat, Cambodia ecarious pontoons and planks linking platforms and houses. Beneath these genuinely mobile homes, small 'supermarket' boats packed with produce plied their trade. Small children played unattended on stilt house decks high above the water, a semi-aquatic lifestyle second nature to these marsh-dwelling people.

The final leg of the journey took us into Tonle Sap, Asia's largest lake. This extraordinary body of water dramatically fluctuates in size between the dry winter months and the summer monsoon. The expansion provides a fantastically fertile environment for breeding fish – half a million tonnes are caught in the waters each year – and the lake is therefore culturally, spiritually, economically and ecologically central to Cambodian life. Even the national currency, the Riel, is named after a silvery carp-like fish from the lake.

Reaching over 6,000 square miles at this point in the rainy season, Tonle Sap was now huge, empty and rather lonely. Suddenly our elderly, listing boat felt somewhat vulnerable on this vast inland sea in the wet, murky weather. A passing tour boat of neatly-seated, life-jacketed Japanese made our rag-tag bunch of locals and lolling, safety-oblivious westerners look like the epitome of nautical fecklessness.

Siem Reap is boomtown Cambodia. The massive lure of the enormous temple complexes a short hop down the road at Angkor made its development perhaps inevitable. There's a definite goldrush air about the place as Cambodians cash in on their historic architectural treasure trove. It was sporting an ostentatious new airport, with a marina in development and an unsightly rash of big, blocky hotels for tour groups that boomerang in and out for their temple fix without bothering with the rest of the country.

We hired bicycles and laboured the four miles or so to the temples along a muddy orange road that the persistent precipitation had turned into a mixture the colour and consistency of salmon mousse. As well as temples, Angkor is actually a huge city, with great walled complexes, palaces and various other peripheral shrines, *stupas* and buildings, spread over a vast area. It was worth recalling that when this civilisation first flourished, London was a modest town of 50,000 or so people. Now, a millennium later, the magnificence, majesty and magic of these constructions lives on thanks to almost a thousand years of constant use. Contrary to popular belief the temples were never 'lost'. Cambodians have always known about and worshipped in the buildings, despite their palpable neglect, and probably feel the same way about their supposed 'discovery' by the West as Native Americans feel about the arrival of Columbus.

We enthusiastically explored the exquisite ruins, scaling piles of lichen-covered rocks and precipitous staircases, and feeling our way through dark nooks, crannies and passageways. The damp, misty air lent further atmosphere to the already powerful ambience of decay and ancient grandeur. Tentacular tree roots of strangler figs writhed over the shiny wet black stones, whilst collapsed cloisters revealed intricately-carved Hindu-influenced reliefs and sculptures. The remnants of the buildings were engaged in a ferocious, ongoing battle with the fertile forces of nature that are attempting to drag them back into the forest from which they sprang.

Whilst Angkor was undoubtedly incredibly impressive, the stones spoke to me about impermanence. Could the visionary, ambitious founders, architects and builders of Angkor have ever envisaged its current dilapidated state? Surely they had foreseen a civilisation and empire of timeless, immutable power and authority? Yet here before us, in the marvellous struggle of stone and jungle, was the evidence of this Ozymandian arrogance. The power base had dissipated, the people largely melted away, and what must have seemed eternal and enduring was now aged and all-but abandoned in practical use. It was a reminder of how even what we may perceive to be unassailable is, in the longer term, actually still fragile and frangible.

With the thoughts of such powerful, sweeping changes in mind, I drew comfort from the possibility that Cambodia may bounce back from the tragedies of its recent history. As Angkor had collapsed so, conversely, might Cambodia as a nation rally again. Admittedly the fledgling, still-weak democracy offered skimpy evidence to support optimism at the

*Strangler fig, Angkor Wat, Cambodia*

*Buddhist monks, Angkor Wat, Cambodia*

current time. The exploitation by much larger commercial forces of the country's development and the people – still browbeaten from their historical sufferings – also pointed in the wrong direction. Yet the lessons of neighbouring Vietnam suggest that a turnaround is not beyond hope. As the raw intensity of recent ordeals fades, so can the light of a better future burn brighter. It is nothing more than the people of this harassed land deserve.

Leaving Cambodia involved taking the notorious 'disco bus' from Siem Reap to the Thai border. According to the slow-travel conspiracy theorists, the appalling state of this road is attributable to a covert deal between a certain airline and the Cambodian Government not to resurface the highway, thereby securing more business from travellers for their 250-mile flights between Bangkok and Siem Reap. Allegedly. It is precisely this sort of short-haul flight that makes my climate-change blood boil – avoidable, unnecessary and almost exclusively to the benefit of tourists flying in and out of Siem Reap. Whereas sorting out the road properly or, better still, building a railway would create a perfectly viable overland route with all sorts of likely economic benefits for local people along the way.

The road did not live up to its fearsome reputation. Though rutted and bumpy, *at least our bums stayed on the seats,* as Fi put it. This was unlike other bus journeys where dubious vehicle suspension and potholed road surfaces combined to create moments of weightlessness. This sensation of 'getting air' was leavened only by the sharp crack of skull on luggage rack above or the fierce gravity-driven reunion of backside and seat. On the Siem Reap bus, we fell asleep.

We were changing countries every few days now, as we headed towards Singapore for our first cargo-ship voyage, to Australia. It was as if each border involved a step change. From the craziness and cultural alienation of China into the cheery, commercial creativity of Vietnam and then the slightly harried and sorrowful hauntedness of Cambodia. Crossing the border from Vietnam into Cambodia, we'd gradually swapped the houseboats and fecund fields of the Mekong Delta, an emerald green landscape criss-crossed by multiple muddy waterways, for thinner vegetation, towering sugar palms and stilted wooden houses on the Cambodian side. The shift in relative poverty had been tangible, akin to the visible differences between China and Vietnam when we'd traversed the Freedom Pass.

Whilst our journey had been continuous through these nations, we had still experienced jolts of transition, the arbitrary nature of a national boundary made obviously apparent by the clearly discernible differences in wealth and lifestyle either side. This challenged the notion of slow, overland travel as being about soft and subtle shifts in culture, context and circumstance. But despite cross-border differences in economics, trans-border commonalities in people, wildlife and linking landscapes made for a relatively smooth elision.

At Poipet on the Cambodia-Thai border we crossed the special Casino Zone between the two border posts on foot. A sort of gambling no-man's land flanked by minefields of prostitutes, touts and scammers, it allows Thais, for whom gambling is illegal, to go for a flutter without having to cross formally into Cambodia. Simultaneously, it protects Cambodians from the iniquities of gambling. It was a convenient, if unsavoury, arrangement. We gave our few remaining Cambodian riels to one of the many beggars who patrolled the strip.

We passed under a crudely-rendered concrete arch of Angkor Wat's towers, over a foetid, stinking creek of heavily-polluted black water that marked the border proper and swapped our dusty, rusty Cambodian bus for a smart new Thai mini-van. As we headed towards Bangkok, the comparative prosperity of Thailand in contrast to its penniless neighbour was immediately apparent. Brick and concrete houses replaced wooden shacks, there were shops instead of stalls. Large numbers of bigger, newer and more expensive vehicles thrummed along smooth roads.

A few days later, on entering Malaysia, a rather fearsome sign on the immigration office wall read 'How to identify an alien with "hippy" characteristics'. Beneath this, the give-away signs were listed, including: 'Wearing singlet without innerwear, unrespectable shorts, sandals (that are not part of national costume), unrespectable silk pants, dirty or untidy hair and an impolite manner'. We looked nervously at each other in our baggy linen trousers and flip-flops, Fi with her sarong slung loosely round her neck. At least my hair couldn't be described as 'dirty or untidy', I wear my balding boldly by shaving my head. It could be described as patchy maybe, but at least it was neat and clean. 'Persons matching this description' the sign continued 'will be immediately deport'. Thankfully they let us in. 'Hippy thinking' is obviously not on the watch list. Yet.

But if the Malaysian border with Thailand had felt strict, the Singaporean border was positively authoritarian. We were herded off the train into a customs hall festooned with huge posters promising 'Death penalty for drug traffickers in Singapore', which seemed weird having just travelled through Cambodia where seemingly half the available agricultural land was under ganja cultivation.

Our Thai driver from Poipet to Bangkok whizzed us along at a cracking pace, our nerves only tested by his repeated and unsuccessful attempts to snatch a mosquito from the air around his head whilst doing 80 miles an hour. As we hit the city he began swerving in and out of the thronging lanes of traffic, constantly seeking the tiniest advantage in the motor-vehicle madness, tutting, sighing and noisily vocalising his frustrations. We flew along raised highways that snaked through the city skyline, then plunged down amongst the gaudy tuk-tuks to roll along tree-lined boulevards dripping with fairy lights past gold-roofed palaces. We found ourselves a room at a quiet guesthouse in Banglamphu. This was run by a very sweet old lady, a retired teacher called Saiyout, who proudly showed us her old black-and-white graduation photo. The room was bare apart from two orthopedically-hard beds and a fan. We also had a midnight curfew. So much for running wild in Asia's city of sin.

That night we went for a voyeuristic gawk along the Khao San Road. Tiny mobile bars sold cheap cocktails and blasted music through distorted speakers as overstretched as the bargirls' skimpy outfits. They were touting for business outside less salubrious establishments while under the naughty neon lights a carnal carnival procession filed past. Hawkers and hustlers hassled, shifty types shuffled and improbably-matched Western-Thai couples sauntered along amongst the stalls selling street food and tourist tat. As I'd noted in Vietnam in regard to the prevalence of 'tourpid' excursions, it was worth remembering that the tackiness of Khao San had not preceded the arrival of mass international tourism, but was rather a response to it. Critical foreign observers would be as well to accuse the proclivities of their fellow visitors for the race to the tasteless bottom of a certain segment of Thai street life, than unreservedly denigrate the Thais themselves.

In the morning we rode the river ferry into town. The swift, narrow, ferry boats lunged against the jetty, which itself was lurching up and down with the boat's own swell, rapidly disgorging and guzzling up passengers before speeding off again. The whole process was co-ordinated through a series of coded whistles from the 'stern man', named after his position on the boat not his disposition, and conducted in a fragrant spray of river water and diesel smoke. Carving through the choppy grey waters of the Chao Phraya was a great way to travel. Smaller, dart-like vessels sliced past, powered by what looked like enormous cappuccino milk frothers, (a hopeless western middle-class simile), churning the river into white foam in their wake. Along the banks, Bangkok's blend of ancient-looking, dilapidated wooden stilt houses and pristine new mirrored-glass developments vied for precious river frontage. Hopping off at the Harbour Department, we asked a security guard the way to Hualamphong Station where we were to collect our train tickets south to Malaysia. Thai men seem to have a penchant for extremely tightly-tailored uniforms, lending a slightly homoerotic air to their outfits. Maybe if American policemen were issued with similarly snugly fitting attire they wouldn't get so chubby.

Thai hospitality and helpfulness are legendary: they've practically turned smiling into a cultural art form. However, this is more complex and nuanced than perhaps many visitors realise, as the smile (*yim* in Thai) is used in a wide variety of ways to convey a whole gamut of emotions or meanings. These range from the usual polite smile *yim tak tai*, used for strangers or people you don't know well, through to *yim mee lay-nai* the smile used to disguise dodgy behaviour i.e. the 'I'm ripping you off and you have no idea' smile. There are apparently 13 different types of smile in Thailand, so understandably naive tourists can often end up misinterpreting superficial smiles while being surreptitiously stitched up, mocked, condescended to or even pitied.

We were completely disoriented on the way to the train station, as no fewer than four different smiling people offered us entirely unsolicited but welcome directional assistance. These of course were definitely *yim tak tai* smiles and not examples of *feun yim* (the forced smile) or *yim yor* (the mocking smile). At least I hope so. In some ways I think I preferred not knowing the potential duplicity of the smiling Thais. Everyone who has visited Thailand will no doubt recall an incident where a question has been answered with a smile and a vocal 'yes' but what they've actually meant is 'no' or 'maybe' – the verbal response being effectively caveated by the type of smile that accompanies it (e.g. the *yim haing* or 'dry smile' that is used in nervous apologies). To avoid further confusion, we fixed a pair of *yim yair-yair* smiles on our faces, the smile used to defuse potentially embarrassing or awkward situations, and hurried on into Hualamphong Station.

Inside was all calm, clean and orderly, completely unlike every other railway station we'd been to in Asia. Where were the hundreds of people lying on the floor? The ragged sacks and bulky piles of miscellaneous belongings? In the air-conditioned ticket office we took a ticket from the machine and waited our turn beneath a sign promising 'Hearty, Speedy, Quality Service'. They lived up to their promise too; that one word summed it up, 'hearty' (defn: sincere and expressed in a cheerful and enthusiastic way). I tried to remember the last time I'd received service that could be described as hearty in a British railway station? Or anywhere in Britain for that matter. It was a deflating thought.

As we hopped on the sleeper train towards Singapore the next day we were now genuinely excited and not a little nervous about our first, and now fast-approaching, big maritime voyage. After the buzzing backpacker circuit of Vietnam and the heavier vibe of Cambodia, the ebullience of Bangkok had lifted my mood again; it was good to be speeding through the now-familiar landscape of lush paddies in central Thailand as we headed south.

In fact we were actually going in almost the right direction for the first time in several weeks. Since Ho Chi Minh City in Vietnam, we'd actually travelled north-west through Cambodia and then west to Bangkok, not ideal when you're supposed to be circumnavigating the planet in an easterly direction. It was even worse in terms of longitudinal progress, as we were still no further east than we had been in Irkutsk, Siberia, almost four months ago. We'd been on the move now for almost six months and, having traversed Europe and Asia, were approaching the equator. We would cross into the southern hemisphere for the first time. It was also a major transition in mode of travel. For five months we'd travelled almost exclusively overland in trains and buses and astride the odd bolshie Mongolian camel. But in the three months to come we were to spend almost a third of that time at sea. This was also likely to reinforce our perception of the world as a 'blue planet'. Flying diminishes the scale of the oceans as we flit from point to point, but 70 percent of the earth's surface is water. We would be crossing huge expanses of briny joy, covering thousands of miles and, with luck, not having to crash crazily over the crest of every massive wave en route to do so.

It was also likely to be a real chance for reflection, a pause in the relentless rhythm of our travel, a moment of stillness in the dancing. While relatively slow and grounded, we had still been moving on every few days at best, so a ten-day voyage on the same ship stretched out in front of us like a haven of contemplative serenity. A chance to take stock at roughly the halfway point of our journey, savour the sensational experiences to date and reinvigorate our appetites for the delights still to come.

After all the colour, vitality and daily drama of our journey so far, Singapore was like being in the film The Matrix. A clean, neat, handsome city, it appeared to have had a partial charisma bypass in which the elements that traditionally bestow a sense of character on a place – the markets, the historic buildings, the earthier, grittier aspects of human nature – had all been evicted, polished up beyond recognition or legislated against. This left me with a nagging sense that if this was what a fully-functioning future city looked like, I wanted none of it.

*Low crime doesn't mean no crime,* boomed one public information notice-board. This wasn't exactly doublespeak, but didn't feel too far from it. It seemed as long as you kept working and kept shopping – the mall complexes lining Orchard Road were like immense temples to the cult of consumption – and kept out of trouble, everything would be fine. It was suffocatingly claustrophobic, not a little Orwellian and simply made me want to get drunk and run down the street naked, shouting *Free love!* But that would probably earn me a thrashing with the rattan cane, the favoured instrument of Singapore's judicial corporal punishment, which wouldn't be the best way to depart, with bleeding buttocks and a criminal record.

So when we phoned our shipping agent, who confirmed that the driver was on his way to take us to the port and deliver us onto the vessel that would take us from Asia to Australia, we were elated. It had been a few days of waiting on tenterhooks, as cargo ships don't run to rigid schedules, being at the mercy of weather conditions at sea. We collected our passes at the port administration building and were driven through mountainous ziggurats of stacked red and blue shipping containers. Enormous yellow gantries squatted above like metallic spiders, hauling the boxes to and fro on web-like cables. Trucks seemed to be speeding around us in all directions as the baffling logistical complexity and co-ordination of one of the world's busiest ports sank in.

After what felt like several miles of dodging amongst this heaving commercial traffic, we pulled up beneath the imposing red bulk of the 600-foot long MV *Theodor Storm*, the hull of which towered several storeys above the quayside. The noise and level of activity was intense. Warning lights flashed and the clanking, banging and resonant crumping thuds of heavy metal on metal as the ship was loaded filled the air. Containers swung balletically overhead, the cranes maintaining a regular rhythm, steadily filling the bowels of the ship with cargo. With the smell of fresh paint, warm grease and the sea in our nostrils we thanked our driver and walked a little warily up to the side of this shipping leviathan. Clambering onto the delicate gantry that was swinging from the deck above, clutching the oily rope that served as a hand-rail, we tentatively climbed aboard.

# HUMAN CARGO

*Twenty years from now you will be more*
*disappointed by the things that you didn't do*
*than by the ones you did do. So throw off the*
*bowlines. Sail away from the safe harbor.*
*Catch the trade winds in your sails. Explore.*
*Dream. Discover.*

—Anon.—

It was with some consternation that we'd boarded the container ship for the voyage from Singapore to Brisbane. I think it was a combination of a number of factors that led to a nervous flutter forming in my gut. Firstly, it was the simple fact of being at sea for a ten-day stretch, an ignorantly pessimistic voice inside me asking if the ship was really safe and seaworthy. After our *Pride of Bilbao* experience at the very start of the trip, we were also understandably not a little anxious about being seasick and all at sea in another major storm. Secondly, were there still pirates in these waters? I'd certainly read enough about the security issues in the Malacca Strait to be at least a little concerned. And thirdly, we were entering a very different phase of the trip, the rather simpler, easier, English-speaking and culturally similar destinations of Australia and New Zealand. After the linguistic and logistic adventures of the previous six months I think I was worried that places might feel a bit flat by comparison.

These initial reservations were heightened when we realised we were the only two passengers on board. Relations amongst the crew seemed entirely amicable but tensions on a voyage at the end of the previous year had led to the Filipino bosun killing the Russian second engineer. I'd found this out by googling the ship's name and stumbling on the court proceedings. *He wouldn't have died,* noted Pavlo the Ukrainian second officer, who had joined the crew since the incident, when we asked him about it later. *But he was left injured for several hours unreported.*

We were given plenty of time to ruminate before sailing, having been encouraged to board somewhat prematurely by our over-enthusiastic shipping agent. Instead of sipping Singapore Slings in town, we watched the loading through our cabin's porthole on the sixth floor of the ship's superstructure, which gave us a vertiginous view into the cavernous hold below, as the giant cranes lowered cargo inside. The ship was essentially an enormous block of 1,500 shipping containers with a hull wrapped around the outside. Thirty six hours of continuous, hypnotic loading activity later, two tiny squat tugs gently edged our vast vessel out from amongst the twinkling port lights and into the cloying, tenebrous evening of the Singapore Strait. We executed a deft and, for a ship of this size, rather tight turning circle as a bright half moon illuminated a night sky ruffled with light, wispy cloud, and we were off.

These were now safe waters according to Pavlo, whose pale complexion, gentle, watery blue eyes and slightly detached deportment seemed quintessentially Ukrainian and genuinely reassuring, most piracy being confined to the nearby Strait of Malacca, to the west. After a rise in attacks in the early 2000s, peaking at 150 incidents in 2003, the Singaporean

*Through the porthole, loading cargo, Port of Singapore*

and Malaysian Governments had stepped up naval patrols to combat the rising threat. While Somali pirates have stolen the headlines in recent years, the Malacca Strait is still of immense strategic importance. About a quarter of global trade and (perhaps more significantly) shipped oil passes through a channel only one-and-a-half miles wide at its narrowest point, creating the world's worst marine traffic jams. Pavlo had seen ships being boarded by pirates in the area but assured us of the Theodor Storm's impregnability: *Normally they attack slower tug boats, but this ship is too fast at 22 knots, and even when the sea is like glass we have a very big bow wave. It's 99 percent safe.*

Modern pirates are much maligned, but perhaps we misunderstand the origins of piracy, which may go some way to explaining why we still simultaneously and paradoxically romanticise them. In his excellent book *Mutiny: Why we love pirates and how they can save us,* Kester Brewin reminds us that the pioneering buccaneers of the Caribbean were a response to the exploitation of the common man at the time. The Royal Navy's press-ganged sailors often found themselves unwillingly at sea for years at a time after a cosh round the head outside a pub. They worked dangerously for a pittance to line the pockets of their officers and the Crown and, understandably, therefore found piracy rather appealing. The 'pirate code' decreed a fair and equal share of proceeds for all the crew and compensation for injury. In comparison the Navy sort of sucked. Brewin argues that piracy perhaps legitimately arises when the benefits of shared common resources become ring-fenced for the few not the many. In particular he focuses eloquently on the challenges of copyright in the digital world and creeping disenfranchisement of the masses. His rallying cry for us all to 'put down our iPads and put on our eye-patches!' is reason alone to read it.

The closest we got to anything pirate-like were the movies of dubious origin in the DVD lounge and the skull on the captain's heavy metal band t-shirt. All the ship's officers and engineers bar one were either Russian or Ukrainian and were, at least initially, a little cool and unforthcoming, a Slavic disposition we were so familiar with from earlier in the journey. Some though, in particular our new friend Pavlo, later thawed as our camaraderie warmed over the passing days. The rest of the crew – greasers, oilers, painters and technicians – were all comparatively garrulous Filipinos, creating a strange hierarchical apartheid based on rank, race and demeanour.

After a smooth first night accustoming ourselves to the background thrum of the ship's engines as we sped through a night as dark as the sea was calm, we went on an orientation walk of the ship, exploring our new home. On the lowest deck, a few feet above the surging ultramarine waters that rushed alongside, we could tangibly feel the speed we were going. Shuffling along the gangway that ran along the ship's side beneath the bulky boxes stacked above, we'd made our way to the bow. Clambering in the dark under the containers, gantries and metal staircases reminded me of sinister science fiction films: the *Nostromo* in Ridley Scott's *Alien* came to mind, where danger potentially lurked in every shadowy crevice. We then stood on the salty foredeck in the hot equatorial sunshine with the wind rushing through our hair and relished the exhilaration of being out on the open sea.

Leaning over the prow we could see the enormous bow wave Pavlo had referred to and that dolphins love to ride, and the bulbous bow itself. This is a torpedo-like protuberance that helps to modify the bow wave, increasing speed and stability and reducing drag and fuel consumption by up to 15 percent. It was also eerily quiet as we were nearly 170 yards away from the engines, with just the splashing of the bow wave and the wind in our ears. So far from the rumble and vibration, it was slightly unreal to be surging so fast, in practical silence with all the enormous mass of the ship behind us.

Later we were formally introduced to Billy, the captain. I commented on our speed and his reply was almost indignant. *This is the Lamborghini of the cargo ship world,* he announced proudly, the *Theodor Storm* being a mere three years old and therefore thoroughly modern in its performance. *We are only doing 21 knots!* he laughed, *and when we hit the current we will be doing 25.* That's almost 30 miles an hour, which may not feel fast in a car, but on a 30,000 tonne cargo ship felt like greased lightning. You can waterski at this speed. Though having seen the titanic jacuzzi effect of the huge propeller at the stern I wasn't sure you'd want to attempt it. We observed how quickly we seemed to overhaul other marine traffic, leaving more sluggish vessels almost standing still in our wake.

Once at sea we quickly found a routine based around meal times, at which we were fed within an inch of our lives; combined with our slightly sloth-like existence, this threatened to swiftly undo the weight loss of the last six months. To stave off the return of looming fatness, we embarked on a regime of intensive table tennis sessions, deck walks and avoidance of the tempting lift, instead making the effort to huff and puff our way up and down the six flights of stairs between our cabin and the galley. We also experienced the weird, unexpected lost hours that you get when shifting slowly through time zones heading east. Unlike on the Trans-Siberian Express, the automatic clock in our cabin would appear almost randomly to advance an hour every couple of days as we crossed the lines of longitude that divide the world into temporal segments.

As guest passengers, we were expected to eat in the officers' mess but, as mealtimes were staggered, often found ourselves eating alone. The captain had his own small table at which he always ate solo. Even when several officers were present they usually didn't sit together, but ate apart grimly and noiselessly. We guessed after months at sea together that most topics of conversation had been rather well chewed over, but this didn't seem to afflict the Filipinos in the crew's mess room next door. We heard their uproarious laughter and enviously eyed their menu of spicy fried fish with okra and other fresh vegetables. Both their company and their cuisine seemed instantly more appealing than the sullen silence and stalwart meat-and-potatoes option we were invariably being fed. *Can we eat with you guys tonight please?* we asked Ronnie, the Filipino chef. *You must ask the captain,* came the reply. So we duly did. *Of course,* said Billy, once he'd turned down the Iron Maiden soundtrack to his stint on the bridge. From then on dining was a rather more engaging experience.

Sonny, the ship's only Filipino officer, was a studious looking man with thick, black-rimmed spectacles and a winning smile. Invariably dressed in immaculate white overalls, he gave us a more formal tour of

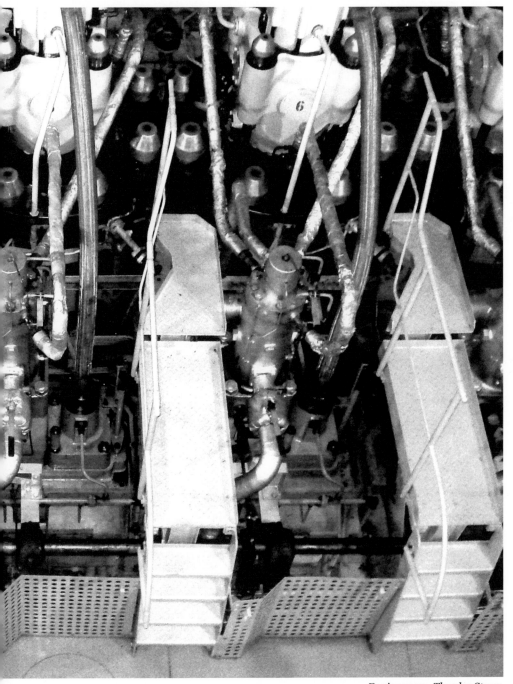

*Engine room, Theodor Storm*

our surroundings with Willy Wonka-ish enthusiasm. The vast engine room was hotter and noisier than a dark drum-and-bass club. The main beast itself was a three-storey high behemoth of cylinders and polished engineering action that thrummed at ear-piercing volume in the sweaty heat. Afterwards it was clear why the Russian engineer who worked in this mechanical nave was so quiet at mealtimes. Twelve hours a day, in three four-hour shifts, in this punishingly loud and uncomfortably hot space was hardly conducive to being chatty. Sonny led us to the metal grille above the massive spinning drive shaft, all gleaming, greasy copper before it passed through the ship's hull to the propeller. Spinning at a bewildering number of revolutions per minute, through complex gearing, the drive shaft spun the giant propeller much more slowly to push the ship around the world. In doing so, the brutal engine burnt up a monstrous 100 tonnes of diesel a day. So much for low-carbon travel, I thought.

Marine shipping actually generates more carbon emissions than aviation, about 4 percent of the global total compared to three. So why is travelling by cargo ship more low-carbon? These issues are never simple, and the devil as always is in the detail. Shipping is actually incredibly efficient in terms of weight moved per unit of energy consumed. So travelling by cargo ship is actually almost 500 times more carbon-efficient than travelling by plane. This has resulted in some shocking counter-intuitive revelations. Eco-conscious European tipplers, for example, concerned about the 'wine miles' their plonk had travelled, started buying only EU wine. That was until Gareth Edwards-Jones, a Professor at Bangor University, pointed out that shipped wine from New Zealand actually had a lower carbon footprint than trucked wine from France. Even more shockingly, his research also showed that driving a mile down to the shop to collect the wine created more carbon emissions than shipping the wine from anywhere in the world.

The other aspect is that marine shipping is ripe for efficiency improvements, by running at optimum-fuel-consumption speeds, changing fuel quality and (my favourite), using giant flexi-foil 'sky sail' kites to effectively pull ships along when the prevailing wind conditions allow. Successful field trials of these have indicated fuel savings of up to

*Navigating the volcanic archipelagos of Indonesia, Timor Sea*

50 percent, and you can bet your bottom dollar that as oil prices inevitably climb, shipping companies will seize on all available technologies to reduce their running costs. Indeed, many already adopted 'go-slow' policies, reducing ship speed and increasing fuel efficiency, when prices previously peaked. But going back to sail power: it just goes to show there really is nothing new under the sun.

Perhaps most romantically, the New Dawn Traders project recently sailed the last existing West Country ketch, the *Irene*, on a fair-trade voyage. Taking organic beer from Exeter to France. Loading olive oil in Spain destined for Brazil. Returning with cachaca, cocoa, coffee, essential oils and superfoods from the Amazon. Their ambition was to explore a truly wonderful slow, low-carbon way of plying global trade without the associated emissions. As they put it themselves, *it's an adventure under sail: trading, sharing, feasting and daring our way to a sustainable future.* Future plans include sailing a Slow Food Circus around the world and experimenting with positive protest through a combination of cargo, crew, craft and creativity.

Over the next few days we spent a lot of time up on the bridge. With the full extent of the ship stretched out below us and an incredible panorama of deep blue ocean beyond, we felt like Masters of All We Surveyed. Or we'd sit on the foredeck enjoying the relaxation of reading in the sun and the pacifyingly simple vista of tropical sea and sky. For the first time in months we could really switch off. We weren't having to move on every second or third day, plan our route, sort logistics, or to worry about timetables, a place to stay or where the next meal was coming from. The ship had embraced us and taken responsibility for all of these things and, as the only passengers, we were an undoubted novelty onboard, bringing fresh conversational meat to the crew's table and revelling in all the joys of a cruise. Only without the crap cabaret and 2,000 other people to have to share it with.

One afternoon we slid past a merrily-puffing active volcano near Sumatra, bulbous gouts of thick grey smoke and grit billowing into the tropical blue skies. Other older, extinct igneous crags lurked along the misty horizon as the sun set, crimson and brooding, through the volcanic dust-laden air. The proximity of these dramatic islands was a bit of a tease and I felt a twinge of frustration that we were simply sailing past and not getting the opportunity to stop and explore or travel among these amazing places.

We'd anticipated one of the challenges of the voyage being boredom so, like the good sea scout I once was, I'd come prepared. Not that boredom is necessarily negative in an 'only the bores are bored' fashion, rather as master of hallucinatory literature Aldous Huxley puts it 'Your true traveller finds boredom rather agreeable than painful. It is the symbol of his liberty – his excessive freedom. He accepts his boredom, when it comes, not merely philosophically, but almost with pleasure'. We were fortunately privileged in our purported tedium and well aware of the fact. Even so, we'd brought dodgy DVDs from Phnom Penh, had a daily Spanish lesson courtesy of the gravelly tones of Michel Thomas via an online course I'd downloaded, and played table tennis in the somewhat optimistically-named ship's 'gymnasium'. This latter was a disappointment unless your idea of a fat burning, cardiac work-out consisted entirely of nothing but high impact ping pong. And, as when I'd crossed the East China Sea, there was karaoke.

The Japanese inventor of karaoke, Daisuke Inoue, never made a penny from his creation, nor did he seek to, deriving satisfaction from the untold joy he has no doubt brought to millions around the world. We inflicted our abject poverty of musical talents on the unsuspecting Filipino crew over a couple of cases of Tiger beer. Clearly karaoke's main contribution to human civilisation is through teaching us all the importance of the tolerance of others.

Fi was initially adamant, *I am NOT singing*. Several bottles of beer from the ship's aptly-named 'slopchest' later she was delivering a challenging interpretation of Madonna's seminal classic 'Like a Virgin' to a room full of bemused sailors who'd been at sea for three months. The Filipinos were wonderful singers. Let's face it, they had plenty of time to practice, melodiously crooning power-ballad standards such as the Bangles' 'Eternal Flame' and the vocal chord-busting strains of the late Whitney Houston's 'I Will Always Love You'. I managed an almost-bearable version of Barry Manilow's 'Copacabana' which made up for my abysmal first attempt at Wham's 'Wake Me Up Before You Go-Go'.

The karaoke DVDs were inexplicably accompanied by what looked like home videos that sought to enhance the audio-visual pleasure of the experience. The one for 'Copacabana' consisted of a pudgy, blonde, red-dressed woman cavorting in a driveway outside what looked like a suburban garage door. This hardly seemed to reflect the 'hottest club north of Havana' imagined in Bazza's original lyrics. But the weirdest was the film for KC and the Sunshine Band's 'Please Don't Go'. This starred a spectacularly be-mulleted Lionel Richie look-alike who mooched about imploring his girlfriend not to leave. The video then cut to footage of his beloved looking mournfully through a wire mesh, apparently trapped in the chicken run at the end of the garden. The lounge also doubled as the DVD room, with an extensive collection of distinctly muscular martial arts movies. Amid the machismo were a few lewder titles, including the spoof porn rip-off 'Lord of the G-Strings'. The cover alone would have had J.R.R.Tolkien spinning in his grave. Everyone knows he preferred a homoerotic subtext.

We found it fascinating talking to the crew about their lives and how spending months away at sea at a time affected them. Pavlo showed us some pictures of his handsome, historic hometown of Odessa on the computer on the bridge, discreetly skipping the mouse over the prominent folder entitled 'Playboy Calendar Album'. I asked him about life in Ukraine following the collapse of the Soviet Union. *For me it's much better. Before, my family had three rooms in a five-room apartment we shared with another family. Now my parents own the whole apartment. But it's not so easy for the elderly people,* he conceded, *they prefer the old ways.*

For the Filipinos a life at sea was comparatively lucrative if *very boring,* grumbled Rene, who was 30 but looked 20, cheerfully. *When we go home we say you are 'millionaire for a day',* laughed his friend Lito, *You make a big party with all your family and friends. After that you must be careful,* he smiled ruefully. *When people come to the house and ask for me I tell my wife to say 'He is at sea!'* he chuckled, thus avoiding acquiring a retinue of hangers-on. They were generous of spirit and with communal support, however. Sonny told us a story about returning home to a disastrous landslide, the result of extreme torrential typhoon rains. These had caused the collapse of the steep volcanic slopes above the town, burying great swathes in mud and rubble. *When my family and I went to see it, we ended up giving everything we had with us to the local people,* he related almost tearfully, *even the half-eaten sandwich I had in my hand.*

*This is a good ship,* observed Rene. *Much better than an oil tanker,* he said, referring to the terrible hydrocarbon fumes and vapours that pervade those vessels. *We call that 'killing me softly'.* They earn around US$1,300 a month, but at some cost to their relationships, especially their reproductive cycles. *My wife gets jealous that I get to see the world, but she knew what the situation was when we got together,* continued Rene. He once went to sea for a 15-month stretch and came back to a year-old daughter he'd never met. Other seamen had problems, or semen problems, conceiving during their short stints at home. Some vow not to return to sea until their wives are pregnant.

Whilst English was the official language of the ship, the range of accents aboard –Ukrainian, Russian, Filipino and Fi's Scots – made for some entertaining pronunciation and comprehension challenges. On a previous voyage, one of the Filipino crew had suffered a serious accident at sea and the ship was met in Brisbane harbour by an ambulance. *Don't worry mate,* said the Aussie paramedic as they carried the patient ashore, *we're taking you to hospital today.* Instead of the expected reassurance, the poor invalid immediately began to panic. Misinterpreting the Australian's Queenslander twang, he'd heard that he was being *taken to hospital to die.*

All the crew had Bay of Biscay anecdotes, calling it the Ships' Graveyard'. After hearing of our joyful experiences there, Alek, the Russian chief officer, described one storm where *We lost 22 40-foot long containers over the side, with another 20 broken loose and shifting dangerously around on deck. A gangway was ripped from the side of the vessel and repairs took over a week. It was lucky no-one was hurt,* he added with considerable understatement. *The best thing was that one of the damaged containers was full of chocolate! And all the crew...* he grinned, gesturing cabins chocka with contraband candy.

I explained to Alek our intentions of crossing the Tasman Sea from Australia to New Zealand on a yacht. I'd managed to make contact with a contract skipper online, and we were planning on doing a competent crew course before joining him in delivering a racing yacht to a client in Auckland. *You are crazy!* he exclaimed. *It is very dangerous that sea, I would not sail it if you paid me money!* This immediately had the effect on us of questioning the risk we might be undertaking. Were we foolish to be even contemplating such a crossing with so little experience, even if we were to be in good, competent hands? The crew's prognosis seemed to be that we were being recklessly naive as to what we might be letting ourselves in for.

To be fair, they had a point. We were being pretty gung-ho about the notoriously treacherous Tasman, and the crew had a fairly good idea of the conditions in the region. The *Theodor Storm* essentially sailed a monthly circuit clockwise round Australia, from Singapore to Brisbane, Sydney, Melbourne, Adelaide then Broome, before returning to Singapore again. As a consequence they were intimately familiar with the Southern Ocean, not least because their last circuit had been particularly rough. This was one of the reasons why the ship had been delayed arriving and departing at Singapore on our current voyage. *There were ten-metre swells,* Pavlo explained, shaking his head at the traumatic memory of it all. This revelation made me shudder, as these were seas even bigger than we'd experienced on the *Pride of Bilbao*. Later I'd asked the Filipinos about the previous round trip. *Impossible to sleep,* sighed Rene. *How did the ship move?* I questioned. *Like this! Like this! Like this!* said Lito gleefully, gesticulating the ship pitching, rolling and juddering violently along with his hand. I didn't fancy the sound of that on a 600-foot cargo ship, let alone a 60-foot yacht.

Five days into the voyage, a pilot joined us just before midnight near Booby Island in the Gulf of Carpentaria. His job was to steer us through the treacherous tidal reefs, narrow channels and shallow shoals of the

Torres Strait between Australia's Cape York and Papua New Guinea. The channel was only ten metres deep in places and the tidal regime at best quixotic. This was due to the interface between the Indian and Pacific Oceans. These have different mean sea levels, so there's a westward 'equalising current' constantly attempting to redress the balance. It'stherefore often the case that at some lunar phases it can be high water at one end of the channel and low water at the other. So careful timing is crucial.

I'd been here before about 12 years previously, in my days as a marine biologist working on a research ship for the Australian Government. We'd sailed from Cairns to Darwin, across the Gulf of Carpentaria, where we'd been conducting pre-season experimental prawn trawling to assess the chronic by-catch caused by the fine-mesh prawn nets. I'd worked 12-hour shifts below decks up to my elbows in dead fish, sifting through the tragic marine carnage, identifying species and counting numbers to evaluate the ecological damage done. It had been fiercely hard work at the time, but I had fond memories of post-shift beers on the back-deck of the research ship. We would pump one of the research tanks full of warm seawater from over the side, grab an ice bucket full of beer tinnies, and lie back underneath a canopy of night sky stars. It felt like the recollections of a different person half a lifetime ago.

*What are you doing on this ship?!* the pilot expressed in surprise when spotting Fi, a perhaps unlikely female, in the darkness of the bridge. *What's wrong with the plane?* came his response after we'd explained. *You must be rich as you have time*, he said after considering a little longer. This is a popular myth about slow travel; whilst our trip certainly wasn't cheap, it wasn't prohibitively expensive from a British perspective either, and the cost has to be seen in the context of its duration. We were to spend around £10,000 each over the 13 months we were away, or around £25 per person per day. We'd saved for years to afford the trip beforehand and calculated the salary hit we'd both take with a year off work. But most importantly we'd made the decision to step off the treadmill of life, make the time, invest in the mental memory bank and spend our money on travel; the one thing you buy that can genuinely make you richer. So rather than the trip being made possible by being rich, it was the investment of limited time and money that would ultimately give us the real, invaluable wealth of irreplaceable experience.

The following morning he pressed me further about the climate-change angle of our trip. *Is it really happening?* he probed sceptically. As he was a marine pilot, I would have hoped he might be a little more aware of rising sea levels. *I think it is just another way to make money,* he concluded, *like drinking milk, they told us to do that too!* I hesitated to point out that failing to tackle climate change will probably have more serious repercussions than not imbibing enough dairy produce. And perhaps the Intergovernmental Panel on Climate Change might be just a little more venerable and august an institution than the Milk Marketing Board. *I went home to Poland at Christmas,* he continued in appropriately ruminative fashion, *and there was no snow to go skiing! It was all grass!* he exclaimed. Go figure, Einstein.

We continued our careful navigation through the narrow channels within what the charts helpfully, or perhaps hopefully, described as the 'Zone of confidence'. This rates bathymetric data in terms of its accuracy and currency. Large, flat reefs flanked the channel, waves shoaling gently over the top, and occasional small, slivers of sandy islets, some sporting mangrove mohawks, dotted the sea. We were in wonderfully placid, azure blue waters now and we soon got our first sighting of the Australian mainland proper, low, arid brown mountain peaks visible in the distance through the hot haze.

Our pacific passage, with a small 'p' as we were actually travelling through the waters between the Arafura and Coral Seas, was thanks to those millions of unselfish shellfish and corals that make up the Great Barrier Reef. This pile of dead chalky animals and its living crust meant we were brilliantly sheltered, the sea almost approaching swimming pool status. When I'd worked in marine research in French-speaking New Caledonia further south, the reef lagoon there had even been known as La Piscine, The Swimming Pool. On the horizon the crest of waves breaking white, frothy and rumbling audibly over the main barrier reef indicated how the sting is taken out of approaching swells. Inside the reef, the sea suffered little more than a bit of wind-chop. We felt protected and safe within its calcareous confines, as did others.

We'd seen frolicking pods of spinner dolphins escorting the ship earlier in the journey, but in the tranquil waters of the lagoon huge humpback whales on their annual migration surfaced languorously around us. Their steamy blow-hole exhalations and the splashing of their pectoral fins and tails were a clear give-away on the calm surface of the sea. Occasionally one of these leviathans would breach, thrusting themselves almost entirely clear of the water before crashing back down in a spray of spume. The playful cetaceans were a joy to watch, and we spent hours on the bridge with binoculars glued to our faces. The experienced crew were remarkably unfazed by the spectacle. *When I am at home I don't want a house with a sea view,* noted Pavlo contemplatively, as his eyes scanned the otherwise featureless blue horizon for the umpteenth time.

As we approached Brisbane on our final evening at sea, the rocky, weirdly shaped volcanic plugs of the Glass House Mountains were silhouetted darkly as a spectacular crimson sunset tore across the sky. What I hoped was an auspicious pod of dolphins swam alongside in the gathering twilight as we entered Moreton Bay. Our ship's berth was occupied, so we lingered rather indiscreetly in the middle of the bay as dusk turned to night and a full, creamy moon lit up the dramatic cloudscape above. Then to cap it all a lunar eclipse began, the moon's disappearance serendipitously coinciding with the end of our voyage.

*If you get hard of hearing mate, let me know,* snarled the brawny Queenslander harbour pilot, who'd come aboard to guide us in. He was aggressively addressing Herman, the Filipino steering the ship, after he'd just possibly failed to catch an instruction through the pilot's thick drawl. A 'runway' of harbour lights guided us up the deepwater channel to the wharf, the closest thing to landing an aircraft we were likely to experience during the year. There was a tense moment as a small fishing boat headed directly towards us. It was possible they simply hadn't seen our huge bulk against the dark night sky. *Give them a blast of the horn,* ordered the captain. The thunderous boom that followed unsurprisingly sent the small, startled vessel scuttling swiftly to safety.

Our delayed docking and customs checks meant it was now almost ten o'clock in the evening and our earlier decision to disembark, which should have been several hours earlier, was now looking unwise. *Is it too late to change our minds and stay tonight on the ship please?* I asked the captain. *Yes,* came the surprising and frankly disappointing reply. So it was that, after saying our farewells to the crew, we found ourselves dumped unceremoniously off the ship, standing on a dark dockside a good 40 minutes' drive from central Brisbane.

Fortunately the shipping agent took pity on us and gave us a lift to a suburban railway station a few miles down the road, where we managed to catch a train into town. All discernment now thrown to the wind, we took a bed at the first place we saw, a huge corporate hostel near the railway station. The bar below was packed with drunk backpackers raucously singing along to corny pub standards. *We're too old for this*, lamented Fi. *Age has nothing to do with it,* I replied as we put in our ear-plugs to block out the noise. *It's a question of taste.*

# ON GUILT

*I did not know that history is like a blood stain
that keeps on showing on the wall no matter
how many new owners take possession, no
matter how many times we paint over it.*

— Peter Carey —

So we'd reached Australia by land and sea like the convicts of old. It had also taken us longer to get there, our journey having lasted six months, whereas the 18th century sailing ships reached Sydney in four or five. We had a profound sense of achievement, and our heads were packed full of the vivid memories of our journey. Our marathon overland travel across Europe and Asia was now topped and tailed by the ships that had taken us from the United Kingdom to Spain and then from Singapore to here, with evocative mental images and experiences that linked every single incremental step of the way. This was the both the challenge and the joy of slower, lower-carbon travel, a rediscovery of adventure and romance in a time when box-ticking itineraries and commodified photo opportunities dilute travel's perhaps more honourable purpose – to unite, connect, inspire and better understand each other and the world.

It still didn't feel entirely real. How could we be in Brisbane without going anywhere near an airport? It struck me that flying to get down under was still a relatively modern phenomenon. Only a generation or so of people have enjoyed the age of affordable international air travel since the oil crises of the 1970s. It was the subsequent price wars and airline mergers in the 1990s that brought prices down and created the budget carriers that have led to such a reckless explosion in short-haul aviation in particular. We had simply revisited a way of travel familiar to most of those who emigrated to Australia prior to those changes. It felt surreal, though, and only became more so during the weeks to come whenever people we met enquired where we'd flown into. Our response *We didn't fly. We came by ship,* invariably being met with appreciative laughter and squeals of delight, slightly confused scepticism or looks of accusatory eccentricity.

We headed north from Brisbane in a converted panel van we'd hired from Wicked Campers, with an oh-so-subtle 'Smurfs' motif spray-painted on both sides. Whilst most definitely cheap and cheerful, Wicked have been widely criticised for a number of aspects of their business, from the questionable roadworthiness of their vans to the more controversial sloganeering of their decor. Perhaps naively, we only learnt about the extremes of this too late, and I would have to agree that their more provocative examples 'Save a whale – harpoon a Jap', or 'Women are like banks – once you withdraw you lose interest' were not just unfunny, but arguably plain racist or sexist. However, Australia is a country famed for its directness in communication where public information campaigns with slogans like 'If you drink and drive you're a bloody idiot' are popular.

In our defence, with over 800 Wicked vans on the road, it's hardly fair to expect customers to be aware of the messages on every single one. But I was mortified to discover this and it's certainly not a decision I am

*The spray-painted legend adorning the rear of our camper van, Australia*

*Safe driving tips for conservationists*

now proud of. We'd opted for the van as opposed to public transport as a compromise for the flexibility it would give. It was not perhaps our finest hour to be associated with such a deliberately contentious, attention-seeking business – that echoed the pre-2014 tactics of notorious short-haul aviation pioneer Michael O'Leary of Ryanair. His strategy always seemed to be to get his advertising banned, thereby garnering free exposure for the campaign at a fraction of the cost, on the basis that there is no such thing as bad publicity.

Our van bore the comparatively acceptable legend 'All I ask is a chance to prove that money can't make me happy' scrawled across its rear end. What would have actually made us happier was a van that worked. To prevent drivers destroying the aged vans' engines through overheating in Australia's often oven-like climate, Wicked fits a warning buzzer. When this sounds you're supposed to pull over and allow the engine to cool before proceeding. As we left Brisbane an occasional 'tweet' emerged from the dashboard, like a cute animal was trapped beneath. An hour into our journey we hit our first steep climb and the 'tweet' rapidly became an ear-splittingly loud twittering shriek as if something was eating our small, cute animal alive. We were forced to stop, with the radiator boiling and bubbling noisily beneath our seats.

Three hours later, a replacement van arrived, this one adorned with a more dubious pneumatic woman against an azure blue sky on the left hand side, heaven apparently, and an equally silicone-enhanced femme fatale amid roaring flames on the other, obviously hell. The 'Flames of Hell' motif was hardly going to allow us to blend in sensitively amongst the foliage of the national parks on our slow journey down to Sydney. Unless we wanted to pose as a forest fire, which was probably unwise given the drought-induced tinderbox state much of the countryside was in. As we were registering at our campsite that evening the old guy on reception asked for the vehicle registration. I glanced down at the key fob where this information is usually found for hired vehicles, *Er, Heaven and Hell*, I replied hesitantly. *A Wicked van eh?* he smiled knowingly. It's fair to say our van was more uniquely recognizable and easily identifiable than any number plate.

We headed north on the Steve Irwin Highway, and it seemed a little odd that you might celebrate a famous environmentalist by naming a monstrous great road after him. Huge hoardings advertising his Australia Zoo bore 20-foot tall images of a wide-eyed Irwin, a mock-shock expression on his face, grappling with a largely uninterested looking crocodile. Above this a cartoon speech-bubble emerged containing his signature exclamation 'Crikey!'

We camped in the Kondalilla National Park and took a rainforest walk as the kookaburras cackled among the trees like a bunch of coked-up PR bunnies in a Soho 'style' bar. Other birds made a 'peeow-peeow' calling noise, sounding like a cheap sci-fi laser battle in the branches above. Strangler figs in various stages of development squeezed the life out of their unfortunate hosts, their thickening, suffocating roots enveloping the helpless tree beneath. The process is almost inexorable from the moment the first tentative tendril descends from the strangler fig seed lodged in the host's branches. When the host is dead and rotted, its demise fertilises the surrounding soil and leaves a hollow ghost-like chamber inside the successful and now well-fed fig. The end results are like multiple tree-trunked cages – nature's climbing frames.

In the forest we struck up a conversation with Geoff, a wilderness-seasoned and just-retired museum worker, *I'm only officially retired,* he clarified. He was merrily dousing *Araucaria* trees with insecticide to collect weevils. Geoff explained that they lay their eggs on the male cones of the tree and their grubs gorge on the nutritious pollen when the cones open up. *The female cones are big enough to brain you if you stand underneath the trees at the wrong time of year,* warned Geoff as our eyes involuntarily scanned nervously upwards. We got talking about what we perceived as the rash of warning and safety signs that peppered the forest: 'Danger: Do not go beyond this point', 'Do not attempt to cross during or after heavy rain', 'Do not take short-cuts'. After what, in retrospect, were our perhaps-risky ramblings over all manner of hazardous landscapes, from Siberian ice to Gobi rocks, in the preceding months, the forest's paths felt rather timid and tame. The signs were perhaps a trifle paranoid. *It's all to protect some petty bureaucrat from being sued,* sighed Geoff

*Great Sandy National Park, Australia*

resignedly. We left him shaking the blue plastic sheets he'd arranged around the trees, collecting the culled invertebrates into a specimen jar. *Happy hunting!* I cheered as we headed off. *Oh yes,* Geoff replied. *Great fun...killing things.*

*One thing I promise is not to get stuck in the sand,* I said to Fi later as we drove along the Inskip Peninsula to camp by the beach in the Great Sandy National Park. Ten minutes later I had the van's back wheels firmly wedged in the soft surface. After a couple of futile wheel-spinning attempts to free ourselves, we resignedly turned in for the night. As I grubbed around in the sand digging out the van in the morning, a voice called out *Need a hand with that?* Richard Hope had spotted our difficulties whilst patrolling the beach campsite with a metal detector. *I'm looking for gold!* he roared gleefully as the machine bleeped at my feet and he triumphantly dug up an inch-long piece of rusty cable.

Beneath his battered leather hat sat a pair of quizzical blue eyes and a brownish red nose expressively wrinkled by sunshine and swollen by booze. He was the epitome of a good old Aussie bloke, suffused with larrikin charm. *I've got 16 grandchildren,* he enthused. *All female! If I lived another hundred years we'd take over this country.* He was deeply proud of his multi-ethnic brood. *My wife's been in heaven ten years. She was Indonesian and when we got married in the 50s it was hard; Australia was a racist country then,* he confessed. *But I was tough in those days and could handle the trouble. Now I've got the whole world in my family.* He grinned happily as he listed the various nationalities and ethnicities his offspring had married into. *Isn't that marvellous? Multicultural Australia? I started it!*

Richard was camped just across from us in a motley but clearly well-established selection of tents and ragged canopies strung around his beat-up Mitsubishi van, not dissimilar to our own Wicked number minus the oddball paint-job. *I'm here for a month,* he explained, indicating his campsite's obvious long-term look. *I've been travelling 20 years. I break horses, I do everything. You've got to work or you just fade away. I've got a job here doing steel fixing starting Monday.* Richard had not left the country his entire life. *I meet everyone here, even though I've never been out of Australia. Never will now. After the war I wondered what I'd do when I met a German. Then I met one and I was like 'Shit! He's just like me!'* After lending his still-impressive septuagenarian strength to helping shift the van we said our farewells. *Enjoy your life!* Richard called as we pulled away. He clearly had.

There was an easy, approachable manner about many of the Australians we met on our travels, an affability that nurtured conversation. I wondered whether the sense of space had anything to do with it, encouraging folk to start a chat because of where you were – in the forest talking to Geoff or on the beach with Richard Hope – rather than who you are. In the fast-fading memory of our London lives such spontaneous conversation was rare, the density of urban dwelling fostering a single-minded privacy and anonymity in people rather than the openness and engagement we were recurrently experiencing in Queensland. These small, personal moments of connection with strangers were peculiarly satisfying. Richard Hope, in particular, lingered in my memory as a big-hearted man who rekindles your faith in the generosity and positivity of the indefatigable human spirit. And as a parting shot *Enjoy your life* seemed about the best instructional goodbye I'd ever had the pleasure of being on the receiving end of.

As we headed south we passed through the unfortunately-named town of Gympie. The drive was a long one by British standards, but probably perceived as pretty pathetic by Aussie ones. In the old days, distances in Queensland used to be measured by the number of beers you would quaff at the wheel en route: *How far's that, mate?* would provoke a response along the lines of *Oh, about four cans.* I wasn't 100 percent certain of the precise can:mile ratio, but suffice to say it's a hot country and driving is thirsty work.

We soon learned that the main hazard on Australian roads is not other drivers but seemingly suicidal wildlife. Evolution has gifted the unique marsupial fauna of the continent with many unusual and specialised attributes to cope with the harsh environment. However, dealing with the very recent arrival of speeding hunks of metal whilst crossing the road wasn't one of them. On the dashboard of the van were two huge stickers that warned us 'Don't fucking swerve for Kangaroos or you'll roll real bad!' and 'Who's going to survive? The Roo, the Emu...or You?!' Clearly, self-preservation comes well before conservation. The stickers were yet another way Wicked had angered people, though the company argued they were about road safety, later incarnations instructing 'Kangaroos – Run the buggers down' drew criticism from animal-rights campaigners. Whilst the sentiment and intent were perhaps laudable, the execution was fairly crude. I guess it depends on your sense of humour. Either way, as a confirmed environmentalist myself being encouraged, nay ordered, to run down the wildlife didn't sit exactly comfortably with my own conservation ethos.

Motoring up a knife-edge ridge road, we climbed onto the Springbrook Plateau. From the top we had spectacular views over stunning coastal rainforest down to the cocky concrete crudity of the notorious Gold Coast. The shoreline strip of fast food, facile theme parks and unfettered and asinine development felt a world away from our serene, green viewpoint and perspective. The wondrous wilderness below us and the adjacent commercial carnage on the coast brought to mind the old Ben Elton line about 'resenting the creation of a world in which beauty is a reminder of what we've lost, rather than what we've got'. While there are many extremely impressive and extensive protected areas of natural landscape left in Australia, it was also sobering to consider how just over 200 years of invasive settlement and development has irrevocably and irreversibly altered this formerly pristine Eden-like continent: upsetting a balance that had sustained indigenous Australian Aboriginals for millennia.

After a few nights of sleeping contortedly and claustrophobically in the back of a van that was most definitely 'compact' but failed to qualify for 'bijou', we stayed with mates in Newcastle. This is a town famous for coal exports, where a flotilla of 35 enormous tankers loitered offshore, waiting to load up with fossil fuel bound for China and Japan. I'd shared a flat with our host Colin, a university zoology lecturer, 12 years previously in Brisbane. A tall, skinny beanpole of a man of sharp wit and pointed opinions, he was a passionate herpetologist even then, and we'd cohabited with a lethargic skink lizard we'd ironically called 'Flash'. Maintaining his interest in all things cold-blooded and scaly, with the accumulating years

Colin had upgraded. Most people get a larger car or build an extension on their house. Colin had got a bigger reptile. A four-foot long carpet python named Oscar to be precise.

Oscar lived in the bathroom, which made for an unnerving shower experience. As you lathered yourself up, always keeping one eye on his gently convulsing coils, he'd return your gaze, flicking out his tongue as if he was mentally sizing you up as a prospective meal. I was glad he wasn't hungry. He'd only recently reappeared after going missing and spending the winter in the loft. *We used to have a rat problem up there,* explained Colin. Now they just have a bigger snake.

Their garden had a lively colony of funnel-web spiders. *They're not that big, but they have serious attitude,* said Colin with almost parental pride. In gangly fashion he demonstrated the aggressive way funnel-webs rear up and gnash their gruesome fangs when threatened, armed with venom that, peculiarly, is toxic only to higher primates. The experience of being bitten by a funnel-web is usually described as 'excruciatingly painful' and compounded by their frankly horrifying tendency to hold on and bite repeatedly. A few days later up in the Blue Mountains we were walking a rough overgrown bush track and one of our companions raised the potential danger of snakes. *Don't worry,* reassured another, *the spiders have eaten all the snakes.*

This is the nature of wild dangers in Australia. Unlike the wolves and bears of Russia and Mongolia or the big cats of Africa, there's nothing to really stalk or hunt you down. Instead you suffer angst about accidentally treading on or being ambushed by lethally poisonous arachnids and snakes, lunging attacks from sharp-toothed crocs and sharks, sting lashings from box jellyfish or, if you're really unlucky, an invariably fatal paralysing nip from the tiny, innocuous looking blue-ringed octopus. As American travel author Bill Bryson says in *In a Sunburned Country,* 'If you are not stung or pronged to death in some unexpected manner, you may be fatally chomped by sharks or crocodiles'. This impressive concentration of dangerous creatures down under led comedian Billy Connolly to conclude that the only explanation was that 'God hates Australians'. So much for it being the Lucky Country!

On arrival in Sydney we received bad news from our prospective yacht charter skipper, Matt, with whom we were hoping to sail to New Zealand. Having made contact with a contract skipper open-minded or wilfully foolish enough to consider us as part of his potential crew, his client, the boat's owner, had decided on a whim to take his vessel to New Caledonia instead. This was a shame as it would have been perfect slow, low-carbon travel, albeit on a rather high-carbon carbon-fibre yacht. Our chances of sailing across the Tasman were now dashed.

We were both bitterly disappointed and simultaneously a little relieved. Actually Fi was immensely relieved. I was gutted that this potential adventure opportunity had been taken away from us, but also secretly slightly thankful we wouldn't have to brave the stormy Tasman on a relatively miniscule boat too. This did create a dilemma, though, as in seven or eight weeks we had to board our already booked and paid for trans-Pacific cargo ship in New Zealand. Somehow we had to get there in time. The thought of having to compromise our no-fly mission to make this sailing filled me with dread. In mild desperation I emailed our cargo ship guru Hamish, who was looking after the bookings for all our commercial crossings. He didn't let us down. Within 48 hours Hamish had secured us a passage on a French cargo ship, the *Latour*, which would take us from Melbourne to Napier on New Zealand's North Island in a couple of weeks time.

Back on track again we could relax a bit and took a trip with old friends Scott and Karin up into the cool Blue Mountains, where the essential oils that evaporate from the eucalyptus trees lend a hazy, purplish hue to the air and gives the mountains their name. We stayed in a lovely wooden house, appropriately named Treetops, in the village of Blackheath. *Drop the beginning and the end, and you get 'lack heat'*, cracked the barman at the local hotel, referring to the relative chill of the area. Sat out on the veranda one night after a few red wines, with a bright, starry and moonlit sky shining down on us through the tree canopy, Scott was coming up with incentives and mechanisms to encourage slow travel. *What about really big clown shoes? How about a ball and chain? Or maybe extremely tight trousers?* he suggested, not entirely helpfully. The friendly, familiar company helped offset the odd feeling of dislocation and subtle homesickness that the strange and unrecognisable celestial constellations above had been having on us every night.

Once these mountain ranges had limited the western expansion of Sydney and were considered impenetrable. Escaped convicts had believed traversing the mountains was the key to freedom and the gateway to China, Australian geography being a bit of an enigmatic mystery to those arriving by prison ship. Subsequently, the pace of rapacious deforestation and decimation of this wilderness accelerated through development and a gold rush. In this context the work of conservationist Myles Dunphy, like the legendary conservationist John Muir in the United States, to protect the area as a National Park in the 1930's for the future prosperity of all seemed remarkably far-sighted and visionary. As Muir himself put it, 'We are not blindly opposed to progress...but we are opposed to blind progress'. We owe these early pioneers an enormous debt of thanks.

Having ditched our Wicked van we took the train back down to Sydney. During the journey we were treated to a display of possibly the most sociopathic bigotry I've ever had the misfortune to come across – a nasty exposé of Australia's unsavoury and unsightly underbelly. A couple of guys in work-dusty clothing boarded the train at Parramatta, heading into town *to a brothel* as one loudly and boorishly informed the whole carriage. He seemed a genuine psycho, like an Australian version of Irvine Welsh's intimidating creation Francis 'Franco' Begbie, pontificating obnoxiously in sexist, racist and misogynistic style. Meanwhile his supplicatory mate, let's call him Doormat, perhaps embarrassed but afraid to challenge him, supplied a half-hearted series of *Oh yeah* responses. The filth that spewed from this man's mouth was unbelievable.

I ground my teeth, wanting to say something to curb his offensive rantings, but this was precisely the response he was trying to elicit. So I fumed in frustrated silence. Their conversation revealed they both had ex-wives, kids they never saw and antisocial behaviour restraining orders placed on them. *I'm done with women,* Psycho concluded. *It's the brothels only for me now. Oh yeah,* Doormat agreed. *It's a shame they've taken themselves off the market,* whispered Fi, *as they're clearly such catches.*

Tiring of city living once again and itching to get moving the next morning, we took a coach deep into the parched New South Wales hinterland. We were heading to sultry Wagga-Wagga to visit our friends Brian and Leonie whom we'd met in Vietnam. En route we had a refreshment stop in Goulburn, a handsome old town that was deserted and shut. It was like walking through an abandoned film-set or the site of a mass alien abduction. The ongoing drought was leading to severe rural depopulation issues in the region.

Brian and his wife Leonie were in their 50s and had come to travel relatively late in life. *We've got backpacks...but we've also got plastic,* Brian informed us. He had a great turn of phrase and was always swift with an incisive comment. Noting that their daughter's new partner was *like Christmas on a stick compared to the last one,* for example. Their relatively sheltered, mono-cultural background in rural New South Wales meant that Vietnam had opened up their world views, something Brian was only too happy to admit. *These Vietnamese people have almost nothing but they're happy. One thing's for sure is that travel combats a sense of lazy racism. A lot of Australians are racist but to meet these people would change their minds. After coming here if I hear someone making a comment about Vietnamese people I'll be pretty upset and set them right.*

Brian and Leonie drove us out through arid countryside to visit their daughter's farm. The crops were shrivelled and dying in the fields due to the failure of the rains for the seventh year running. Their farmland was curiously green, however, due to the precipitation effect of a nearby ridge that brought some moisture in this otherwise sun-bleached terrain. On the side of the track to their property lay the battered carcass of a highly venomous red-bellied black snake that their daughter had run over the day before *about 40 times in four-wheel drive – just to make sure.* The homestead was a huge wooden building surrounded by a low dry-stone wall, allegedly built by an elderly one-armed Englishwoman. It must have been quite a limb and, judging by the size of the slabs she'd shifted, you wouldn't have wanted to arm-wrestle her.

I rode in the 'ute' with their son-in-law Chris and, as we toured the property, bombarded him with questions about the farm. He was a classic Aussie farmer, baseball cap jammed low over his eyes, curly blonde locks protruding from under the rim and a rolled up cigarette on his lip. All alone he looked after 3,000 sheep and 300 cattle on 4,000 acres of undulating hills. *Eight thousand if you rolled it flat,* observed Chris. Their 'hands-off' approach meant they expected to lose 3 percent of their stock each year to disease and injury. We talked about climate change, the drought and the impact on the farm. *You know Opera?* asked Chris. *Opera?* I replied quizzically, momentarily wrong-footed by his cultural query and wondering what the hell it had to do with climate change and agriculture. *Yeah, Opera, the black sheila with the TV show,* Chris clarified, explaining he'd seen a guy interviewed about global warming on Mrs Winfrey's programme.

The drought was having major impacts on farming. Water shortages across much of this massive, arid continent meant constraints on abstraction, the construction of new dams, and cities looking to dramatic shifts in water efficiency. Some places were experimenting with previously unpopular grey-water use, water recycling and even desalination. Goulborn had typified the rural exodus, and farmers across Australia were simply locking the gates on unproductive, barren farms and taking more lucrative work in the booming coal and mining industries. The paradox of the climate change-facilitated failure of one industry then supplying labour to an industry exacerbating climate change wasn't lost on me.

Before leaving the next day, Fi and I took a bike-ride round the hot, dry and dusty streets of their local town, concurring with Brian's assessment of being *a nice place to live but not to visit.* It was great to see a corner of Australia that could scarcely be described as a 'destination', catch up with mates and understand the challenges that these thirsty outback borderlands face. *Wagga is probably the closest you can get to a town that still embodies the traditional Aussie values,* explained Brian. It was very, very white indeed. Leonie confessed that her mother was not without her prejudices, either. *She refers to the 'Ese' people,* she admitted embarrassedly, *Chin-ese, Japan-ese, Vietnam-ese, Leban-ese,* and was convinced there was *a Muslim conspiracy to take over Australia by out-breeding the white population*. During our stay there, we barely saw an Aboriginal face. *Try the prison*, Brian suggested with a mixture of sadness and realpolitik.

Not for the first time, the irony of white Australian racism reared its unattractive head. Brian and Leonie were boat-like beacons of open-mindedness beached in a parched Aral Sea of prejudice. In a nation dominated by immigrants, it seemed ignorant to display discrimination against more recent arrivals, when the vast majority are themselves incomers. During the Cronulla Beach race riots in Sydney in 2005, banners such as 'We grew here, you flew here' were waved, and the intolerance of fresh waves of migrants was just as sharp as in mixed-race communities like in London's East End. There, successive waves of French Huguenots, Irish, Jews and Bangladeshis each reacted defensively to the arrival of the subsequent population influx with the usual protests around threats to jobs, culture, religion and housing. The ongoing hypocritical attitude to immigration is therefore by no means a uniquely Australian problem. But the real tragedy down under is the persistent marginalisation and ignorance of the continent's genuinely original inhabitants, the Aborigines, and their rich, unique culture.

Where collective memories appear woefully short and highly selective, how can reconciliation occur between the justifiably aggrieved and disenfranchised, and those who deny either personal or mass accountability for the wrongs of the past? In his softly seething travelogue *Terra Nullius: A Journey Through No-one's Land* Sven Lindqvist asks the following question: 'Can we feel contrition for other people's crimes? Can we feel contrition for crimes we have not committed personally, but have subsequently profited from? How can we formulate the criteria for contrition to make them applicable to collective responsibility for historical crimes?'

In early 2008, then-Prime Minister Kevin Rudd publicly and symbolically apologised for the 'stolen generations' of Aboriginal children removed from their families over a century or so of Australia's chequered history. This practice was only ended in the late 1960s. Building on the

Mabo Ruling of the early 1990s that enshrined 'Native Title' or indigenous land rights into law, Australia is taking clear steps to address the injustices of its past. Lindqvist's own solution to his question seems to suggest this is a landmark moment: 'We freely admit that our predecessors have done wrong and that we are profiting from it. We ask forgiveness of those who were wronged and of their descendants. We promise to do our best to make amends to those who were wronged for the effects that still remain. The larger the collective, the more diluted the personal responsibility. The less intimate the contrition, the greater the risk that it will just be hollow ceremony.'

But support is by no means unanimous, and the sense of contrition in Australia certainly not, as Lindqvist proposes, sufficiently 'intimate'. Hopefully Australia can, like Vietnam, achieve some degree of closure on what has come before and look to a more just, equitable and integrated future in a fashion that goes well beyond 'hollow ceremony'.

For me this is symptomatic of our dilemma with climate change. Its planetary scale and huge differences in impacts between nations – in which a typical Indian's lifestyle emits a mere fraction of the carbon emissions of your average European's – challenge our notions of what global equity and responsibility means. Emitting carbon is not a crime; we all do it to a greater or lesser extent. But the differences often involve an order of magnitude, between say Africa and America, not just relative ratios. The current generation of citizens of developed nations in particular have massively benefitted from the enormous improvements in quality of life that the post-industrial revolution world has delivered, with all the carbon emissions this has entailed. Should we feel contrition for the climate change legacy this is already bequeathing the world?

I would argue no. Much of this carbon was emitted before we perhaps really understood its full implications. However, there is genuine culpability, in my view, once we continue to burn our way through our fossil fuel reserves in the knowledge of what this means for us and our planet. We have conscious, aware choices now. Shame on those who know the consequences but fail to act, or worse, wilfully obstruct, decry or dismiss the corrective actions of others. This was a clear criterion for our slow, low-carbon trip. How could we see the world without disproportionately contributing to climate change in the process?

This is why I believe climate change is a personal issue as much as it is a political and planetary one. The larger the collective, the more diluted the personal responsibility. Comparisons between whole nations muddy the waters. I've lost count of the number of people I've heard discounting the benefits of personal action 'because of China', despite the fact the average UK citizen still has a carbon footprint significantly larger than the average Chinese. In the United Kingdom we can attempt to hide behind national emissions figures, as with 'only' 60 million people our collective footprint is obviously relatively small in total compared with China's 1.4 billion.

This is the Bystander Effect at its most challenging. If you fall over and hurt yourself in the street, you're better off if there's only one person around to assist. They'll think 'Oh no, he's fallen over in the street, I'll step in and help him'. Whereas when there's a crowd, people shift nervously, look at each other and think 'Oh no, he's fallen over in the street, I really hope someone else steps in and helps him'. The climate change Bystander Effect is pernicious, as people think 'this is such a big, urgent, scary problem, someone must be doing something about it, right?' without fully acknowledging that that 'someone' is all of us – individually and collectively.   Psychologists identify three criteria for overcoming the effect. First you have to notice the problem. Second you have to interpret it as pressing, urgent and needing attention or intervention. Finally you have to take responsibility to act. The climate change Bystander Effect is a huge problem, as tackling it often fails at all three hurdles: we deny the scientific evidence; we believe it is something which happens to someone else, somewhere else, tomorrow; and, lastly, we dodge our own responsibilities.

International comparisons also mask the major discrepancies within the country depending on lifestyle. The fact remains that personal carbon footprint is largely tethered to income. The more we earn, the bigger our impact, as a general rule. This leads us to the paradox where a supposedly educated, engaged and concerned British citizen is accountable for significantly larger emissions than an apparently disconnected, allegedly uninterested one. Those who purport to care more about climate change, emit more. This is where it gets personal.

One of the key reasons I gave up flying on holiday was climate change. I've not owned a car in 15 years, I live in a shared flat – one of the best ways of cutting your own carbon is co-habitation, as you split your domestic emissions from heating, lighting and other utilities among all residents – and cycle to work. As a result, my footprint is well below average at around about three tonnes per year, including the tonne or so emissions we all share from the provision of public services. The international target for a 'safe' level of emissions per capita is around two tonnes to 'contain' global temperature changes at or below 2°C, thereby hopefully avoiding runaway climate change and an accelerating, possibly one-way journey towards a much hotter, less hospitable world. And herein lies the problem.

As soon as you get on a plane, you ruin your carefully-calculated personal carbon budget. So a return flight from London to Malaga will emit two-thirds of a tonne of carbon per passenger, to New York around two tonnes, (approximately my entire controllable carbon footprint for the year) or to Auckland about six and a half tonnes. This is a big deal. Whilst the aviation industry argues that its contribution to global carbon emissions is small at about 3 percent, the real truth is that most people on the planet don't fly, so it is a minority of us who create this impact. In addition, flying is one of the major elements of carbon emissions that is voluntary or optional. Much of it is non-essential.

Science fiction writer William Gibson describes jet-lag as a sort of 'soul delay'. A female character awakes after a flight from New York to London feeling 'that her mortal soul is leagues behind her, being reeled in on some ghostly umbilical down the vanished wake of the plane that brought her here, hundreds of thousands of feet above the Atlantic. Souls can't move that quickly, and are left behind, and must be awaited, upon arrival, like lost luggage.'

In a climate context in which we all are, or at least should be, acutely aware of the repercussions of aviation, I think flying also induces a more

*Bottom of an island continent at Norman Bay, Wilson's Prom, Australia*

worrying form of 'soul lag'. The tensions we experience between the values we proclaim to hold, such as 'I care deeply about climate change' and the high-impact behaviours we practice, like frequent flying, induce powerful cognitive dissonance. The resolution of the discomfort this dissonance generates is usually to change the belief or value: 'actually I don't care that much about climate change', ignore or discount the evidence of climate change and aviation's significant, and your personal contribution, to it. Or we hype up and defensively exaggerate the benefits of flying; 'I need a holiday, air travel connects the world, how else will that eco-tourism resort in Kenya get visitors, everyone else is doing it so why shouldn't I?' etc, etc.

We find it relatively and liberatingly easy to post-rationalise a behaviour we ought to know in some ways is morally tricky or at least hard to absolutely defend. It makes us feel better. In doing so, we somehow leave our souls behind in the trail of our own self-justification. Our conscience remains unconscious. We give in to our more selfish reptilian urges at the very literal expense of others as we emit far more than our share of global carbon in an atmospheric Tragedy of the Commons.

With some of the highest per-capita carbon emissions in the world, Australia is in many ways a country experiencing profound denial. Perhaps the transition from drought through floods to the firestorms that swept devastatingly across parts of the country in 2009 – and again in 2012 and 2013 – may break the impasse. Former Prime Minister Julia Gillard explicitly linked these to climate change; the Australian Met Office has had to add new colours to the nation's temperature map as the mercury hit 54°C. Maybe we are finally reaching a tipping point?

Impaled and twisting painfully on the fork tines of a cognitive dissonance that we all experience to some extent, Australia tries to reconcile massive coal mining with climate change, and its often ugly colonial history with modern multiculturalism. Deny the scientific and historical evidence and you are relieved of the responsibility to act. Contextualice your position – 'we're a big, spread-out country, far from the rest of the world, that needs a lot of aircon' or 'Terra Nullius' – and take the sting out of the potential ethical conflicts. Rebalance priorities onto the economy and social stability, and you kick the ball for action further into the longer grass.

Don't get me wrong, I'm not being exclusively hard on Australians here. It's just that the country serves as a useful cipher for many of the individual and collective psychological knots that relatively wealthy people and their nations tie themselves into on issues such as climate change and international equity. Only by skilfully unpicking these uncomfortable inconsistencies can we hope to reconcile our dissonances in constructive rather than destructive ways. In this sense slow travel is a positive opportunity that emerges as opposed to continuing to 'fly-blind' to the consequences of our actions.

On our penultimate evening in Australia I stood on Norman Beach, close to the Australian mainland's southernmost point. The rain was icy and stung my cheeks. But when the sun broke through the billows of cloud in bright, burning shafts, everything felt illuminated in an ethereal glow. I strode amongst the stranded clumps of surf-shredded seaweed, with the wet sand sparkling underfoot in the soft, sunset light. Gazing out across the rolling surf and into the Bass Strait, one of the most notoriously rough sea channels in the world that separates Australia from Tasmania, I mulled over what the Tasman would have in store for us during our second cargo-ship voyage of the trip. It could be pretty hair-raising at that time of year apparently, catching, as it does, the swell from the Southern Ocean and the 'Roaring Forties' winds that blast straight off Antarctica.

Our five weeks in Australia had evaporated faster than its rapidly-diminishing water supply. Not for the first or last time, we were at the mercy of shipping timetables. As transit beggars we really could not afford to be choosers. As I'd anticipated on the *Theodor Storm*, Australia hadn't matched up to the intensity of our travel experiences through Russia, Mongolia, and China; the cosy, familiar cultural connections and simple ease of doing things meant this was never likely to be the case. But the drought, mining, biodiversity and racial tensions had provoked deep thoughts about the nature of responsibility and the attraction of denial that I carried with me, like excess philosophical baggage, as we prepared to set sail once more.

Back in Melbourne making final preparations to board our cargo ship, the *Latour*, we were accosted in the street by a chugger (charity mugger). *Would you like to know how you personally impact climate change?* he asked enthusiastically. Don't get me started...

# TABLE-TENNIS
# WITH DENIS

*Long voyages, great lies.*

— Italian proverb —

Boarding the *Latour* in Melbourne, we met Roy, a wild-eyed, Panama-hatted and extremely wrinkly 77-year-old Tasmanian. He was disembarking, having sailed all the way from the United Kingdom. *Why a cargo ship?* we asked curiously. *Because I smoke!* came Roy's reply. It was an impressive commitment given that his 60-a-day nicotine habit involved nearly two months at sea rather than 24 hours on a plane. Just so he could have a fag. *You'll probably smell the smoke in your cabin!* Roy added gleefully. We did. It was like sleeping in an ashtray.

*You don't smoke do you?* asked Dick, another of our fellow shipmates, in haunted fashion, obviously having been exposed to Roy's fumes for the past seven weeks. Dick, a strapping, bald bear of a man, and his wife Isabelle, a grey-haired and gregarious granny, were newly retired and on their way to visit their daughter in New Zealand. *Would you consider emigrating?* I asked. *That's why we're going for six months,* smiled an eager Dick. Isabelle looked more sceptical. They both waxed lyrical and enthusiastically about their voyage so far: the Panama Canal, the shoals of flying fish accompanying them across the Pacific and the marvellous mollycoddling of mealtimes onboard. Fi wondered out loud about whether her parents would consider travelling by cargo ship, concluding that though her keen sailor dad would probably be up for it, it would definitely take her mum out of her comfort zone. *Comfort zone?* laughed Dick, *The ship's like a womb – and one with a view at that.* Dick had worked in Health and Safety and pounced on my teasing remark about the right-wing media's cliché of over-regulation or 'Health and Safety gone mad!' *It's those wilful bloody idiots in local authorities,* Dick grumbled, *they understand a quarter of the law, an eighth of the principles behind it and a sixteenth of the science of risk!*

*You're much younger than most passengers on these ships,* noted Gerald, the fifth and last of the travellers onboard, another 77 year old. He had a jowly, hangdog expression and a taste for badly-knitted jumpers. *Usually it's older, retired folk like me,* he added, and the distinctly grey demographic of cargo ship cruisers was something we were fast coming to understand. *I don't like flying. It's not for me. I can't stand heights,* he explained in his no-nonsense Yorkshire burr. *I went on a plane once, to Norway for a stag night, and that was enough.* He used to run a factory making promotional gifts and costume jewellery in Sheffield but sold up due to competition from China. *Twenty eight pence for a gold-plated, four-colour embossed key fob!* exclaimed Gerald. *Same thing would cost me two and a half quid to make.* Gerald became very animated when talking about key fobs. He enjoyed soliloquies on a range of classic subjects including 'Britain Going to the Dogs', 'The Death of Manufacturing' and 'The Problem of Immigration'. Gerald was also a little melancholy, as this was likely to be his last trip, most ships placing a 75-year-old age limit for passengers. Gerald was only aboard this ship having passed a special medical examination. Lord only knows how the ferociously fuming Roy had got through this particular test. *I don't have sympathy with the dopeheads,* opined Gerald, *but giving up smoking is hard.*

We sailed at two in the morning, crossing placid Port Philip Bay and entering the belligerent exposed waters of the Bass Strait at dawn. I woke just after five o'clock, as we hit the incoming 10 to 15-foot swell at 45 degrees. The ship began pitching and rolling in queasily languorous fashion. The memories of Biscay came creeping unpleasantly back. *I changed course to give everyone some sleep,* one of the officers later informed me as we ran with the swell rather than across it, the motion in the ocean subsiding to a more regular, gentle rhythm. For the rest of our crossing, the Tasman Sea was on its best behaviour. Despite this superficial calm the choppy, grey surface still had a brooding menace. It was as if, in an inverse of seduction, it might slip into something less comfortable at any time. I was reading Annie Proulx's *The Shipping News* and her description of 'the ocean twitching like a vast cloth spread over snakes' was suitably apt. Tiny storm petrels whirled around the ship, swooping and arcing low over the rising peaks and troughs of the waves in which blooms of dark red jellyfish bobbed just beneath the surface. On deck, thick, dirty salt encrusted the hand-rails, and the horizon was a blurred smear between sea and sky in the misty weather. We were sailing around the bottom of the world and it felt brilliant.

*You are our angels,* joked the captain as he formally welcomed us aboard. *Normally the weather between Melbourne and Auckland is very bad. On the way here there were very big waves and we were pitching into big holes.* A burly, thickset and deep-tanned Croatian with dense silvery hair and an enthusiastic manner, the captain always gave off the air of someone who had just enjoyed a good drink, his red-rimmed eyes shiny and a little glazed. *I missed lunch!* he would complain, lighting the next of a constant stream of Marlboro Lights, *but for me it's not a problem,* he guffawed, slapping his hands on his ample belly.

*Maro and I engaged in high intensity offshore ping-pong, Tasman Sea*

*Relaxing in the Latour's bar. Maro, the Chief Engineer and Denis*

Later we were summoned to the bridge for an emergency drill, where the captain, fag as ever in hand, took us through the procedures in characteristically louche fashion. In his 'cattle-grid' English, he rumbled swiftly and confidently over any gaps in grammar or vocabulary. On deck, the crew were tackling a simulated fire in the paint store. Standing next to Dick, whose decades of experience in safety inspection included involvement in a major explosion and fire at the Texaco refinery in Milford Haven, it was clear he could barely contain his excitement. As the crew unrolled hoses and donned breathing apparatus and fire-resistant suits to tackle the 'blaze' we were ushered towards the lifeboat. *They won't ask us to climb in,* revealed Dick, *more people get injured doing that in fire drills than anything else!*

The voyage on the *Latour* was very different to our last cargo ship. Yet everything seemed somehow familiar and we swiftly made ourselves at home in our compact cabin once we'd defumigated it from Roy's puffing. But the atmosphere aboard, the camaraderie amongst the crew and the presence of other passengers made for a contrasting experience to the one on the *Theodor Storm*.

It being a French vessel, we dined on *haute cuisine*, and a cornucopia of cold cuts, cheeses and limitless carafes of complementary wine accompanied every meal. Perhaps fuelled by the fine food and libations there was a real bonhomie amongst the largely Croatian officers and Filipino sailors, as typified by Captain's Drinks at Sunday lunchtime. Not that the captain needed much of an excuse to break out the booze. Crew and passengers gathered for pre-victual quaffing, as the Filipino Singing Chefs from the ship's galley strummed guitar and serenaded us with a selection of their favourite mournful love songs. Mercifully, there was no karaoke.

*Without this,* smiled Denis the third engineer, gesturing across the contented faces in the Officer's Lounge, *four months at sea can feel like four years.* Unlike the Russians and Ukrainians on the *Theodor Storm* and their solitary dining habits, the Croatians ate heartily together, laughing and joking uproariously. We sat drinking 'diesel', a foul concoction of beer and coke, with Denis and Maro, the very, very tall, young and

*Aotearoa - Land of the Long White Cloud, New Zealand from the Latour*

handsome third officer, whose dark eyes and amazingly long lashes got Fi rather excited. *I never eat lunch* boasted Denis boozily, *and on Sundays no dinner either*, apparently gaining sustenance from the glass in his hand and the procession of cigarettes he was marching militarily into his mouth.

After those of us who actually ate lunch had dined, we played a rather riotous doubles table tennis tournament. Fi was partnered with a by-now highly vocal Denis, and I with Maro, but it was Dick and Isabelle who, after weeks of practice during the voyage from the United Kingdom, uncompromisingly wiped the floor with all of us. The not-so-sprightly Gerald spent the afternoon, as he seemed to spend most of his time, playing patience in the passengers lounge.

Denis later gave us a tour of the engine room, pointing out the myriad monitoring and early warning systems that controlled the vast inter-connected series of boilers and heavy machinery. *It's very hard to fuck things up,* he grinned whilst explaining that if no-one responds to an engine room alarm signal within five minutes, the general alarm sounds. He told us that the ship's funnel was currently billowing out clouds of steam due to a leaking and faulty seal in the auxiliary boiler. This would mean draining it and working overnight to re-weld it in Auckland the following evening, a job Denis was clearly not looking forward to.

Up on deck in the morning, we got our first glimpse of Aotearoa, 'The Land of the Long White Cloud', as we passed Cape Reinga on New Zealand's north western tip. Ragged pinnacles of black rock raked the sky and tufts of cumulus clouds shrouded the highest peaks. The weather was now warm and sunny as we sailed along the north-east coast of the North Island through highly amenable waters. As we approached Auckland from the east, the Filipino crew member responsible for passengers, Sparky, came to see us in our cabin. He had a benign but reptilian and bulgy-eyed look about him, accompanied by an arid sense of humour and a somewhat inscrutable face. *If you have whisky you must declare it for New Zealand customs,* he explained. *Even if it's an open bottle?* I asked. *Maybe you finish it before we arrive?* suggested Sparky. *If not, just empty the rest over the side.* He obviously saw a look of horror sweep across my face. *Wait a minute. What sort of whisky do you have? Ten-year-old Talisker single malt,* I replied. *Do not throw this one over the side,* Sparky instructed in deadpan style.

The Auckland skyline was just lighting up in the gathering dusk as we cruised through the low-lying harbour islands and in to the dock for an overnight stop. This was for cargo loading and unloading only, we were officially disembarking at the next stop in Napier, so stayed on the ship. A weasel-like jobsworth of a customs officer came aboard to check our documentation and created a tight-lipped song and dance about the lack of evidence for our later departure from New Zealand. The fact that cargo ships don't issue tickets didn't seem to cut much mustard with him. He also insisted we ring immigration to clarify we had enough money to support ourselves while in the country. Fi made a pointless telephone call, during which an immigration officer asked about the balance of our bank accounts. She could have placed her little finger in the corner of her mouth in 'Dr Evil' fashion and said *One million dollars!* for all the evidence or proof we could actually offer over the phone. Mr Pinched-Face customs officer seemed to be appeased. But this still didn't stop him sitting there rolling his eyes, tutting and explaining in dramatic fashion exactly how 'lucky' we were and bemoaning the fact that 'these difficult evenings' always happened to him.

We had now officially 'entered' the country at least. *It's not like home is it?* chuckled Gerald, *there it's 'come on in, get your benefits and join the party',* he griped sarcastically. *Great company,* he commented about CGM, the shipping firm who owned the *Latour. Shame it's bloody Froggy!*

The sea was a calm, slick black beneath a hazy sky the following morning. Watery sunlight sparkled on the surface as we left Auckland, bound for Napier further down the North Island's east coast. There we would leave the ship to continue its voyage across the Pacific. The captain was looking forward to this. *It is more relaxing,* he said comparing it with the often rough conditions of the Tasman. *Nice weather, sun-bathing,* and we understood now how his mahogany skin tone was cultivated. Denis appeared looking like a coal-miner, distinctly red-eyed and not a little battered around the edges following his night of boiler repairs. He'd had to climb inside the uncomfortably small and filthy chamber in order to make the necessary welds. As they were time-pressured they couldn't even let it cool down properly so the walls had still been scaldingly hot. All in all it sounded like a thoroughly unpleasant experience.

We spent our final afternoon onboard chatting with him and Maro. Denis told us the story of the prominent scar that ran right down the middle of his forehead. He'd driven his car off a 100-foot cliff back home. Remarkably, he was not badly injured given the height involved, but his sister's dog, also unhurt, was thrown out of the vehicle during the crash. *Now the dog won't get in a car with me!* cackled Denis in mock surprise. He told us how he had been drafted into the Croatian army and forced to fight in the Balkan war before coming to sea. *Total madness, and now we all have to live together again. I just want to have a good time in my one life.* He'd started smoking whilst in bunkers on the front line for eight months. To stifle the boredom they'd either smoke or put out bread and cheese, and shoot mice with their semi-automatic weapons. *At the start I was very, very scared. Because of snipers at night we had to smoke like this,* he demonstrated, cupping his fists tightly around the cigarette. *I had to scrub my hands as they were completely yellow. Now as soon as I wake up I smoke,* he laughed through teeth the colour his palms no doubt used to be. *When they bury me they must put ten packets of Marlboro and two lighters in with me so wherever I end up I can smoke,* he proclaimed. *You won't need a lighter where you're going,* quipped Maro shrewdly.

Our *Latour* cruise had been brief, only four days, but the creature comforts of the cuisine, the gentle seas and the companionship of the crew and other passengers made us sad to leave. As Dick and Isabelle had also departed the ship in Auckland, Gerald was now the sole passenger left onboard for the long trip back to Europe. He was going to be playing a lot of patience.

# ISLANDS OF HOPE

*A traveller without observation is a bird
without wings.*

— Moslih Eddin Saadi —

New Zealand has more species of flightless birds than anywhere else in the world, which seemed a suitable reflection of our similarly-grounded travelling ways. A flight-free lifestyle hasn't been great for iconic species like the kiwi and kakapo, though. Both the birds and their eggs are extremely vulnerable to predation from colonising peoples and the mammals they brought with them. The immigration of wildlife and humans had a devastating effect on the ecology of the islands that had been evolving in splendid isolation for the best part of 80 million years.

Indicative of this impact is the story of one of the world's mightiest trees, the New Zealand kauri. Reaching heights of 150 feet, girths of over 60 feet, and with a reputed lifespan of up to two millennia, these giants of the forest once covered thousands of square miles on the North Island prior to the arrival of humans. Two hundred years of logging and burning for land clearance has left just tiny fragments of this once-magnificent woodland. These are now protected, but the kauri's low growth rates mean it will be generations, if ever, till these habitats are restored. Channelling my inner tree-hugger, I embraced the immense trunk of one of these beauties: its venerability, stature and sheer mass were imposing, intimidating and awesomely, in the true sense of the word, inspiring. The kauri's destruction was a classic snapshot of our short-term avarice and unthinking behaviour, in ignorance and defiance of the long-term ecological consequences. But there is a positive note to be struck here too.

There is now renewed interest in planting kauri trees as a carbon sink, to absorb and lock in atmospheric carbon dioxide, and help to mitigate climate change. The trees' prodigious size and longevity means kauri forests have the highest carbon sink potential of almost all forests, at over 1,000 tonnes of carbon sequestered per hectare. Rejuvenating these magnificent arboreal titans and tackling climate change would seem to me a rather straightforward 'win-win'.

As arrivals by sea, we felt like a rare and endangered species of traveller as we made our post-Tasman landfall in Napier on the east coast. Almost entirely destroyed by a major earthquake in 1931, which was actually less powerful than the one that devastated Christchurch on New Zealand's South Island in 2011, the city was rebuilt in a uniquely coherent fashion in the cultural style of the time, Art Deco. The dominance of the beautiful classic clean-lined buildings through the centre of town gives the place an oddly-unreal feel, a little contrived even, like some imagined, idealised vision of what a 30s city should look like. Or a film set. Napier is the real deal though, its heritage genuine and authentic. Perhaps the jumbled diversity of conflicting architectural styles that typifies most historic cities, and arguably adds to their appeal, makes us see well-preserved examples of a consistent style as somehow a little chocolate boxy. Like a clichéd

*Maori mask, Rotorua, North Island, New Zealand*

Cotswold yellow-stone village of neat houses and floral gardens, Napier had a clear integrity of polite traditional architecture that was almost too good to be true. Its vernacular spoke in an easily comprehensible and monolingual fashion, not a muddled and confused polyglot. But after the crude American suburbanisation and strip-mall development of many Australian cities we'd visited, it felt stylish, classy and really rather cool.

Our cargo-ship guru, Hamish, picked us up at the port. A companionable expat Scot of some 40-odd years, it was his expertise in 'container cruises' that was enabling us to traverse the world's oceans in such fine style. A former merchant seaman himself, Hamish runs a small travel company that specialises in arranging cargo cruises. With a mop of white hair, a dedicated beer-drinkers' physique and a rogueish, clubby charm, Hamish was a hugely generous and welcoming host as he gave us a whistle-stop tour of town in his car, which sported the rather apt registration plate 'FR8TER'. As we drove, we discussed the pros and cons of living in the United Kingdom versus down here on the bottom of the planet. *In New Zealand we read the news, in Europe you are the news,* observed Hamish pointedly.

There were some logistics to finalise for our next voyage, to 'Fortress' America. So Hamish took us back to his suburban office to sort out the details. Arrival into the United States by ship requires a visa, regardless of nationality. As you might guess from our track record, we didn't have any. The on-going security paranoia in the aftermath of 9/11 means that it's easier to stuff a whole caravan of camels through the eye of a needle than to obtain a US visa in New Zealand. Even as Brits. We'd need to call a premium rate number, fill in an online form, book a face-to-face interview appointment at the US Embassy in Auckland, subject ourselves to fingerprinting and a retinal scan and probably promise our first-born child to the Land of the Free.

*You could just get off in Ensenada,* advised Hamish sympathetically. We'd originally planned to go as far as San Francisco on the ship but it obviously wasn't to be. The irony was it would be perfectly possible for us as Brits to leave the ship in Mexico and then cross the border by land into the United States without a visa. We just couldn't arrive there by sea without one. So we took Hamish's invaluable advice, disembarking in Mexico being infinitely preferable to wrestling with Uncle Sam's po-faced immigration services.

Hamish had an encyclopaedic knowledge of freighter routes that came across as organic and experiential rather than systematic. As his business was up for sale, I worried that his expertise and the company would effectively retire with him. The increase in bureaucratic obstacles wasn't helping either. It turns out that it is precisely the type of immigration rigmarole outlined above, plus the paperwork and unnecessary hassle that accompanies it, which is causing several of the world's major shipping companies to end their traditional practices of carrying fare-paying passengers. Bluntly, it's just not worth the potential logistical headaches involved. These were sad thoughts if they would deny others the travelling opportunities on merchant ships that we'd already been privileged enough to enjoy. It could mean the effective end of hundreds of years of commercial marine passenger travel, leaving the crass opulence and ostentatiousness of cruise liners as the only alternative. On a more positive note, we also discovered we'd be getting a no doubt unbearable stop-over in the isolated, island idyll of Tahiti en route to Mexico. *It's not the end of the world, but you can see it from there,* advised Hamish.

Napier is the heart of the internationally famous Hawke's Bay wine region, so we took a tour of local vineyards. Expecting to get an inside track on the wine-making process, instead we got a colossal insight into the product, tasting a cirrhotic 33 wines at half a dozen different wineries. I know you don't have to drink every wine, but I was brought up not to spit and, as a good environmentalist, abhor waste of any kind. At the boutique Moana Park Estate we met an improbably Irish vintner called Sean who spoke poetically about the subtle intricacies of astringency, aroma and flavour. 'Talking phenolics', he called it. Sean introduced us to the attractive sounding concept of a light 'breakfast wine' and an almost perfectly clear, crisp and refreshing white that was *perfect for business meetings*, he explained drolly, *as it looks just like water.* He was passionate and knowledgeable about his wines without being pretentious. *It's wine. Not life and death,* noted Sean with an admirable sense of perspective.

*Pohutu Geyser, Whakarewarewa Thermal Valley, Rotorua, North Island New Zealand*

There was an undoubted humour about the Kiwi winemakers that was part of their appeal, a fact that hasn't gone unnoticed amongst their European rivals. The rash of 'amusingly' named wines such as Chat en Oeuf and Old Fart is an attempt to repackage stuffy French vin in the more populist and accessible ways of the New World. At the Hatton Estate we sampled a fine selection of typically straightforwardly named vintages that had graced the tables at celebrity chef Gordon Ramsay's restaurants in London. EC2 or Eat Crayfish Too, a delicate white to complement fresh crustacean; the BSR or Big Steak Red with all the rich full-bodied pepperiness you'd expect; and The Doctor. The last one is, of course, not named after any recommended food it should accompany, but because of its price. At 60 Kiwi dollars a bottle it cost exactly the same as a doctor's appointment. *We've thought about making one called The Dentist too,* joked the owner, *but we haven't yet produced a wine expensive enough for that.*

The next morning found us waiting in the brilliant early morning sunshine on the handsome Napier seafront for a bus headed inland to the volcanically volatile Maori heartland of Rotorua. It was a beautiful day, waves lapping onto the gravelly beach and a low-hanging mist draped casually over the canyons and valleys of the rugged Cape Kidnappers headland to the south. The scenery along the way was almost perfectly rounded 'Teletubby' green hillocks with lightly forested slopes. The road wound through the steep-sided valleys that meandered between these verdant lumps and occasionally over the top of a lower one. Our route would slice through the top of the brow in a carved scar-like groove, and then the next valley would drop away beneath us down slopes carpeted with lush pasture.

As we rounded the shore of Lake Taupo, distant volcanic cones lined the horizon. The volcanoes around Taupo, itself the remains of a vast super-volcano's collapsed caldera, are dormant, not extinct. This is a sobering thought when the last major eruption in 180AD, a blink of an eye in geological time, threw around seven cubic miles of rock into the sky and turned the skies red as far afield as Italy and China. The nearer we got to Rotorua, the more fuming holes appeared by the roadside, spewing clouds of steam into the air from between the thick vegetation, as the very earth boiled beneath us. Thermal springs and bubbling hot mud pools belched toxic sulphurous emissions into the air. Even the golf course had exposed vents billowing clouds of pungent fog, and bunkers of broiling sludge – the ultimate hazards, though not ones you could easily retrieve your ball from.

At Hell's Gate geothermal park and spa, a stark, grey lesion of crusty, crystallised minerals, scalding mud pits and a lunar-like surface of cracked stone amidst the luscious tree ferns, we were given an unsolicited upgrade to a private mud bath. *Because you're not French,* the Maori woman advised in a conspiratorial sotto voce, the wounds of the All Blacks' Rugby World Cup defeat to France a few days beforehand obviously still raw. We slathered our bodies in the thick, fragrant ooze and were then poached to soft-boiled perfection in the hot pools. It was simultaneously invigorating and soporific; we were aglow yet lethargic, humbled and vulnerable having experienced firsthand the vital, elemental power of the earth itself. It felt like an insight into how much of the world once was, hundreds of millions of years ago, a raging tempest of inhospitable fire and rock.

Frolicking in the volcanic effects of a magma spike is not the only way to get stimulated in New Zealand. Nowhere in the world are they so keen to twang you around on giant elastic, or to chuck you out of a plane, off a vertiginous bridge, down a precipitous white-water canyon or into a gaping cave. *Even my shit was scared,* read the quote of one presumably satisfied customer on the poster for an improbable activity that involved swinging hundreds of feet on a piece of string into the maw of a yawning gorge. Extreme adrenaline sports are enormously popular. Maybe this is a consequence of the wonderfully diverse and inspiring landscape of the country – from windswept, glacial and fjord-riven mountains, to sheltered, sub-tropical, palm-fringed beaches – inspiring ever more creative outdoor pursuits? Or perhaps it's fuelled by a competitive and self-reinforcing national obsession amongst commercial operators: each coming up with ever more loopy activities, from jet-boating (basically a giant multi-passenger jet-ski), to fly-by-wire (a sort of tethered personal propeller-powered missile) in order to bring in the punters. This booming industry was triggered by the rise of bungee jumping in the 80s, but I couldn't help feeling some of these pursuits actually undermined potential enjoyment of the stunning countryside. The staggering beauty of New Zealand didn't require additional embellishment, or a white-knuckle experience bolted onto it, to make it rewarding. For me the landscape itself it was intrinsically satisfying, but I wasn't entirely able to resist at least a taste of this cultural phenomenon.

Our no-flying policy, perhaps thankfully, ruled out skydiving and the various flimsy and bizarre excuses Kiwis have to jam you into a helicopter. Heli-kayaking seemed to be faintly ridiculous, like 'cave-sailing'. So we opted for inherently un-sensible Zorbing. Only in New Zealand could they have devised a form of entertainment that entails rolling you down a steep hill in a giant rubber ball. If you've ever wondered what your washing feels like whilst on 'hot wash' at the launderette, then be curious no longer. Our 'Zydro' Zorb meant they also added some gallons of lovely geothermally heated water, effectively recreating that 'inside of a washing machine' effect as we hurtled along. Entry and exit to and from the Zorb required wriggling through a small hole like a puckered red sphincter. At the bottom of the slope, I popped out with surprising force, wet and elated, like an improbably big, fat, hairy white pea from a pod. It was definitely low-carbon travel, but not perhaps as we'd ever quite known it before.

Leaving Rotorua on an infinitely more conventional mode of transport, a coach, we headed south towards Wellington in heavy rain. We sped over broad mountainous, moorland plateaus of scrubby brown grass flanked by the cloud-shrouded peaks of active volcanoes, and followed the rift-like valley of the Rangitikei River, crossing the many green, leafy chasms of feeder streams that ran into the main watercourse below. Before Wellington the road hugged the west coast of the North Island and the islet of Kapiti, which local boy and film director Peter Jackson used as King Kong's island in his labour-of-love remake, squatted darkly and tantalisingly on the horizon across a brightly sun-dappled sea.

Not wishing to be solely reliant on public transport, and wanting to meet some Kiwis, we decided to try our hand at a spot of hitch-hiking on the South Island. I hadn't really hitch-hiked since university days, and mourned the demise of the culture of thumbing for and giving lifts back home. A combination of hyped-up safety fears, dodgy horror films and perhaps a rising selfishness seemed to have killed hitching stone dead in Britain, with drivers increasingly seeing hitchers as free-loaders rather than free spirits. To be fair and on a positive note, it does appear that a more formalised form of lift-sharing via the internet is on the rise, but whilst still great for meeting people, cutting fuel costs and saving carbon, it lacks the slightly gung-ho riskiness, mystery and excitement of hitching random lifts from strangers. But maybe that's the whole point. In a time of increasing scepticism, insularity and risk-aversion, what should be an entirely innocent practice is somehow tarnished, marginalised and socially unacceptable.

We'd heard that hitching was still alive and well in New Zealand, however, and what better way to meet a few friendly locals than by trying to cadge a lift? We had 200 miles to travel between Picton and Christchurch so, after taking the inter-island ferry across the Cook Strait, we deployed the inherently sexist tactic of Fi proffering her thumb on the roadside whilst I lurked discreetly on the verge trying to make our baggage look small.

Our first lift came within minutes from a retired Geordie engineer called Fred, who regaled us with the details of his forthcoming marriage to a Chinese woman he'd met online. Thankfully they had also actually met in person too, spending four months travelling around China together earlier in the year; *As a test like,* outlined Fred in his still strong 'Toon' tones, *and there weren't too many battles, so here we are.* Unfortunately Fred was only going as far as Blenheim, a mere fifteen miles down the road. On the outskirts of town we formed an orderly hitching queue behind another bloke heading in the same direction. Half an hour later, with him successfully picked up, we scored another ride, this time with two Korean guys working at a local vineyard. *How far are you going?* I asked hopefully. *Er, Seddon?* replied the driver uncertainly, pointing hesitantly at the first destination on the road sign in front of us. Another 15 miles: so far, so slow travel.

As we breezed through Seddon, Fi nudged me, *They said they were going here*, she hissed furtively. *Where* are *you guys off to?* I reiterated. They laughed a little nervously, exchanged a conspiratorial glance then replied, *It's hard to explain.* There was a weird, uncomfortable silence as we travelled another 15 miles, the road being more or less devoid of viable destinations until Kaikoura, which was well over 100 miles away. Finally they dropped us in Ward, a tiny last-chance saloon hamlet where our arrival probably doubled the number of inhabitants.

Following this 'lost-in-translation' experience, we were two lifts, two hours, zero Kiwis met and only 45 miles down the road. As we gathered ourselves to charm another passing vehicle, a bus pulled up with 'Christchurch' emblazoned on a card in the window. Not in the habit of looking serendipitous gift-horses in the mouth, we got on, bringing our unsuccessful hitch-hiking experiment to a close.

The drive south was impressive, as the bus driver threw himself with gusto into the journey, man-handling his speeding vehicle in a fashion as ambitious and dramatic as the scenery we passed through. Gently rolling hills of dry-looking, regimented vineyards led to the coast, where the road shared a narrow, rocky ledge between the mountains and the sea with the main north-south train line. The snow-capped peaks of the Southern Alps towered above us as we wended our sinuous way around inlets and bays lapped by intensely blue-green, almost teal-coloured waters. Small rocks topped by shaggy wigs of leathery kelp fronds glistened as they surfaced through the undulating swell, and the odd sea lion popped up its head to watch us as we rumbled past. We crossed swollen torrents of turbulent brown rivers in spate, and at one point a small, rickety train appeared alongside us on the track parallel to the road. Our driver then began a multi-modal race with it as it intermittently disappeared into tunnels and we skirted headlands, our routes inter-weaving now and again to give each other the seafront position. And all the while, the sun blazed down from a perfect blue sky above as we whizzed delightfully along.

The weather was very different the next day when we took the Trans-Alpine railway across the mountain range that forms an icy spine down the South Island. The day started wet, grey and miserable as we crossed the Canterbury plains and, climbing into the foothills of the Alps, the temperature dropped dramatically. A biting, icy wind whipped sleety rain across our faces as we stood in the open-air observation carriage. It was bitterly cold and the forests that lined the track were now frosted with a fine dusting of icing-sugar snow. At Arthur's Pass we plunged into the five-mile long Otira tunnel which, when it opened in 1923 after 17 years of construction, was the longest railway tunnel in the British Empire. After the frozen eastern flanks of the Alps, it was very weird to emerge at the western end of the tunnel into a warm sun-kissed green valley beneath the snow-capped peaks. I half expected a bunch of nuns to skip over the brow of the nearest hill, trilling tunes from a well-known musical. On the valley floor, a bewilderingly bright blue river, milky with suspended glacial deposits, wound its way across broad grey gravel beds and, on the pastures beside the twisting watercourse, young lambs head-butted their maternal ewe's udders enthusiastically like small, woolly Glaswegians. It was utterly idyllic.

The spring-like climate didn't last long, however, and two days later and a little further down the west coast of the South Island, the rain was back with a vengeance. Despite the 'dreich' conditions – Fi's Scottish word for dull, overcast, drizzly, cool, misty and miserable weather – we kitted up for an expedition onto the frozen crags of the Fox Glacier. We drove to the glacier's lower end in a gorgeous old reconditioned 1978 Bedford bus in immaculate burgundy livery. *This is John's first time driving since the accident,* announced our guide, Malcolm, about his colleague hunched over the unresponsive steering wheel. *But it's OK, because this is his lucky bus – it's the only one he hasn't crashed yet,* he reassured. Under the circumstances, his buoyant charm was essential. *We're going to get very cold and wet today,* Malcolm informed us pragmatically, *so we're going to need a sense of humour to get through.*

We trudged up the steep glacial valley, its sheer sides scarred by the scouring action of grinding ice. The Fox Glacier is almost unique in terminating amongst temperate rainforest only 300 yards above sea level. We were walking through fertile bush festooned with ferns, lichens, orchids and exotic epiphytes. Often cited as one of the climate change

*Climbing a giant fragmented mint, Fox Glacier, New Zealand*

*A billion tonnes of broken ice heads seaward, Fox Glacier, New Zealand*

'canaries in the coal mine', glacial retreat has, internationally, been a matter of increasing concern, demonstrating tangible evidence that the planet is warming. Ironically, the Fox Glacier and its neighbour the Franz Josef are among the very few glaciers in the world that have advanced in recent years, though this is largely to do with short-term environmental shifts associated with an El Niño event, rather than any cause for unsubstantiated climate optimism.

Malcolm ushered us swiftly across an active rock fall of broken stone, known affectionately as The Gun Barrels, as it shoots out rocks so often. Below, we could see a huge, half-buried boulder protruding from the river bed. Its recent descent had left deep impact craters on either side of our path, where the megalith had bounced on its way down. *Rock falls are most likely after heavy rain and seismic activity*, Malcolm muttered drily as we hurried on nervously in the torrential downpour, remembering the news reports of last week's sizeable earthquake in the area.

Donning crampons, we stepped out onto the gritty exterior of the ten-mile long river of ice. Like fissured quartz, the glacier was criss-crossed with fractures and cracks where the ice had broken as it poured over ridges in the valley floor beneath. Immense pressure forces had then fused the enormous chunks and fragments back together, creating a splintered, uneven pavement underfoot. Occasional glimpses of sunshine through the rolling clouds instantly illuminated the crystalline surface into a million tiny sparkles. Glistening icy blue moulins – vertical shafts in the ice – gurgled as rain and melt-water runoff drained into the frigid channels running 200 yards below. The more frequent formation of moulins on the Greenland ice cap gives cause for concern to climate scientists as the melt-water percolates to the base of the ice sheet and lubricates its movement over the rock below. This accelerates the rate at which it is sliding off the land, calving more and bigger glaciers into the sea and speeding up the disintegration of the ice cap itself. But in New Zealand, it was a misty, moody and magical experience as we rode the 14 billion tons of slow-travelling ice down the glacial valley towards the sea.

Bitten by the outdoor bug, we headed further south to Queenstown and made preparations for 'tramping'. This has nothing to do with

*The 1200m high cliff faces of Milford Sound, South Island, New Zealand*

unfortunates of no fixed abode but is a term used by Kiwis to describe wilderness trekking. Many of the 'Great Tramps' were closed due to the threat of avalanches following late-season snowfalls and the recent earthquake. So we opted for the relatively benign Greenstone Track, a three-day route used by early Maori to collect *pounamu*, the revered jade-like rock found on New Zealand's west coast.

Leaving under the threat of a severe wet-weather warning, we were blessed by surprisingly clement conditions, hot sunshine and cloudless skies, as we hiked carefully along a crumbling cliff-side track high above a rain-swollen river. Around us stood impossibly dense, fertile ancient forests. Thick trunks of long-dead trees decayed swiftly in the moisture-laden air, supporting a carpet of lustrous lichens and mosses. The logs provided a growing platform for tiny saplings, young replacing old in a timeless cycle of renewal.

That night we shared the smart trail hut with an assortment of other trampers, including a Spanish bloke wearing lycra trekking trousers so tight they were positively indecent. A feral cat prowled around outside. 'Needs shooting' read a terse entry in the visitors book. Judging by the large pile of well-thumbed copies of *Rod & Rifle* magazine on the table, some hut guests would be only too happy to oblige. In the morning we awoke to the promised cool, wet weather front. *Colder than a witches tit,* murmured one of our trail-hut compatriots as he surveyed the conditions. Six hours of challenging, bedraggled tramping later, through bleak, drizzly and very boggy river valleys, over precarious wire bridges spanning frothy river canyons and along muddy paths criss-crossed by knotted, twisting and extremely slippery tree roots, we made it to the second hut. We weren't the only ones.

The interior resembled a Chinese laundry, as a motley crew of clammy trampers attempted to dry their kit over the welcoming pot-bellied stove. As darkness crept in and the temperature plummeted, the perpetual rain turned to snow. Suddenly the door swung open and a sodden Irishman strode through. *Anyone mind if I bring my dog?* he, appropriately, barked. We'd probably have objected more if he'd left the poor beast outside in the freezing deluge. A cosy camaraderie built up as the fire burnt down.

The purely-medicinal bottle of whisky I'd lugged for the last 18 miles did the rounds – an excellent way to make friends and get people under the influence. Which was good, given there were nearly 20 of us sharing four giant communal beds. Before we retired, the full moon popped out from behind the dark mountain ridge above, illuminating the delicate dusting of snow on the trees of the upper slopes. We slept in neat rows, the hut air damp from drying clothes, scented by foetid socks and rent by the Irishman's buzz-saw snore.

I loved it all. The sense of space in the wild mountains, the distance from the nearest road, the fecund vegetation and the easy company meant that, despite the bone-chilling dampness that had soaked us to the skin, we were elated. Even three days of just walking had completely altered the pace of our experiences which, despite our overall slow-travel approach, could still lead to a fairly relentless, if laid-back, itinerary. Apart from short stints at sea we'd been moving along more or less every other day for months now, so the chance to sling much lighter rucksacks on our backs and just walk through the forested valleys was both liberating and restorative. Honest, base pleasures were appreciated, and the simple wistful wonder of being alive felt like a hedonistic celebration. But inevitably, joltingly, the clock was ticking, and our cargo ship to Mexico was sailing within days. So, having completed the tramp, the onus to move northwards returned once again.

The relative ease of travel in Australia and New Zealand had, as I feared, lulled us into a sense of slight laziness since the challenges of Asia. Heading to Mexico and Central America meant new linguistic and cultural wranglings, and I felt a little exhausted and daunted by the prospect. A terrible feeling of ingratitude gripped me almost immediately and I knew that, as soon as we made landfall on the other side of the Pacific, my curiosity and passions would be stirred again. I forced myself to reconsider the purposeful philosophy of our travel, which as Marcel Proust suggests is when 'the real voyage of discovery consists not in seeking new landscapes, but in having new eyes'. Our trip had never ultimately been about where we would go but rather about how it might irreversibly change us. But right now I was filled with ambivalence towards the final phases of our journey and the challenges, both mundane and meaningful, still to come.

Our last few days in New Zealand were spent in and around Auckland, making final preparations for our Pacific crossing and catching up with old friends. Plus, I had a few meetings to attend to and a talk to give on climate change and our slow travel adventures. After sessions with Oxfam, Greenpeace and the Environmental Defence Society I was primed for my meeting with the New Zealand Tourism Association. There I pitched the notion of qualitative rather than quantitative growth as a way of developing their industry without dramatically increasing its carbon footprint. Of marketing a visit to New Zealand as a 'once in a lifetime' experience that you owe it to yourself to make the most of and stay as long as possible. Underpinned by a very real truth that a fortnight can never do its wonders justice.

Essentially only the airlines benefit from an increase in classic 'two-week' tourists; by focusing on tourists who might stay twice as long and therefore spend twice as much money, the industry could become much more sustainable and more profitable at the same time. The flights tourists take to and from New Zealand are by far the single biggest component of the industry's carbon emissions, but the real benefit to the national economy comes from how much visitors spend while there. This seemed to stretch the creative imagination of those in the room to breaking point, the idea being met by an air of resignation that suggested such radical change simply wasn't possible. It was frustrating and disappointing that such plausible, practical options were so swiftly dismissed.

I also came across a real fatalism among some of the environmentalists I met. There is a growing movement of morbid resignation to our impact on the planet and our likely fate, as embodied by the Dark Mountain project in the United Kingdom. One of its founders, Paul Kingsnorth, a campaigner of some 20 years standing whose writing I have found touching, inspiring and superbly insightful, recently officially withdrew from the struggle. Arguing our civilisation as we know it is doomed, Kingsnorth hopes that by accepting this inevitability we might hope, dare and dream of doing things differently. On this I agree, but am unsure that what is in many ways a defeatist approach is necessarily the best way to galvanise change. Admittedly, patching up the status quo in a dishonest way and denying the gravity and immediacy of our challenges is unlikely to be effective either. Instead, I prefer to think not of 'Doom and Gloom', but 'Doom and Bloom', recognising the severity, urgency and scale of the reality in which we find ourselves and using this to inspire and accelerate positive change.

In New Zealand I encountered several Kingsnorth acolytes, 'Survivalists' terrified by the prospect of horrors like urban cannibalism in the face of environmentally driven economic and societal meltdown. Some had fled the United Kingdom as a result, fearing the long, slow, nasty deterioration and collapse. *It won't be quick,* one told me earnestly, having decamped from my own neighbourhood of Brixton for a new start in Wellington. *Here I'm just waiting for the big earthquake,* he half-joked, perhaps preferring his chances in a swift, natural and unpredictable disaster to those in a stalking, predictable man-made one.

This worried me. It felt somehow like giving up, dropping out. Simply by believing we will fail in the process of our essential reinvention and transformation, we increase the likelihood of disastrous collapse. Conversely, having faith, hope and belief in the possibility of a world in which humanity transcends its lizard-brain desires enhances the chances of us realizing it. In the context of what we as environmentalists know about the state of the world, I find it impossible to even consider somehow opting out, retiring.

I feel this responsibility profoundly and have spent most of my career attempting to align my personal sense of purpose with my work, to walk my talk and hopefully to do so in an inspiring fashion. In Robert Frost's poem 'Two Tramps in Mud Time' he describes this elegant interweaving of job and destiny:

*But yield who will to their separation,*

*My object in living is to unite*

*My avocation and my vocation*

*As my two eyes make one in sight.*

*Only where love and need are one,*
*And the work is play for mortal stakes,*
*Is the deed ever really done*
*For Heaven and the future's sakes.*

Frost's eloquence on acting for the greater good and tackling the false dichotomy between our labours and our purpose make me frustrated at the notion that anyone in the full knowledge of what faces us can consider withdrawing from the fray. Whilst the scale, complexity and urgency of our problems is admittedly daunting and intimidating, we can take lessons from the Serenity Prayer, accepting what we can't change, having the courage to change that which we can, and being wise enough to know the difference. We can all do something to change the world in our own small way every day. Absconding to the undoubtedly beautiful country on the bottom of the planet to avoid the supposedly inevitable apocalypse probably isn't it.

The journey towards solving the conundrum of sustaining civilisation is like skippering a yacht. The route is seldom direct and will involve dramatic meanders as we tack and jibe in the right general direction. Conscious navigation is crucial if we are to reach the destination we want. An unconscious course brings to mind the Chinese saying, 'If you don't know which direction you're going in you'll end up where you're headed'. We cannot just drift passively along and hope for the best. The world is constantly changing, and we all need to be on the transition team to steer it to where we want and need it to go. The reward for success is priceless, the cost of failure incalculable, and there is still everything to play for. As my dear friend Paul Dickinson, founder of the Carbon Disclosure Project says, if we get this all right 'the infinite promise of the future is ours to keep'.

# GRUMPY OLD MEN

*Travelling is almost like talking with men of
other centuries.*

— René Descartes —

Our accommodation aboard the *Hansa Rendsburg* was probably
the most spacious we had enjoyed so far. Cargo-ship cabins, in our
experience, were at best like glorified Travelodges, clean and simple but
not exactly luxurious. On the The*odor Storm* to Australia, we'd had the
Owner's Cabin. Containing a table, sofa, fridge and television with DVD
player, it felt very much like a floating hotel. The *Latour*, which had
taken us to New Zealand, had been much more compact, just a bedroom
and en suite bathroom, and laced with the smoky aromatic legacy of
Tasmanian Roy's fags. But on the *Hansa Rendsburg* we had a suite – a
bedroom, bathroom and living room, with coffee table, DVD, fridge and

*John, Chief Engineer of the Hansa Rendsburg, at home in his engine room domain*

even enough space to entertain guests. As crossing the Pacific would take 16 days or so, we were glad of the additional creature comforts.

The same couldn't quite be said about the rest of the ship. According to John, the chief engineer, it had been built in a Chinese shipyard that had previously constructed only wooden vessels. As a consequence, the 'experimental' boat had initially failed to find a buyer. After languishing in the dock for a few years, rusting away nicely, it was finally picked up at a bargain price by its current owners. *They all want the best ship at the cheapest price,* grumbled John, *which can't be done.* A white-haired and bearded Kiwi with a curmudgeonly view to offer on practically anything, John was particularly scathing about his own ship. *The engine's bloody deciduous!* he exclaimed. *Pieces come off in your hand, or you go down in the morning and find a part on the floor and you've no idea where it's come from.*

Les, the captain, another Kiwi, was equally dismissive of his apparently rickety vessel. This wasn't exactly heartening to hear as we embarked on a trans-oceanic crossing. However, over the coming weeks at sea we were to realise that Les and John never let the precise details of the actual truth get in the way of a good old salty seadog yarn. We suspected the origins and the seaworthiness of the ship were perhaps a little exaggerated for comedic and dramatic effect. Prior to departure, ruddy-faced and nicotine-wrinkled Les had taken us through a few port and safety drills with a weary air, fag in one hand and a beer in the other, muttering about the irritations caused by passengers who forgot this was a working cargo ship, not a cruise liner. *Some mornings I have six emails to deal with,* Les moaned in regard to his workload, and we wondered how he ever found time to steer the ship.

Together Les and John made quite a double act. If other cargo journeys had been about singing karaoke with the Filipino crew, or drinking and hearing war stories from the Croats, the *Hansa Rendsburg* was all about the Les-and-John Show. Sitting down to dine with them both, thrice daily for over a fortnight, meant we covered huge tracts of conversational ground. We discussed everything from ship safety to Indian port practices, penal colonies to black-box flight recorders. A chat about homosexual stewards at sea made them shift uncomfortably in their seats, but they were both extremely animated when it came to taxes, pension funds and superannuation. John alluded to offshore bank accounts in Switzerland and Hong Kong. *With a government like ours you have to hide your money somewhere,* he growled.

This obsession with grey finance was perhaps because both John and Les were close to, if not past, retirement age. This also led to some striking inter-generational differences in attitudes that, like deep-sea methane clathrates (frozen gases that when released cause global warming), occasionally bubbled up to the surface to accelerate a swift change in the conversational climate. Coupled with the allegedly dilapidated state of the ship, their dated views made the voyage feel a little like time travel. *Welcome to 1971,* I joked to Fi after one particularly retro conversation where John and Les had expressed distaste for women who smoked and swore. This must have involved a sense-of-irony bypass, as Les puffed away and John opined, *I can't bloody stand it.* This later provoked, from a furious Fi, *Makes me want to start smoking and swearing constantly.*

Their opinions weren't that unusual amongst a certain demographic in New Zealand. One grey-haired taxi-driver in Auckland had even grilled us on whether we would ever buy a German-built car. *From our enemies,* he added with a conspiratorial wink. He'd just had a young Irishman in his cab, *I told him he had no right to be here as his country didn't back the UK in the war. What was his response?* I pressed. *Said he wasn't born then,* grouched the driver, *but that's no excuse.* Like the Japanese soldiers who continued fighting the Second World War on remote Pacific islands, some Kiwi attitudes were a remarkably long way behind the zeitgeist.

John had worked as a mercenary on tugboats on the Mekong during the Vietnam war. There he'd met his Vietnamese wife, *a dynamic woman with a mind like a steel trap,* he smiled fondly, his eyes wrinkling expressively around the edges. They'd been married for 30 years but had recently separated as John explained, with more than a hint of sadness. *Not divorced. Just separated,* he clarified, *which means you take your respective shares of your accumulated wealth and spend it on what you want for a change. What do you do with your share?* I enquired. *Mostly give it to her,* John laughed.

As the only two crew members for whom English was their first language(the rest of the Hansa Rendsburg's contingent being a mixture of Russian, Filipino and Kiribati), John and Les were clearly starved of chat. Obviously rather bored with each other, they relished the chance to pontificate and recycle their numerous anecdotes on some fresh victims. To begin with this, was all rather one-way, John and Les revelling in their captive audience and the imposition of their distinctly politically incorrect perspectives. They would effectively tag-team each other in a conversational wrestle, flinging subjects back and forth without allowing us to get a word in edgeways. It was the same at every meal, made worse by us crossing the International Date Line not long after departure. This meant we experienced Friday 11 November 2007 twice, reinforcing the whole *Groundhog Day* sensation of long sea journeys, where individual days blend inextricably together even at the best of times.

John had a tendency towards a slightly pompous delivery and was keen on rather grand, sweeping statements as provocations for discussion. *Another ice age will control population growth,* he'd state, before segueing seamlessly into a range of rambling generalisations such as Negro farming methods, Asian spending habits (*they don't understand saving for winter)* and the lack of qualified engineers versus financial consultants: *You can BE somebody in the city, but DO nothing.* I was actually inclined to agree with him on the last one, but it was often dangerous to actively encourage him.

He also had a gift for turning the conversation round to sex. John regaled us with colourful stories about a certain middle-aged female passenger who had horizontally 'entertained' most of the crew during one long voyage. A mention of Tasmania provoked a wistful response. *It used to be 'ABC' down there,* he recalled with a leer *'Apples, Beer... and something else'.* A few days into the trip Fi and I had commented on the lack of other shipping we'd seen from the bridge. *It's good, we like the ocean to ourselves.* said John. *Very Garbo-esque – we want to be alone* I noted. *Now she was a raving lezza,* beamed John. He'd even described his wife's bosom to us in maritime terms as a 'big sail for a small craft'.

*The Hansa Rendsburg at anchor in Papeete harbour, Tahiti, French Polynesia*

John was a chuckler, whose friendly round face would scrunch up amiably beneath his thick white beard, roguish eyes a-twinkling as he made a lewd or suggestive observation. Les, on the other hand, would punctuate his own stories with gasping, wheezy bouts of watery-eyed laughter: thrusting his head forward, open-mouthed, his liver-spotted skin reeking of ill health and his voice hoarse and gravelly from too many ciggies.

Les had empathised with our US visa hassles in New Zealand. He'd had to fly into San Francisco to captain a ship. *Do you intend to enter the United States to commit terrorist acts?* enquired the immigration form. Having avoided that cunning trap in the subsequent face-to-face interview at the US Embassy in Auckland, he was asked *Why do you wish to enter the USA? Because I have to for work,* was Les's weary reply. *You should have said 'It is God's will',* I suggested mischievously.

They'd both seen dramatic changes in merchant seafaring over the course of their five-decade long careers. The sordid shore leave of yore, in which sailors would have several days in each port to souse themselves and seek out houses of ill-repute whilst the stevedores laboriously swung cargo on and off the ship were long gone. The modern mechanised efficiency with which uniformly-sized containers are loaded and unloaded meant that dock time for ships is now seriously curtailed, usually lasting less than 24 short hours. In the Port of Brisbane, we'd noticed half the dockside was fully automated, remote-controlled robotic gantries selecting and transporting containers around at the behest of some centralised computer system. There was scarcely a unionised dock worker to be seen. My late grandfather had been a 'big man' on Southampton docks, the last of a dead or dying breed. Les and John bemoaned the fact that in the early years they had genuinely seen the world, now they just saw the harbour and not the joys of other local pleasures. *I've never been to a brothel in my life,* protested Les. *Lying bastard!* John shot back in credible disbelief.

One evening, however, it all got too much as Les over-stepped the mark. Originally from Kent, Les had emigrated to New Zealand decades ago. He was relating yet another lengthy anecdote about returning to the

United Kingdom for a visit and being greeted at Heathrow customs by a turbaned Sikh. *And do you know what he said?* gasped Les: *Welcome to our country!* There was an awkward silence before I pushed Les as to why this was either odd or funny. *I think you've been in New Zealand too long,* I suggested. Les was guilty of that typical expat sin: bemoaning changes in Britain, despite the fact that they themselves had abandoned the country by seeking a better life elsewhere. This is then compounded by a prejudice for those who have done exactly the same thing in reverse by immigrating to the United Kingdom. As in comedian Stewart Lee's classic line 'You know who I hate? Emigrants!', I pointed out the almost perverse hypocrisy of the situation. This was met with much huff and bluster about how the United Kingdom wasn't the same any more and again, irony of ironies, the 'problem of immigration'. As expressed by expat migrants! It was a heated and tense debate, fuelled by our defence of the multicultural Britain we knew, loved and passionately believed in, and not helped by John's darkly veiled warnings about the dangers of 'being too liberal'.

Although difficult at the time, the altercation proved to be a turning point. This was a relief, as we had another ten days to go on the voyage that could have been miserable if the atmosphere of confrontation was sustained. It made me think about the discipline of tolerance required on a ship in mid-ocean. This was something John himself had commented on when explaining why he often preferred to work alone at night in the engine room. *No-one around to bloody annoy you,* he said testily, before adding that *You have to be nice to people at sea or they can make your life hell.* Or indeed kill you, if the murder on the *Theodor Storm* was anything to go by. When I told John about this incident, he didn't seem surprised. *Russians and Ukrainians often seem to think they're superior to supposedly 'sub-ordinate' races like the Filipinos, who obviously don't believe that they're inferior!* Judging by some of the thoughts expressed by him and Les, it seemed to me a little rich for John to be accusing Eastern Europeans of having a superiority complex.

The day after the dinner argument, Les made a concerted effort to clear the air, commenting on how refreshing it was to have passengers of a different age group. Though the conversation continued to cartwheel from topic to topic, and the tennis-like to-and-fro between the ship's most senior crew members went on, at least now there was an attempt at dialogue and interaction as opposed to the one-way verbal deluge of before.

Apart from the social rollercoaster around the dinner table, we were otherwise well into our now-accustomed ship-based routines: Spanish lessons, reading, writing and plenty of calorie-burning table tennis to get some exercise. Our cabin was also on the seventh floor of the vessel's superstructure, and there was no lift. This meant a daily scramble up and down countless flights each day just for meals in the deck-level galley, which naturally helped keep the weight off. We were used to the juddering and vibration of the ship too, which was made worse by the vessel's relative age, its construction and design. A key quirk of the *Hansa Rendsburg* was the fact that the nine-storey block containing accommodation, culminating in the bridge, was positioned directly above the engine, ensuring we experienced the maximum possible vibration effects.

John gave us the obligatory tour of the engine room and its famous 'part-shedding' centrepiece. It had a distinctly chaotic, haphazard feel about it and was much grubbier than others we'd seen. By now, we felt like we were fast becoming amateur enthusiasts about cargo ship design, layout and propulsion. Dirty baked-bean tins from the galley hung on wires to catch oily drips from leaking pipes, and a sense of mechanical clutter pervaded the hot, noisy space. It reminded me of an old man's shed with all the accumulated curiosities and acquired objects, both useful and useless, you'd expect to find there.

The benign Pacific weather meant we spent considerable time on deck, soaking up the sunshine and watching the silvery flying fish that fluttered like giant marine dragonflies out of the breaking bow wave. They'd glide for surprising distances between the wave peaks of the rolling blue sea, in a similar fashion to the storm petrels of the Tasman, eventually plunging back into the water after their unlikely airborne excursions. We'd stand, Titanic-style, on the small platform on the prow of the ship, rather naffly spreading our arms out like a wannabe DiCaprio and Winslet. While at the bow, we noticed the metal plating on the bow-deck was buckled and broken in places. We later found out from Les this was the work of a previous captain who had forced the apparently less-than hydrodynamic ship too fast into an extremely heavy swell. It was hard to believe you could actually bend a vessel of this size, but the evidence was right there before us. *You weren't doing bloody Titanic impressions at the bow were you?* asked Les. *Of course not*, we sheepishly lied. *Good*, grunted Les, *a cargo ship lost two passengers recently when the wife fell off doing that nonsense and the husband jumped in after her.* We nodded obediently at the thought of such foolishness.

Shortly afterwards, while we were walking on deck, Fi had an altogether different accident. Ducking beneath a metal gantry in a peaked cap she'd worn to keep the blazing sunshine out of her eyes, she misjudged the height and caught her head hard on a sharply protruding bolt. A few steps in front I heard her cry out, and turned to find her in tears and bleeding profusely, the blood pouring dramatically down her face. I gasped and must have looked horrified at the sight. Fi was most definitely in shock as we edged, arm in arm, along the narrow open gangway that ran the length of the ship's side. We had scant protection from the racing sea only a couple of feet below. It was a scramble of nearly 150 yards, and I was paranoid that she was going to collapse and we'd both tumble unnoticed into the water, with an untimely end in the middle of the Pacific.

As we reached the main superstructure, Fi really did faint, slumping like a dead weight in my arms on the final set of steps. Her eyes were half open but she was out for the count, blood all over her face that was now a grey colour, a shade beyond even her normally pale Scottish skin. Thankfully we were then spotted by one of the Kiribati crew who was painting on deck. Between us, he in his respirator mask, sunglasses and overalls looking like an 80s rave refugee, we manhandled Fi into the dining room. There we laid her in the recovery position on the cool lino floor. This seemed to bring her round, and the Filipino second officer and I managed to get Fi up to the ship's 'hospital' to patch her up. It was a modestly-equipped medical room where you'd be reluctant to perform anything beyond minor first aid. I was seriously concerned and not a little shaken by the whole experience, as of course was Fi. But once we'd wiped the dried blood from her face and head, the actual wound was almost pathetically small. Actually, it was laughably so. We then did laugh, long and hard, as much from relief as anything else. *It's your fault*, giggled Fi in mock accusation, through tears of laugher this time: *It was your face that made me freak out.*

After five days at sea, we reached Tahiti, the peaks and ridges of the island of Moorea protruding from the sea like the shards of an enormous broken bowl. It was hot, misty and muggy, without a breath of a breeze as we slid gently into Papeete, French Polynesia's main port. A flotilla of traditional out-rigger canoes and modern kayaks flanked our enormous bulk, and it took skilful piloting to ease us between the low fringing reef and narrow breakwater that frame the harbour entrance. Along the shore, the town itself was a cute clutter of low buildings stretching up from the waterfront and onto the lower slopes of the thickly forested volcanic mountains above. Boisterous cumulus clouds billowed around the island's crags, like smoke from the long-extinct caldera.

Our Tahitian shipping agent, who went by the unlikely name of Harry Cowan, gave us a lift into town in his car. *My grandfather was English,* he explained, dropping us off for a teasing few hours ashore in this island paradise. The pristine beaches of one of the world's most exclusive holiday destinations, the beach-lined crater of Bora Bora, were only a short distance away. However, Papeete is the lethargic administrative and commercial hub of French Polynesia. While it lacked the flashy looks of its idyllic neighbour it had a rough and ready charm about it. But our very limited shore leave could only ever give us a glimpse of the wider archipelago's possible delights.

Snake-hipped transvestites sashayed between the bars on the portside strip as we sipped insanely expensive beers, Polynesian prices being as high as the women are famously beautiful. Even the men were gorgeous. We had a swift poke around a market that felt suspiciously aimed solely at passing cruise tourists: gaudy shell necklaces, traditional wooden carvings and vibrantly coloured sarongs galore. Buying three plump, juicy pineapples from a Gandhi look-alike on the roadside, we then ate a meal on the quayside. After the uninspiring fodder on the ship, we were spoilt for choice amongst the harbour *roulottes*, food caravans that offered a range of tasty options like a mini gourmet festival. We devoured crispy gallettes stuffed with oozing cheese and salty ham, followed by a sweet 'Martinique' of rum and raisin ice cream and crème chantilly, praising the hallowed Gods of French cuisine for their mouth-watering blessings.

Around midnight we were underway again, with the last containers having been swung onboard. A few of the crew had been skipping dangerously about beneath the huge swaying loads to guide them into position on the already-stacked deck. It was not a job for the faint-hearted, and I'd watched with concern from our cabin window. Our stop-over in Tahiti had left us with a strange taste in our mouths, which wasn't just from the gallettes or the expensive beer. We'd had an insight into how cruise liner passengers generally experience the ports they call into: trekking ashore, perusing the trinket markets, maybe having a quick drink and a meal or a very brief cultural excursion before returning to the ship. There was something innately frustrating about the superficiality of such a fleeting time-limited visit. It was almost pointless, like admiring the fire exit of the National Gallery while being denied a decent peek at the paintings inside.

Contrasting cargo ships with cruise liners seemed like comparing trucks to limousines: they might both get you to your destination, but only one has a champagne fridge and leather seats. Cargo-ship travel felt contemplative, unrushed and unfussed. We were freed from the distractions of telephones, the internet and the modern world that permeate even the remotest holiday resorts these days. At sea, our minds could wander, ruminate and we could truly escape. As a working ship, the *Hansa Rendsburg* also had a purpose, a practical function, transporting the fruits of world trade around the globe. Not simply shipping tubby tourists around a series of global holiday hotspots for a quick onshore shuffle. The luxurious pampering and clientele of clubby retirees are all part of the cruise liner experience and come with a price tag to match the prestige. Cargo ships are very much the 'no-frills' option.

We were also gaining a fascinating insight into the logistics and mechanics of the way much of the world's commerce is conducted, which is sobering when you see first-hand the scale of maritime shipping operations and the challenges involved. Cheap oriental Christmas decorations are suddenly seen in a new light when you appreciate how they've reached the United Kingdom. There is also a downside of course, depending on your view of some aspects of global trade. I'd asked one of the Ukrainian crew on the *Theodor Storm* what was in the containers. *Crap!* he gruffed. *It's all cheap, crappy, plastic crap from China!* There were around a thousand boxy metal containers on the *Hansa Rendsburg*. These were full of dried-milk products, white goods, fruit and, in the 150 or so refrigerated containers, fish, meat and ice-cream. We'd even got a hazardous cargo of 'low specific' radioactive material going to Canada that meant we were likely to acquire a Mexican naval escort for the final approach into Ensenada.

A few days later we were utterly, totally and completely isolated. We'd crossed the equator. *Did you feel the bump?* cracked Les for, no doubt, the thousandth time in his shipping career, and were now at the mid-point of the world's biggest ocean. At almost 65 million square miles the Pacific is nearly as big as the other four main oceans combined. And we were slap-bang in the middle of it. On our other ships and ferries we'd never been far from land. Crossing the Bay of Biscay we were basically hugging the French coastline; from Singapore to Australia we'd slithered between the many islands of Indonesia, East Timor, Papua New Guinea and the Australian continent itself. Even in the Tasman, we'd only ever been a day and a half or so offshore.

Now Tahiti was 2,000 miles behind us and Mexico 2,000 miles ahead. We weren't quite at 'Point Nemo', the oceanic Pole of Inaccessibility or remotest point from all land, named after Jules Verne's submarine captain. Point Nemo is 1,670 miles from any land, and is located midway between Pitcairn and Antarctica in the southern Pacific. But we were similarly lonely. I had never felt quite so thrillingly isolated, vulnerable and humbled. It was inspiring to think of the vast expansive space around us and, at the same time, slightly unnerving. We were somewhat beyond the reach of the RNLI after all, and it was best not to dwell too deeply on the consequences of a real mid-ocean emergency. Despite these irrational fears, it was a sense of freedom and humility the like of which I'd never felt before. I understood the addictive qualities of marine travel properly for the first time. The words of Mirosawa, the Japanese gentlemen with whom we'd shared our train compartment from Mongolia to China, came back to me. *Ship, ship, ship. You love ship!* And at that moment in the middle of the Pacific I genuinely, passionately did.

All great journeys inevitably come to an end, and by the time we were in Mexican coastal waters we had both started to go a little stir-crazy after 16 long days at sea. *Get me off this ship!* Fi ranted, from which I inferred she'd probably had enough. Such was the sense of anticipation that we even got up before dawn to watch the approach into the port of Ensenada. An underlying swell rolled gently beneath us as we got closer, yet the surface of the sea was mirror-calm in the still morning air. It was cool, but the rising sun was already fiery behind the dark Baja hills, and the promised Mexican naval escort for our nuclear cargo was conspicuous by its absence.

Leaving the ship for the final time we had genuinely mixed feelings – palpable relief to be on dry land once again after over two weeks at sea, but with a pinch of regret that the shipboard routine was now over. We'd become institutionalised worryingly fast. Four months of travel through Central America loomed large in front of us. New cultures, new language, new challenges; it felt invigorating, but intimidating at the same time.

We bade our sad farewells to Les and John. Through the lively dining table discussions, we'd built up a peculiar fondness for the odd couple, who still remained more or less entirely unfazed by the unfashionable nature of their opinions. We'd enjoyed taking them to task on their unreconstructed views though, and when we left, it was in a spirit of genuine friendship and mutual respect. I'd been reading Naomi Klein's *The Shock Doctrine*, in John's eyes a potentially 'dangerously liberal' text with its troubling warnings of Milton-Friedman-esque 'disaster capitalism'. In it, Klein argues that radical free-market economists and neo-conservatives have united in a multi-faceted ideological mission that uses violent disruption and disorder, from South Africa to Iraq, to establish what would otherwise be unacceptable, ruthless financial systems – the 'shock therapy' of the title – on resistant economies. I'd lent it to John who had been politically provoked and stirred by it. *Did you it make you angry?* I asked him, noting it had both reinforced my own concerns and certainly radicalised me. *I'm bloody livid!* he said. We'd found our common ground. *I'm an old man but hopefully I can still influence people like you. That matters,* rumbled John, somewhat poignantly.

One side of Ensenada harbour was undergoing extensive and expensive redevelopment, with new quays and jetties under construction. On the other, the half-sunk hulls of a couple of rusting ships jutted up from the oily marina. It looked like the two different sides of Mexico. We had to take an uncomfortably long step from the ship to the quayside, carrying our now strangely heavy-feeling rucksacks, in order to make our first landfall in the Americas. As I looked anxiously down into the watery gap below it felt like a big step into the unknown, but one more closer to home.

# DUST, DRUGS AND DREAMS

*My own journey started long before I left, and
was over before I returned.*

— John Steinbeck —

*Which hotel are you staying at in Ensenada?* asked Eyan, the dapper
young Mexican shipping agent who'd picked us up at the dock office.
*The Ritz,* I replied, at which Eyan burst out laughing. *There is no Ritz in
Ensenada,* he chuckled before I gave him the address of our hotel which
was trading libellously on the reputation of its ever so slightly more
prestigious London namesake.

After our long Pacific build-up to Mexico, we were swiftly engaged by Ensenada's seedy charm. Fi was just glad to get her feet back on terra firma. Like many port cities Ensenada was fairly rough around the edges. The centre was an array of bars and tat-touting tourist shops full of Mexican wrestling masks and cheap pharmaceuticals. These were clearly aimed at the North American cruise-ship passengers that spilled into town on a daily basis from passing vessels. A few blocks further on, the scene was very different. We sidestepped around dubious, loitering characters and working girls who hung outside swinging saloon bar doors. Passing a hard-faced man preparing to inject himself outside one brothel-cum-bar, we resolved to get back into our comfort zone. *Maybe he was diabetic?* Fi offered rather charitably.

Along the seafront, fishing charter boats jostled excitedly for business. In the adjacent Pescado Mercado, slabs of oily smoked tuna sat in sticky, tar-like piles. An ice-cold Corona with a slice of tangy lime amidst the equally refreshing chaos of Ensenada, and our appetite for travel adventure was returning.

You could hardly walk anywhere in Ensenada without tripping over a mariachi group. Splendidly moustachioed geezers in leather jackets with snakeskin trim and Stetsons, armed with guitars, violins and not-so-portable double basses lurked round every corner. They conducted a form of musical guerrilla warfare by ambushing unsuspecting tourists with their folk classics and close harmonies. With the sound of 'La Cucaracha' ringing in our ears back at the Ritz Hotel, we wrestled the grubby cover from the bed as it seemed to be providing an attractive dance floor on which the song's eponymous beasties were enjoying shaking a leg or six.

After acclimatising for 48 hours or so, cranking out our creaky Spanish we prepared for the transitory life again after our long Pacific voyage. We were keen to head south down the long Baja California peninsula, so caught a bus towards El Rosario. As we left the outskirts of town, we entered a parched, dusty landscape strewn with glass and plastic rubbish. Impromptu fences of wooden pallets and old tyres collected wind-blown debris and divided the dirt into graveyards of decaying vehicles, abandoned buildings and piles of unkempt junk. Scrawny dogs prowled through the filth. The many abandoned buildings seemed like painfully visible reminders of unsustained and now long-dead hope – the former optimism of their construction as retrospectively improbable as the likelihood of their future restoration. The initial thrill of being back ashore was rapidly wearing off. Gazing out the window I wondered what the hell we were doing in this apparently joyless and derelict destination.

After the depressing desolation of Ensenada's suburbs, and a couple of hundred miles of similarly bleak surroundings further south on the bus, we arrived in Catavina around dusk and found a room. Catavina wouldn't quite qualify for the dizzyingly aspirational status of a 'one horse town'; the best they could probably rustle up would be a few scraggy canines. The linear hamlet sprawled for a few hundred yards along either side of Highway 1 in dusty dribs and drabs of aged and mostly boarded-up buildings.

The setting was magnificent, however – a rugged valley of massive broken boulders, some house-sized and squatting threateningly in precarious piles beside the road. This cluttered scene stretched on to a skyline of dark, venerable volcanic cones and distant rocky ridges. Among the fragmented rocks grew several varieties of enormous cactus. Their sparse but crudely even distribution lent a curiously stubbly texture to the landscape.

Besides the classic *cardón* cacti, instantly recognizable from cowboy films, there were bizarre and unique endemic species like the *cirio*. Round and broad at the base, these distinctly odd-looking succulents tapered like an inverted 20-foot high root vegetable to fine-pointed branches bearing a small yellow flowery growth. The surface of the narrowing shaft was covered with strange little projecting leaflets, and their presence made us feel we were on a low budget *Star Trek* set of an extraterrestrial planet.

*Cirio* are also known as Boojum trees, inspired by Lewis Carroll's nonsense classic *The Hunting of the Snark*, an epic rhyming tale about the pursuit of a fictitious beast from his feverishly-imagined menagerie of Jabberwocks and Bandersnatches. In the poem a Boojum is a particularly dangerous form of Snark, the descriptions of which Carroll left deliberately vague and ambiguous, concentrating only on its character and demeanour –its predilection for 'breakfasting at five o'clock tea' and constantly carrying around bathing machines – rather than its physical form. Although he does explain how a Snark might taste 'meagre and hollow, but crisp...With a flavour of Will o'the wisp'. These weirdly conceived attributes allowed Carroll to unleash the reader's own imagination in conceptualising the strange beast, by far the most effective of unnerving literary techniques. Our own creative fears were similarly inspired by Catavina's odd surroundings, wondering what furtive danger might lurk behind the hunched rocks and alien flora.

That night a huge full moon illuminated the surreal panorama in bright monochromatic light. We slept fitfully in a roadside cabana, regularly awoken by the monstrous, resonating air-brake flatulence of passing trucks. Up at dawn, we were treated to a serene scene of simultaneously rising sun and fat waning moon, the soft, warm, early light picking out the protruding cacti from between the shadowy rocks. It was strikingly beautiful. Suddenly the appeal of Baja began to make sense in this random truck-stop of a town in the middle of stony nowhere.

There was a sense of direction to our journey that travelling down a long slender peninsula inevitably dictates. Without our own vehicle to get off road, we were obliged to adhere closely to the main artery of Highway 1 and the bus routes that plied it. I liked this restriction, as it lent a certainty to our travel that was similar to the journey we'd made from Bangkok to Singapore. It was as if the relatively narrow isthmuses of Malaysia and Baja pointed us on a specific trajectory, without the temptations or distractions of tangential meanderings. The limited choice liberated us from travel decisions: there was only one way to go, and that was south.

Almost immediately after we left the Catavina valley, the landscape changed. The creepy cacti and rubble of boulders disappeared, and we drove across a broad dry plateau. As the sun set, the silhouettes of distant volcanic peaks melted away into the gathering darkness, only to be picked out again a few minutes later when the appearance of the full moon flooded bright, bleached light across the scene once more. It was past 11pm when the bus dropped us in the dark on the main road near to San Ignacio.

Centre of the seasonal grey-whale-watching industry, the turning was marked by a huge whale skeleton glowing ghostly white in the moonlight. We'd arrived before the tourist-luring cetaceans, and after everything had apparently shut for the night. Walking boldly off into the pitch black we luckily stumbled across the Motel Fong and secured a room.

The sun was searingly hot in the morning as we ambled into San Ignacio along a palm-fringed road, sticky dates pressed into the sandy verge underfoot. The town centre was a gorgeous shady plaza of huge leafy trees offering respite from the midday heat, dominated at one end by the imposing 15th-century Mission building. The Jesuits and subsequent waves of missionaries had once dominated Baja during Spain's colonisation of the region. Despite being rebuffed by fierce native Cochimis on their initial attempts, they were eventually successful and established their first Mission at Loreto in 1697. Their proselytizing was met with continued resistance from the indigenous inhabitants, who were perhaps understandably reluctant to give up their itinerant, semi-naked, polygamous lifestyles. The Jesuit message essentially being *Believe in our God, stay here, put on these clothes, and stop having sex with everyone else*. It reminded me of old-school environmental lecturing, of telling people what to do, castigating their 'normal' way of life, of imposing values on others, rather than inspiring audiences to aspire to something better.

Whilst initially – depending very much on your perspective – 'successful', the Missions ultimately scored a most spectacularly tragic own goal. God does indeed move in mysterious ways, as the Old World diseases the Missions had imported with them rapidly reduced the indigenous population they hoped to convert from 40,000 to 4,000 souls in less than a century. I imagined an emissary's report back balancing the good news, 'The conversion of the locals is complete', with the rather bad, 'But there's only a tenth of them left'. Despite the historic violence with which the Missions had coerced and converted the indigenous people, San Ignacio was the first really handsome town we'd come across in Mexico. Its sleepy off-season feel was a welcome departure from the edginess of Ensenada and remote weirdness of Catavina.

Back at Motel Fong we sipped cool Pacifico beers on the veranda while we waited for the next bus south and were entertained by the proprietor himself. Manu Fong's father was Chinese, hence the distinctly un-Mexican surname, and beneath the weathered cowboy hat you could just detect a trace of oriental ancestry in his eyes. Excited to fetch his battered 34-year-old eight-string Spanish guitar to play us some tunes, he cut the back of his hand on the cupboard door. As he plucked out a few old favourites for us as his captive audience, crooning his way wheezily through 'La Bamba' and 'South of the Border', I watched mesmerised as a thick trickle of dark red blood oozed its way across his knuckles.

On the bus we had to pass through a series of military checkpoints that are a regular feature of travel down the Baja. Bored recruits in sandy desert fatigues hunched uninterestedly over sand-bagged machine gun nests, long, live-cartridge belts hanging menacingly beneath. Strangely, even though we were stopped around half a dozen times, they never shook down the bus for drugs. Mexican 'narcos' clearly travel in classier fashion. The checkpoints were a sobering reminder of the vicious war being waged across northern Mexico. The US State Department suggests that 90 percent of cocaine in the United States comes through Mexican narcotic networks. As a key transit route between cocaine production in South America and the voracious US drug market, trafficking is now a major Mexican industry that leads to thousands of murders a year, chronic police corruption and the headless bodies of executed gang members littering the countryside. Baja is one of the most violent Mexican states as a result.

Since the implicit relationships between the authorities and the drug cartels began to break down in the 1980s, the wholesale trade, estimated by some experts to be worth up to almost 50 billion dollars a year, has become ever bloodier. Over 45,000 troops are involved in battling the cartels, who themselves are battling each other for control of the lucrative trade. The lethal combination of poverty, lack of opportunity and rapid wealth accumulation has led to ever more extreme violence. Summary executions appear on YouTube, body parts are thrown into crowded nightclubs, and public hit lists of targeted police officers are picked off

*Vintage fire engine, Santa Rosalia, Baja California, Mexico*

one by one by drug cartel assassination squads. The carnage created by cocaine in Mexico alone, never mind the humanitarian and ecological disasters propagated in countries like Colombia, where production fuels civil unrest and generates horrific pollution, are powerful arguments against the dismal failure of prohibition policies. Yet these continue to be mindlessly rolled out by politicians all over the world. While the profits of the drug trade remain so high, despite the bloodshed involved, this is an industry that is only ever likely to grow, with all the social and environmental costs that this entails. At an estimated 60,000 deaths and counting – in Mexico alone since 2006 – that line of cocaine on a mirror in London or New York has one hell of an ethical footprint.

The remnants of one of Baja's biggest former industries littered our next stop, Santa Rosalia. The French 'El Boleo' copper company had founded and dominated this town that nestled in a steep, rough-sided valley topped by graveyards and towering crosses. The French had left in 1954, but the works were in use by a state-owned company up until the 1980s. They were then finally abandoned, but typically not dismantled. Instead they stood as a heritage reminder of former glories. Vast rusting complexes of defunct pipes and ducting filled broken-windowed warehouses, the once-busy smelting plant being now thick with the dust that seems to settle on every static thing in Baja. We were distracted from the sad legacy of Santa Rosalia's industrial decline by its brightly painted wooden houses. In brilliant combinations of purple and green, or orange and blue, the clapperboard buildings were uplifting in the otherwise pervasive atmosphere of decay. The presence of a hundred-year-old French bakery also cheered us as we ate authentic crusty baguettes with salty white cheese, fat, juicy tomatoes and soft avocados beside the long-retired railway station.

Copper was the cocaine of its day for the Baja economy. Miners were lured in by the prospect of money to what was a difficult, dangerous and dirty business. Fatalities were common in the extraction of the lucrative ore that helped supply the global industrial revolution, as they are now in the trafficking of the even more profitable powder that supplies a more problematic worldwide habit. But if the blossoming whale-watching businesses around San Ignacio were anything to go by, perhaps eco-tourism can provide a safer, cleaner income for the region?

Baja is certainly blessed with a richness of biodiversity to enjoy. Another short bus hop along the eastern shore, past numerous rocky islands lolling lazily in the calm blue waters, took us to Mulege, a small town sleepier and dustier than a sloth in a flour-sack. Here Baja's wildlife was really putting on a show. As we walked along a rough dirt track towards the beach, a sea eagle flew past gripping a large, live, twitching fish in its talons, which it then proceeded to dispatch on the tall stump of a palm tree. By the small, crude concrete lighthouse at the head of the arroyo, we watched as magisterial frigate birds whirled overhead, flanked by their aerial henchmen, the black vultures. Below us in the surf, the 'Mexican air-force' was in action. Synchronised squadrons of brown pelicans, gannets and cormorants plunged headlong into the fertile, fish-laden waters, and behind us a pair of elegant white egrets prowled the mangrove fringes. After hundreds of miles of inhospitable terrain it was remarkable to see such abundance.

Other parts of Baja that had virtually no permanent population were wilder in a rather different way. There was a definite *Mad Max* feel to many areas, the dry waterless soil, merciless sunshine and scarcity of people adding to the post-apocalyptic air. It resembled a hot, arid version of the similarly bleak but boggy swathes of Siberia we'd seen many months before. Informal trailer parks of American motor-homes sat parked up defensively, like the modern-day circled wagons of survivalists, on some of the more attractive bays. The biggest of these road-beasts were the size of static caravans, and towed cars as large as SUVs behind them. One even had a quad-bike in the back of the SUV; heaven forfend the occupants might actually have to walk anywhere. There were also a few small secure enclaves of newly built villas and condominiums for expats from north of the border, with signs threatening armed response units and guard dogs to uninvited guests. It reminded me of South Africa, where the moneyed few live in fear of the many poor, where even a holiday house can be a fortress with a contradictory lack of freedom.

Attempting our first hitch-hiking since New Zealand, we were picked up by Vin-Diesel-lookalike Mario, all bulging muscles, thick bands of tattoos like road markings, shaven head, mirrored sunglasses and wide-boy banter. *Are you English?* he shouted back a little incredulously to us as we squatted in the rear of his pick-up. *No, Scottish!* Fi hollered back, perhaps marginally too triumphantly. Turned out he was from Haringey, 'Norf Lahndahn', and had been in Baja on and off for ten years, absorbing perhaps just a tad too much UV and certain locally-plentiful combustible herbs. *I'm not thick, I just talk slow,* he drawled whilst drawing on another hefty reefer.

Mario dropped us at a *palapa* – an open-sided palm leaf-roofed hut – on Coyote Beach where we could camp for the night. We set up the tent while Mario rolled joints, regaling us with stories, as brown pelicans dipped in and out of the shallow water along the tide-line. They were skilfully scooping small fish into their leathery pouches from the huge nursery shoals seeking shelter against the shore. *You can see why they named the bay Bahia Concepcion when you see how much life is born here,* observed Mario, channelling his outwardly-unlikely inner Attenborough.

He'd bought a piece of land in one of the valleys above the bay, where he was building a house in the form of a geodesic dome. He told us of his past as a party organiser both here and back in London. He'd had a minor novelty hit record with a song about 'being a Mexican and drinking tequila in the sun'. *I wrote that before I'd even been to Mexico too!* he laughed huskily. *Folk in London want a bigger house, in a better neighbourhood, or a bigger car – I had all that and it's meaningless,* Mario philosophised. *But this,* he gestured, waving his hand across the broad sweep of the sparkling blue bay to our left, flanked by reddish rocky headlands, *this is aspirational.*

After a stiff night's sleep on the hard, sandy beach, we arrived in La Paz in the rain. To enhance the damp ambience, the main drag was being resurfaced, creating an obstacle course of wet cement, open man-holes and drains, piles of new metal street furniture and the odd dangling electrical cable to add to the excitement. Ravenous, we ate a spicy *sopa mariscos* in a very local cantina, complete with obligatory blind guitar player strumming away in the corner, and made plans for the ferry crossing to the mainland.

Many years ago, one of the books that had first inspired me to become a marine biologist was John Steinbeck's *The Log from the Sea of Cortez*. It's about a trip he made with his friend, the celebrated American scientist Ed Ricketts. Those were the days when field work was all about catching bizarre new species and shoving them into glass jars of formaldehyde. The book chronicled their relationship and philosophies in a way that I'd found provocative when I first read it in my late teens. Considering the timing of the book, its evocation of man's place *within* nature rather than mastery *over* it and its passionate concerns about our ability to find a balance between greed and need were unusually premature. Sustainability, stewardship and the notion of interdependence were all powerfully evoked. Between them, Steinbeck and Ricketts were putting forward ideas that modern environmentalists would instantly recognise, but in the 1940s were seen as distinctly avant-garde.

Now La Paz was the focus for Baja's burgeoning tourism industry. Steinbeck had mourned the construction of the first holiday hotel during their visit: 'Probably the airplanes will bring week-enders from Los Angeles before long, and the beautiful poor bedraggled old town will bloom with a Floridian ugliness'. He wasn't wrong. La Paz did have elements of that crude everglade-style development, but at least we'd arrived by land and sea, a journey of which I hope he would have approved. Gazing out over the same azure blue waters that had so moved him and Ricketts, I wanted in.

Our snorkelling boat took us out to Los Isolotes, a series of pinnacled crags jutting out of the sea and home to Baja's biggest colony of California sea lions. The journey through the choppy waters was bumpy as we wove between barren but unspoilt islands and past deserted white sandy coves lapped by turquoise waves. The rocks of Los Isolotes were red but topped by a thick white crust of dried guano – 'shite-washed' by the resident seabirds. As we approached, we could not only hear but also smell the feral pungency of the sea lions as they honked away at us like oceanic dogs from beneath the cliffs. In the water, they demonstrated the millions of years of evolution that separate us from our marine mammal cousins, gliding elegantly around our flailing limbs in mutual curiosity. The sleek young pups swam right up to our masks, barked in our faces and swam rings around us. As well as the sea lions, the water teemed with colourful parrotfish, surgeonfish, groupers and jacks. On the rocks above, massive bull seals aggressively defended their harems of breeding females from adolescent males attempting to sneak in for a crafty shag. As we bounced back across a rolling, darkening sea to La Paz in the dying light, I paid a silent tribute to Steinbeck and Ricketts and the natural beauty and bounty of Baja, and thanked both for their ongoing inspiration.

It was our nine-month anniversary of being on the road the next morning as we set off for the ferry to Topolobampo. The straightforward linearity of the journey, the simple quiet towns and vast wilderness of Baja were over, and the buzzing life of the Mexican mainland beckoned. At the breezy port a slow-moving queue of passengers shuffled through the security check and we boarded the ferry for the six hour, 300-mile crossing to the mainland, the penultimate major boat journey of our trip.

An email from Hamish had also confirmed our cargo ship across the Atlantic. We'd be leaving Costa Rica in around four months time. Having this date fixed was significant. We now knew the final leg of our trip was confirmed, and we had been given something to aim at. Our sailing from Singapore to Australia had decided our itinerary through South-East Asia, and this new departure date would hang over our Central American journey in similar fashion. In some ways I resented these impositions; as Steinbeck himself observed, 'A journey is like marriage. The certain way to be wrong is to think you control it'. Dates and destinations created delusions of control, dictated times and trajectories of travel. If we weren't careful we were in danger of becoming divorced from the purpose of our travel: a new way of viewing the world, not simply seeing its sights.

# ENNUI

*He gave the impression that very many cities*
*had rubbed him smooth.*

— Graham Greene —

A vintage bus with enamelled fittings, bakelite console and a driver of comparable antiquity bumped us through the darkness from the ferry port at Topolobampo to Los Mochis. Arriving in a strange city after nightfall is never an entirely relaxing experience so, after losing ourselves in the gloomy streets, we made the unfortunate knee-jerk choice of the Hotel Los Arcos. Our room was clean enough but reeked of cheap Brut-like aftershave, a bit like sleeping in Henry Cooper's armpit. The shower head had a built in heating element to warm the water which was wired to the mains. The constant fear of electrocution was definitely one way of encouraging shorter showers and water conservation.

An alarm bell should have rung in our heads on arrival when we'd seen the bar next door, 'Chicass [sic] & Beer'. The clientele seemed to be having a contest to see who could make the loudest, most irritating noise throughout the night. The competition was intense: early contenders started on slightly obvious tactics such as playing Mexican pop at speaker-destroyingly loud volumes on the stereo of your parked car, demonstrating your new air-horn to your friends or shouting to people half a mile away down the road. These initially promising performances were later trumped by what sounded like two guys ululating into a microphone followed by the enormous crash of a heavy object being thrown from an upstairs window into the street below. However, the winner by a clear lead, for sheer bravado alone, was the silencer-free motorbike that was ridden repeatedly at high, roaring revs along the pavement outside our room. The challenge was concluded just before 4am, when everyone seemed to have had enough and finally, mercifully, headed off home.

Two short hours of sleep later, and we got up to catch the famous Copper Canyon train to Creel. This grand railway achievement took over 60 years to complete, being fully opened in 1961, its construction surviving both bankruptcy and the Mexican Revolution. It was originally conceived by the great American railway entrepreneur Arthur Stilwell as a route to connect land-locked Kansas City with the Pacific Ocean, but now runs between Los Mochis and Chihuahua. There were two daily trains, a 6am 'first class' and a 7am 'second class', the primary difference being that the early train cost twice the price and was marginally faster. Needless to say, we had an extra hour in bed and took the latter. It was an 11-hour journey over 37 bridges and through 86 tunnels, the astonishing track winding its way up and through a seemingly impossible landscape of narrow dead-end valleys, pointed pinnacles onto a cool, piny mountain plateau.

Climbing from sea level to over seven and a half thousand feet at Divisadero, where it crossed the continental divide that decides into which ocean the rivers will finally empty, the train's engine had its work cut out. It was an incredible feat of engineering. We stood between the carriages, sticking our heads out of the window and playing 'chicken' with approaching tunnel walls as the train rattled along its way. Sadly, bar the

*Riding the Copper Canyon railway to Creel, Mexico*

specialist tourist-oriented services such as the Tequila Express that runs a mere 20 miles or so from Guadalajara to the distilleries at Amatitán, the Copper Canyon line is the last remnant of regular, reliable railway in Mexico. The decline of a once-extensive network has been rapid and dramatic following withdrawal of government support at the turn of the millennium. Annoyingly, my personal bugbear of short-haul flights and the admittedly rather good Mexican bus system are now taking up the slack.

In Creel we were at the heart of the Copper Canyon system, a series of valleys in the Sierra Tarahumara mountains, four times larger and at points deeper than its far more hyped relative, the Grand Canyon a little further north. It was so cold at this altitude after balmy Baja, we were glad of the carbon monoxide-spewing 'death machine' gas heater in the corner of our room. A slow, lingering poisonous demise seemed preferable to being frozen into hypothermic unconsciousness. As the heater warmed up, it performed a passable impression of Rolf Harris on a wobble-board, as its casing buckled and boinged with the heat. To stretch our legs and get beyond the shabby, unattractive streets of the town, we hired bikes and set off to see some of the local wind-eroded rock formations. The Valleys of the Frogs and Mushrooms were a little underwhelming. I think someone had been on the peyote when they mistook the blobby boulders for amphibians, although the mushrooms did look vaguely fungal. Marginally more impressive was the Valley of the Monks, where huge vertical rock towers stood sentinel-like in meditative groups along a narrow chasm.

But the rides and the sights left me as cold as the bitter weather. Sigmund Freud said that 'dying is replaced in dreams by departure, by a train journey'. It felt like a part of my travelling mojo had died on the Copper Canyon railway. I was feeling weary of supposed 'attractions' that usually led to disappointment; local communities invariably but entirely understandably over-hyped their immediate, meagre assets in pursuit of tourist dollars. To put it bluntly, the problem was that we were jaded. A little tired and even bored with travelling, I was no longer seizing every moment, wringing every last drop of joy from it, before moving hungrily onto the next. After nine long months on the move, I'd reached a sort of saturation point which, despite my guilty thoughts about how scandalous this attitude was in the context of our privileged liberty, I was finding it hard to shake off. Like depressed creative types who take prozac to alleviate the mental gloom, I felt like I'd lost my edge. I was going through the motions of travel without the same thrills as before. The tangible end-date for the final ocean crossing we'd confirmed with Hamish hadn't helped either. Instead of a target to focus on, I felt like we were now simply filling in or killing time before leaving and heading home.

Chatting to a Swiss guy who was cycling from Alaska to Patagonia, in Creel I felt humbled, our trip somehow belittled by his taut-thighed efforts. I resolved to find a way to chase off this malaise, overcome our sense of pathetic ingratitude and reinvigorate the trip once more. Lying in bed that night, I realised I tended to enjoy myself most when we were in the nondescript places, the accidental destinations, the things we stumbled upon en route rather than those we actively sought out. The Tao of travel would reinforce this idea of the rewarding journey not the destination or, as Lao Tzu proposes, 'A good traveller has no fixed plans and is not intent on arriving'. While we had a plan to leave from Costa Rica in four months time, nothing in-between was set. There was still plenty of scope to be free range and flexible over the coming weeks and re-sharpen our blunted edge, even if the notion of 'planning to be more spontaneous' in itself felt more than faintly ridiculous.

Next day we caught the bus to Hidalgo del Parral. We never actually made it. The bus was rammed with country folk and carried the heady aroma of earthy, unwashed bodies and wood smoke. I didn't expect Raramuri people, the canyon's indigenous inhabitants, to be on the bus. From what I'd understood they were famed for their stamina, the name Raramuri literally meaning 'runners on foot'. Living in settlements separated by long distances, Raramuri traditions involved the competitive running and kicking of wooden balls, sometimes for days, and the aptly named technique of 'persistence' hunting, where prey is chased to exhaustion by super-fit pursuers. Maybe this was why they got motion sickness on the bus. Shortly after departure, the tortuous winding mountain roads did for one Raramuri's stomach and added a pungent piquancy to the already-fragrant cocktail of fires and flesh. We spun around the crenulated edges of steep canyons, enjoying broad vistas across the huge drops below. Groaning and creaking on the punishingly steep ascents, the bus threatened to run away from the driver's control on the alarmingly fast descents. Then the bus broke down. To this day, we're not entirely sure where or why – our Spanish vocabulary certainly didn't stretch to mechanics – and we spent an unplanned night in a roadside motel.

Thanks to Michel Thomas, we could conjure up enough survival Spanish to ask directions, book accommodation and shop politely. The only downside was that our superficially-fluent delivery of the basics tended to open the flood gates of conversation with perennially chatty Mexicans, leaving us utterly befuddled and confused. My response was usually to try and answer the question I guessed they might have asked. Fi mistook this for innate linguistic talent rather than the seat of the pants blagging it quite blatantly was. At breakfast in our random roadside motel, a Stetsoned *hombre* greeted us and – we guessed – asked where we from. He followed this up with, I assumed, a question about how long we were visiting Mexico for. *Dos mesas,* I confidently replied. (I didn't realise that this means 'two tables'; the word for months is *meses.*)

After finishing our *huevos, chorizo* and *frijoles*, we caught the next bus on to Parral. The sun popped out as we arrived, and it was pleasantly warm after the frigid mountains of Creel. Parral was a handsome if nondescript mining town and we embraced its comfy normality. After checking into the ominous sounding Room 101 at a cheap hotel, we ate fibrous but tasty chicken in the tiny cantina next door, accompanied by a pile of soft tortillas kept warm wrapped up in a dirty towel. Stepping out, we admired the paint-peeling shutters, rusty window grilles, cracked plaster and exposed brickwork of beautiful old buildings that had seen better days, mulling on the appeal of genteel dilapidation. We enjoyed the anonymity of feeling like locals in the tourist-free town: a guy even tried to sell us a dog, at which point, for a moment, we felt like we genuinely belonged.

Dawn broke the next day, turning the low clouds a glorious bright pink as we roused ourselves for the bus to Durango, the home of the Mexican film industry. The road consisted of long, flat straights over parched plains scarred by river canyons, before weaving up and over a succession of ridges. Hefty flat-topped mountains punctuated the horizon, thrusting up from amongst plantations of barren-looking olive trees and prickly-pear-like cacti. Bright crimson flowers budded like licks of red flame on the edge of their succulently fleshy and leafy lobes. Patches of brittle dry scrub burned or had been burnt beside the road, like a black charcoal tongue lapping along the verge, and ghostly blue-ish smoke billowed on the breeze. We were in cowboy country now, as men on horseback with many-galloned hats herded dusty brown cattle and the thermometer at the front of the bus crept up to 27°C degrees as the day grew hotter and we approached Durango.

We stayed at the Hotel California, which wasn't exactly as I'd imagined it from the lyrics in the Eagles' song. I'm sure Don Henley didn't have to sleep on a plastic sheet for a start, and its location was less 'dark, desert highway' than 'dingy, suburban backstreet'. But it was cheap, central and run by a smiling woman with an impressively engineered set of monumental dentures like she'd eaten a small piano. Durango was the setting for a slew of classic westerns such as *A Man Called Horse* and *Geronimo*, and much of the central architecture had been spruced up, the city ironically investing heavily in its historical buildings to keep the place looking authentically old. We explored streets lined with heavy wooden doors and shutters that hid mysterious courtyard houses beyond. In the Plaza Centenario we spotted our first Christmas tree of the season. Strung with lights of such gaudy flamboyance they were almost Chinese, the tree created a brief pang for far-away friends and families. At least its presence was timely, with only a fortnight to go till Christmas, in contrast to the appearance of municipal decorations back home in late October.

Durango's merry festive spirit was infectious, and we mingled unselfconsciously with the Mexicans as they bought colourful paper star-shaped piñatas to fill with sweets and goodies. We must have caught someone's eye, however, as, the following day, a truly bizarre set of coincidences aligned themselves. Catching the bus to Zacatecas we bought a small roast chicken and some tortillas to sustain us on the six-hour journey. Lacking napkins and wishing to avoid an on-the-bus grease-fest, I bought a random newspaper to wipe our mitts. After devouring our delicious bird and sacrificing a couple of oily sections of the paper in the process, I was idly flicking through the remnants of the local rag. Attempting to exercise my modest Spanish reading talents, I spotted a familiar-looking couple in a picture accompanying an article about tourism in the city. *We're in the paper*, I deadpanned to Fi. *What on earth are you talking about?* she retorted. So I showed her the half-page image of the two of us outside Durango cathedral that must have been snapped unbeknownst to us the previous day. The paper's photographer was probably briefed to go and 'snap some tourists' and, being about the only ones in town, he'd stalked us. It was one of those brilliant travelling moments when a whole series of improbable events combine to create a satisfying but highly unlikely outcome. It seemed implausible that we were photographed in the first place without our knowledge. But that we then bought the right newspaper as an impromptu napkin and then actually read the thing, only to find ourselves in it, was almost incredible.

Besides my own regular column in the *Observer* and other articles I'd penned en route, it was not the first time our trip had hit the international media. The *Pride of Bilbao* voyage at the very start had made the front page of local paper *El Correo*, such was the ferocity of the storm we'd encountered. We had also appeared in the *Grevesmühlen Zeitung*, under the headline 'Weltreisende besuchten Grevesmühlen', (World Travellers seek out Grevesmühlen). The article, written by the friend we'd stayed with (a former journalist), sought to explain why we'd ended up in that pleasant but somewhat somnambulant corner of Germany as part of our global circumnavigation. So we'd lied a little. But now we could add our unexpected splash in *El Sol de Durango* to the list.

The generally reliable Mexican bus system conveyed us efficiently south through the sun-bleached dusty highlands and plains. The only discomfort was the fact that our seats were often stuck in 'full recline' position. The sensation was not dissimilar to travelling along in a speeding dentist's

*Valley of the Monks, Creel, Mexico*

*Making news, our unexpected appearance in 'El Sol de Durango', Mexico*

chair as we entered the colonial heartlands. We were certainly in the right place to pick up a few cheap fillings. The extraordinary architectural wealth of the Mexican 'silver towns' is based on the rich seams of precious metal-bearing rock that have been mined for almost half a millennium. Spain did rather well out of this exploitation; the records at one mine alone, the Alvarado, show output between 1548 and 1867 of nearly 800-million-dollars-worth of silver at today's prices.

In Zacatecas we visited El Mina, plunging deep into the hillside down a rough-hewn tunnel on a rickety little train. We explored the huge cavernous gash, from which the valuable ore had been excavated, the chasm dropping away from the grille beneath our feet into dizzyingly deep misty darkness. There was also a nightclub, which brought new meaning to the expression 'All back to mine', and a small museum of rocks and minerals that managed to achieve the impressive feat of making geology seem sexy. Fabulously coloured crystals from across Latin America included violet fluorites, vibrant orange creelites and viridian green malachites that shimmered and twinkled in the artful lighting.

The riches generated by the mine were plain to see. Dominated by the ornate pink sandstone Churriguera-style cathedral, the heart of town was a compact maze of attractive narrow streets and alleys, opulent merchant houses and well-to-do shops. In the early mornings the sharp, clinical smell of bleach filled the air as shopkeepers and maids mopped their steps and street frontages clean. This diligence was a far cry from the laidback, dusty feel of the Mexico we'd seen so far.

In the Museo Rafael Coronel they had a mind-blowing display of over 3000 masks. Housed in a warren of rooms among the atmospheric ruins of an old convent, the masks ranged from bestial and ceremonial types to a whole room full of red-lit devilish *Diabolo* disguises. We were confronted by hundreds of grinning skull-like death masks from the energetic Dia de Muertos (Day of the Dead) celebrations and almost-comical carnival headgear with long blonde straw wigs and Carlos Valderama afros. There were moustachioed gringo masks, a menagerie of animals including crocodiles, leopards, pigs and cows, often using real skulls, and strange shamanic, witch-doctor masks made of bundles

*The view over Zacatecas, Mexico*

of twigs. The masks ranged from those which were obviously ancient, through to the entertainingly modern, incorporating cast-off sunglasses and other contemporary ephemera, proving that the art of the mask was alive and well.

The purpose of masks is to hide and conceal intentions, disguise identity or assume different characteristics. Mexican mask-making goes back millennia. Earliest examples include the vertebra from a now-extinct species of llama that was carved around 10,000BC to resemble a coyote's head. By around 1000BC, masks made of clay and stone were becoming more common. These were eyeless, probably death-masks; the founders of Mesoamerican civilisation, the Olmecs, made jade, onyx and quartzite masks of hybrid man-birds and other mongrel human-god combinations. The Aztecs focused on ceramic, half-flayed, fleshless and half-living masks, denoting the many-layered reality of life. These durable masks are the ones that have survived, and it's almost certain there were other styles and variations of more fragile materials that failed to be preserved.

Animal masks proliferated in pre-Christian Mexico through the belief that each child born had a *Tona* or soul guardian, an animal counterpart with whom their fate was inextricably linked. I immediately thought of Phillip Pullman's *His Dark Materials* and the 'daemons', their animal familiars, that every human is metaphysically connected to. People were meant to be able to transform into their *Tona* at will. This reflected the notion of interconnectedness that bound humans to their environment and the natural and supernatural worlds – an idea that many modern environmentalists endeavour to rekindle.

Like most conquerors, the Spaniards co-opted the Mexican traditions of dances dedicated to various gods that featured masked participants as birds, insects, and other animals such as jaguars, and matched them to their Christian beliefs. The 'Dance of the Moors and Christians', following the expulsion of the Moors from Spain, was introduced to Mexico as an example of Christian superiority. Mexicanised versions of 'Conquest Dances' followed, depicting Spanish victories over indigenous people. The modern Dio de Muertos rituals also combine old Aztec festivals in honour of Mictecacihuatl, the goddess of the underworld, with the

*Traditional mask, Museo Rafael Coronel, Zacatecas, Mexico*

Catholic holidays of All Saints Day and All Souls Day. Other traditions included the 'Dance of the Old Men' where doddery walking 'dancers' in geriatric masks stagger along to the general amusement of the watching crowds.

That evening, a 70-strong brass band was playing a seasonal selection of yuletide classics in the Plaza de Armas near the cathedral, next to a Christmas tree irritatingly decorated solely with Coca-Cola insignia. We perched ourselves on the steps behind three sturdy sousaphone players and hummed along to familiar tunes. 'Jingle Bells' and 'Frosty the Snowman' felt particularly surreal in sunny Zacatecas. When the band finished, we strolled through the softly lit night-time streets, as in Durango, enjoying the festive feel of a Mexican Christmas. A smartly dressed woman approached us at one point; she strode up, smiling from ear to ear, greeted us warmly and welcomed us to Zacatecas, before melting away into the crowds, leaving us with a lovely, fuzzy feeling of contentment as we headed back to the hostel.

There they were having a 'Margarita night', an initially slightly forced affair. It's amazing what tequila can do towards oiling the wheels of conversation among the guests. I'd earlier been impressed by the Spanish talents of a huge flame-haired Irish-looking bloke, who, it unpredictably turned out, was actually Mexican. *They call me El Churro Rojo!* (the Red Cowboy) he roared, *I am Mexican inside! Outside? I don't know!* he said shaking his broad, red, sunburned head topped by a tuft of bright ginger thatch. He looked about as Mexican as Mick Hucknall. El Churro Rojo explained that his parents had emigrated from the Emerald Isle before he was born, which went some way to explaining his extremely Celtic looks.

In the queue at Leon bus station the following day we met 'Doctor London'. He was a bizarrely baby-faced bloke with jet black, probably dyed hair who looked to be in his early 50s. His American accent belied his supposedly Ukrainian roots and he looked at us through the type of calm, slightly glazed eyes you usually associate with members of cults. Like us he was headed to Guanajuato, where he now lived, so we enquired as to what he did there. *I run Mexican tourism,* he replied humbly, *among other things. They say I'm one of the best educators in the world,* he continued, warming to the heat of his own fevered ego. *I am a very powerful man, if I have a problem I just call up the President of Mexico or the President of the United States,* he intoned solemnly. *You must have an amazing phone book,* I observed, but there was no stopping him now. *I can literally send people to Hell,* the Doctor informed us gravely. *Literally?!* Fi exclaimed unable to suppress her incredulity. Sensing he was perhaps just a little delusional, we edged slowly away. For all his supposed success it can only have been Doctor London's inherent modesty that led him to be catching the bus with a couple of skint travellers like us.

On arrival in Guanajuato we were instantly disorientated, as most of the roads that run through the city centre are underground. They're buried in tunnels that used to carry the city's river, long ago diverted into a natural cave system to reduce flooding. We hopped off the bus in a dark passageway and climbed a small stone staircase to emerge blinking into the sunshine of a city largely un-invaded by cars. Why can't it always be like this, I thought as we wandered the convoluted narrow alleyways that twirled between buildings painted cheerfully in an understated palette of pink, lime and purple.

The removal of cars meant that a vibrant pedestrian street culture flourished in Guanajuato. There was something timeless about the absence of the all-powerful motorcar, a resurgence of a human-oriented pace of life and use of space that vehicular traffic usually kills stone dead. It wasn't just that the air was cleaner as a result, except of course in the rather fumy tunnels below; the place felt different. As I used to say when I'd worked as environmental manager at London Transport many years ago, it didn't matter if we all drove clean, green electric vehicles, we'd still all be sat in clean, quiet traffic jams. In Guanajuato it was possible to see the tangible effect of excluding cars almost completely, and it was overwhelmingly positive.

People walked unhindered and uninhibited by the threat of traffic, plazas became calm, leafy havens of social activity. Resplendent mariachis in starched white suits serenaded drinkers and diners beneath the trees, shoppers wandered freely in and out of the quiet cobbled streets without fear of speeding motorists. We were even spared the popular Mexican promotional tactic of large car-mounted tannoy speakers blasting adverts, offers, information about events or political posturing and slogans to an involuntary streetside audience. They could still do it in Guanajuato, but they'd be underground, out of sight, out of mind and most importantly of all, out of earshot.

I relished this pedestrian liberation as we huffed and puffed our way through the narrow *callejons* and alleyways that riddled the city's buildings as they crept up the steep sides of the valley. It seemed an inversion of the priorities we'd seen in other places like Moscow, where it's the people who are effectively buried, forced to use underpasses and subways to go beneath rather than simply across roads. Guanajuato had turned this logic on its head and was an infinitely more lively, lovely and ultimately successful city as a result. It was a rare example of far-sighted urban vision that transcended the short-term mobbing of the motoring lobby that hobbles so many other cities around the world.

While the impeccable urban transport policy undoubtedly deserved commendation, there were other aspects of the city that raised questions about the notion of good taste. We continued the subterranean theme of the road tunnels with a visit to the city's famous Museo de las Momias. Instead of mummies of the carefully prepared ancient Egyptian variety, Guanajuato's are the relatively young, naturally desiccated cadavers of townspeople whose families were unable to pay the local grave tax. Failure to pay meant the deceased's body was exhumed and placed on public display. Tours of the grisly remains began surreptitiously in the late 19th century, when a glimpse could be had by slipping the custodians of the tomb a few pesos. Now the museum attracts almost a million visitors a year and the substantial profits go to municipal funds, coffins now contributing handsomely to coffers.

There were over a hundred leathery mummies inside, preserved by the region's uniquely dry climatic conditions that avert normal decay. Dried skin was cracked and taut over straw-like muscle fibres protruding through tears in the tanned hides. Eye sockets sat sunken, hollow and empty, while long yellow teeth lined the edges of mouths from which the lips had long retreated. Some mummies had macabre stories associated with them. The damage to the fingers and forehead of one woman had led investigators to speculate she may have been buried alive whilst in a cataleptic state, only to recover underground. This victim of the most visceral of nightmares sent shivers down my spine. Similarly the tiny bodies of mummified babies, like damaged, discarded and delicate dolls, were especially distressing. The most recent corpse was that of a drowning victim who'd only been added to the collection in 1984 – not even a lifetime ago, let alone the millennia we associate with the more conventional idea of mummies as preserved Egyptian Pharaohs.

We had never seen so many relatively 'fresh' dead bodies, and the effect was quite moving. This perhaps reflected the healthy Mexican attitude to death as demonstrated by the veneration of the departed on the Dio de Muertos. On the first and second of November every year Mexicans – together with Catholics in many countries – celebrate and remember late ancestors and friends, in a positive party spirit more akin to a wake than a funeral. Perhaps in light of this approach, the museum managed to maintain a respectful, contemplative and poignant tone in what could easily have been a crudely voyeuristic, ghoulish or exploitative exhibition. Sadly this reverence evaporated outside in the car park, where enterprising vendors were hawking 'Candy Mummies' to the sweet of tooth for whom looking at dozens of dead bodies was an appetite-stimulating experience. Or where, for ten pesos, you could have your photo taken posing with two faked-up life-size female mummies, complete with skimpy skirts and vest tops constraining their bulging embalmed bosoms.

Our experiments in activities of questionable taste continued that evening with a night out at the Lucha Libre, the 'Free Fight' that is Mexican wrestling. Very much a family affair, we joined groups comprising several generations of locals as we all shuffled into Guanajuato's Parque Beis-Bol. We'd arrived ridiculously early, so sat impatiently on our concrete bench in 'The Pen', behind a chicken wire fence that separated us from the ring. Our sense of anticipation increased in direct proportion to the loss of feeling in our buttocks. The first part of the bill consisted of wrestlers or *luchadores* who looked like your dad had decided to have a go. With podgy bodies clad in string vests, budgie-smuggling Speedo swimming trunks and cast-off old tights, they grappled with each other in amateurish style. One even looked like he was about to go fishing, wearing camouflage shorts and a khaki green body warmer, more J.R. Hartley than Giant Haystacks. And of course, continuing the Mexican traditions we'd seen in Zacatecas, all the wrestlers were masked.

In between bouts, the gargantuan stereo system pumped classic bass-heavy Mexican two-beat rhythms into the stadium. During these breaks, a wonderful array of hawkers descended upon us, touting everything from wrestling masks to strawberries and cream, though any similarities to Wimbledon ended there. One hugely fat man flogged nuts, cakes and biscuits from a heavily-laden round tray perched atop his plump, bald head. We were impressed by his deportment and balancing skills, but when he paused and offloaded the tray to pat his perspiring brow, we realised how flat and plate-like the top of his polished pate was. He was either born to do it or had been doing it far too long.

As the evening wore on the combatants grew bigger, were in better shape in an Arnold 'body like a condom full of walnuts' Schwarzenegger sort of way, and no strangers to body waxing and tanning salons. The costumes were also a little more sophisticated, looking a little flashier than something their mum had apparently knocked up on a sewing machine at home.

It wasn't so much about the winning as about taking your opponents apart. Dirty tricks were integral, and the crowd only became truly enlivened when what superficial rules existed were transgressed with a sucker-punch to a distracted opponent or by kicking a man when he was prostrate on the canvas. The acrobatic, gymnastic choreography of throws and holds was all stirring stuff, but the Royal Shakespeare Company couldn't have been better rehearsed. It was clear that Lucha Libre maintained the 'fourth wall of theatre' through *kayfabe*. This is the practice by which the activities in the ring are presented as real and in which disbelief is suspended. The origins of *kayfabe* go back to the travelling fairs in which wrestlers once starred and mean any technique, from sleight of hand with a pack of cards to snake-oil medical solutions, which used illusion to pull off confidence tricks.

Just when we felt the comedic bitch-slapping slap-stick had reached its zenith, there was a special round for what the politically correct would call 'vertically challenged' wrestlers. These diminutive brawlers were a case study in small-man syndrome viciousness, going at each other in a febrile frenzy of aggression. Having three-man tag-teams is essentially an excuse for a brawl. The violence was then unexpectedly leavened by outbreaks of simulated sex on incapacitated opponents. One burly masked midget suffered the repeated indignity of having his pants yanked down to reveal his G-stringed buttocks, like a tourniquet tightly bisecting a bronzed ham. This was invariably the cue for another member of his tag-team to be flung face first between his perspiring cheeks, to the crowd's delirious roar of approval.

The final headlining match featured the wrestlers whose masked faces adorned the posters that had first drawn our attention to the night, plastered as they were across the city. In the red corner we had El Hijo del Santo (the Son of the Saint), in fetching white tights and silver hood, and Gronda XXX, a red body-painted demon complete with horns and massively steroid-induced muscles that looked more inflated air than pumped iron. Their opponents were the Blue Demon Jnr, a vision in shades of cerulean, and his partner, Dr Wagner, whose popularity with the baying mob the audience had by now become was secured by the hilariously camp, homoerotic mincing of his muscular bulk around the ring.

Twice the action spilled out of the ropes into the crowd, and once even into the stands, a wonderfully unlikely eventuality in that it involved both wrestlers clambering precariously up on a metal chair. This was a more conventional use of the chair, as usually they were beating each other over the head with it. The bout culminated in final submission moves executed on top of a white van conveniently parked next to the ring. The delirious crowd roared a mixture of happy approval and angry regret, depending on their allegiances. By the end of the evening we were numb of cheek and somewhat emotionally exhausted. But we did end up buying wrestling masks of our own, which have become popular fancy dress items back home. Lucha Libre came across as a perfect outlet for social aggression, though I would question whether the semi-comedic ultra-violence was really wholesome family entertainment. That said, the 'fighting' couldn't have been more pantomime without actually involving a wrestler called Widow Twankey.

After scaling such dizzy cultural heights, we left Guanajuato and headed for the madness of the megalopolis that is Mexico City, one of the biggest, busiest and dirtiest conurbations on the planet. It's less a city than a medium-sized European nation of 20 million souls jammed into a place built almost entirely on a drained lake-bed. These uncertain boggy foundations cause a structural engineers' nightmare of wonky, squint buildings with highly questionable perpendicularity. Throw in the odd earthquake to rearrange the substrata and it makes for a somewhat irregular skyline. We got tantalising glimpses of the extent of the smoggy, suburban sprawl as our bus approached the Terminal del Poniente in the west of the city, the metropolis melting off mysteriously into the misty air. Outside the terminal building, two rather elderly looking dogs were unselfconsciously executing a desiccated coitus by the taxi rank, as commuters hurried in studied ignorance around them. We hustled ourselves onto the metro at the Observatorio station, noting the clever use of symbols for each stop aimed at illiterate passengers. Onboard, blind music vendors, wearing blaring speakers around their necks like over-sized medallions, paced their way carefully through the carriages selling cheap pirate CDs. I bought a Sonia Lopez compilation from one, to get us properly into the Mexican musical mood.

Emerging from the clean, efficient metro at the Zócalo, the first thing that struck us was the wall of noise from the festive street vendors. Like a football crowd caught between renditions of recognisable or co-ordinated chants, where every fan is roaring out their own thing, the hawkers competed in a deafening, cacophonic bedlam to be heard. From cuddly toys to bath towels, lingerie to hardware tools, T-shirts to cheap plastic gimmicks familiar from Shanghai, everything was for sale in this one lairy, loud street. We sought sanctuary from this pre-Christmas commercial gauntlet by checking out the Diego Rivera murals in the expansive Secretaria de Educacion building. It was a hulking stone edifice with a double courtyard inside and three gloomy gallery floors of murals. We'd visited Rivera's old family home in Guanajuato, a grand townhouse full of dark wooden furniture and personal effects. There we'd seen an exhibition of his simple black line paintings that brought caricatures and scenes to life with an incredible economy of strokes. But the murals at the Education Secretariat were an order of magnitude more impressive, the highly politicised slogans a stirring reminder of ideologically simpler and more idealistic times. My favourite was one which read 'True civilisation is when men live in harmony with the earth and with each other'.

Other propaganda pieces included a great image entitled 'The Capitalists Dinner', depicting honourable workers offering up produce to the ugly, stern-faced bourgeoisie. They were sat humourlessly around a banqueting table, accompanied by a crying child. The underlying messages were certainly not cryptic; Rivera was a famous Communist who had lived in Moscow and hosted Trotsky in exile. Another panel showed a beaten and bleeding member of the gentry surrounded by triumphant labourers, entitled 'The Defeat of Capitalism'. More confusing was another called 'The Workers Will Eat', which featured an artist on his knees, the tools of his trade – books, painter's palette and harp – scattered beneath him and a worker's boot firmly planted on his backside. It seemed to suggest that simple honest toil would be rewarded but weak creative types would not, which seemed ironic from Rivera's perspective. After getting our fill of this somewhat unsubtle but beautifully executed and creative cant, we wandered a little aimlessly through the adjacent streets. In the Centro Historico a grid of grubby avenues stretched hazily to the distant mountainous horizon through the claggy air. The cobbled streets reverberated to hordes of cute green VW Beetle taxis of untrustworthy and now unlicensed origin – a sure-fire route to a rip-off apparently, though still cheaper than a London black cab, I'll wager. Eventually we stumbled on the building formerly used by the Spanish Inquisition. Now nobody expects that.

Huge, noisy and filthy – we loved Mexico City. Where else is your metro station built around a restored Aztec temple?

Christmas was fast approaching, so we negotiated the heaving hectic hordes at the TAPO bus station for our journey down to the Veracruz coast. We were heading to stay with Omid, a British-Iranian friend of a friend we'd never met before. *Look for the guy who seems most Taliban* were Omid's instructions on how to identify him at the bus station. We'd effectively invited ourselves to spend Christmas with strangers, so were a little concerned about the randomness of it all. But our reservations melted away quicker than a bankrupt celebrity's entourage, in the face of the warm welcome we were to receive.

As we left, we rolled through the scrappy suburbs of Mexico City on high-flying overpasses, a constant clutter of crude concrete houses crouched below. The city seemed to be spreading like a grey rash as far as the eye could see and up into the foothills of the surrounding slopes in every direction. Descending into Veracruz from the high plateau of central Mexico, there was a distinct shift in the climate and the bus was enveloped in a thick bank of mist. We wound round sharp twisting loops and bends, passing sacks of oranges piled on roadside stalls, the fruits of the verdant sub-tropical jungle around us.

The Veracruz coastline had an unspoiled charm. Brown sandy beaches, scattered with beautifully worn and bleached driftwood, faced out onto the warm waters of the Gulf of Mexico. Every few days, stiff *Norte* winds would whip the murky surf into white peaks, dump more wooden debris onto the shore, and make the beleaguered palm trees thrash back and forth ferociously. Lacking the white sands and blue seas of Mexico's Caribbean coast, the stretch of beach around Monte Gordo, where we were staying, was almost entirely undeveloped. Large sections of natural frontage were still left between the villas standing intermittently along the shore. It was wild, wonderful, and far from the madding crowd.

Italian author Cesare Pavese describes travelling as 'a brutality. It forces you to trust strangers and to lose sight of all that familiar comfort of home and friends. You are constantly off balance. Nothing is yours except the essential things – air, sleep, dreams, the sea, the sky – all things tending towards the eternal or what we imagine of it'. Omid, his girlfriend Vania, and her family the Costellos were consummate hosts, welcoming us unquestioningly into their extended celebrations over Christmas and New Year. The mutual trust of relative strangers mitigated the unfamiliar absence of our loved ones during the festive season and rebalanced us, and the feral beauty of the rugged coast stirred our spirits. Easing for the first time in months Pavese's 'brutality' of travel, and overcoming the sense of ennui that had recently stalked us like a shadow.

During the two weeks we stayed in Monte Gordo we enjoyed blazing beach bonfires, bountiful banquets, and long, loud laughter into the night. Our stay built up to a climax on New Year's Eve when, amidst the firework celebrations, one of the family cousins added to the pyrotechnics by emptying his pistol into the air, thus ensuring we saw in 2008 with perhaps more of a bang than we intended. We, meanwhile, were continuing our Lucha Libre with the Spanish language, merrily mangling the pronunciation of *Año* (year), wishing everyone *Feliz Ano Nuevo,* or a 'Happy New Anus'.

# PROSPECTING THE FUTURE

*And I wondered, with mounting anxiety.*
*What am I supposed to do here?*
*What am I supposed to think?*

— Alain de Botton —

Our inaugural journey of the New Year was a cross-country bus mission over to Zihuatanejo on Mexico's Pacific coast, 150 miles north of the tourist hordes undoubtedly 'going loco' down in Acapulco. A former fishing village on a beautiful horseshoe bay of rocky, forested headlands and a series of sleek, sandy beaches, 'Zihua' was our first real taste of a mass-market holiday resort in Mexico. Unselfconscious North Americans waddled along the shoreline, while Mexican beach dudes with tans the colour of expensive, antique furniture touted various serenity-rending activities. The air was filled with the squeals of parascending vacationers and the nasal whine of waspish jet-skis.

We stayed in a hostel run by a Canadian-Mexican couple. I explained our slow-travel trip to Greg, the gringo half of the partnership. *You're in the right country,* he winked. We'd also admired the lovely white sheet on our bed that had a striking red striped strip along one edge. Very Mexican, we thought, and asked Greg where we might buy one. Turned out the sheet was unique, he'd bought it in a second-hand shop in Vancouver. The label said 'Made in Pakistan'. The bed linen was as well travelled as we were.

Greg illuminated us with regard to the increasing influx of North American cruise ships to Zihua, as an improbably huge white gin palace squatted awkwardly in the small bay. At present passengers are ferried ashore from their giant liners by a flotilla of small boats but plans were afoot to build a proper cruise ship terminal, with questionable benefits to the local economy and ecology of the bay.

*For 500 years things have been done in the same way here, a controlling elite makes the decisions and it's backhanders all the way. You can't even find out who's behind the jetty project. There's no such thing as what we might call 'transparency'. It's just 'they're going to build a terminal', and to whose advantage?* fumed Greg frustratedly. *Ask the traders,* he explained, referring to the bustling craft market around the harbour. *Cruise ship passengers don't buy much, as they stop in so many different places,* reinforcing our own suspicions from our short stop in Tahiti. *A lot of them are simply bussed to resorts in Ixtapa [Zihua's highly commercially developed neighbour], where they can lounge by the pool for the afternoon! We had over 80 cruise ships in Zihua last year alone, and resistance to this proposal is growing. $10 million to build something of dubious provenance that will wreck the fragile ecology of the lagoon – couldn't we spend that better on improving the six sewage treatment plants that empty into it?!* In some parts of the bay the sewage sludge on the seabed is apparently several feet deep. *Another case of badly misplaced priorities,* he grumbled justifiably.

Mexico experienced an explosive growth in US-originating cruise ship tourism from 3.2 million passengers in 2000 to 6.4 million in 2007, although scare stories about shore-based crime, robberies and even murders and mysterious disappearances onboard have since led to a decline. It is a big, highly profitable business worth multiple billions; ships are run by largely unregulated, un-unionised staff who are often paid only a few dollars a day and live in hot, squalid under-deck conditions. It is a murky, often exploitative industry that seems to have coerced the Mexican authorities with the lure of further tourist revenues, excluding local people and often marginalising their economies.

The jetty plans were generating stiff local and wider national opposition, even bringing the enigmatic Zapatista leader Sub-Commandante Marcos to Zihua for a tub-thumping pipe and balaclava speech in solidarity. The stakes were high, as the initiative threatens the finely balanced mix of local family-owned businesses and limited corporate tourism that makes Zihua so attractive in the first place. There is, and should be, room for both.

So it was with some joy and relief that I later learned that the vociferous campaigning, lobbying and protesting of Zihua's 'People in Defence of the Bay Coalition' had successfully fended off the massive development threat to their environmentally overwhelmed lagoon. For me, it felt like a relatively small, hard-fought but symbolic and important victory for a more people-focused form of tourism: not blind to the significant income and jobs that visitors generate, but equally wide-eyed to the potential for a locally led, appropriately scaled version in which residents and the fragile ecology carry equivalent weight to the previously all-powerful dollar. *It's their town, their village,* one visiting American said. *I would have that come first.* And, inspiringly, Zihua is taking the first tentative steps in that direction.

Sat in the bus station a few days later, a guy selling tiny, handmade artificial roses approached us. *Hello honeymooners!* he grinned as we groaned. *You know how I know?* he continued unabashed. *Because she*

*Getting up close and personal with a Monarch butterfly, Angangueo, Mexico*

*Traditional mask, Museo Rafael Coronel, Zacatecas, Mexico*

*looks happy and you look tired!* It was not the first time we'd heard this corny line in the touristy town. I smiled agonizingly; Fi just looked weary. We headed for the hills.

A series of buses of ever-diminishing size and roadworthiness took us up into the Michoacán mountains and the little village of Angangueo, strung out along the side of a high valley. We'd come to see the over-wintering grounds of the monarch butterfly, where millions of these *mariposas* gather in the cool, mist-shrouded pine forests after a monumental migration from as far north as Canada. An impressive travelling feat in itself, the journey is even more astounding when you find out the butterflies that return from one season to the next are the great-great-grandchildren of those that left the previous year.

Quite how these brilliant, bright orange butterflies navigate these enormous trans-generational distances is still not entirely understood. It's humbling when nature challenges the limits of our knowledge. Like sea turtles that return to their ancestral nesting beaches, the mechanism by which the descendants of an individual butterfly navigate their way home is thought to be at least partly genetic. Flight patterns are inherited, and the butterflies use a time-compensated 'sun compass' based on a circadian biological clock located in one of their antennae. Combined with the ability to orientate to the Earth's magnetic field, this suite of tools allows multiple generations of butterflies to pilot their way successfully up and down the length of the North American continent. As with the amazing navigational abilities of the bluefin tuna, we're just not sure how they do it.

After a wheezy climb through the thin high-altitude atmosphere, we were treated to one of nature's truly great spectacles. The branches of the pines were bent heavily with the sheer weight of butterflies, encrusting the trees like incongruous dead brown leaves amongst the dark green needles. As the sun warmed up the slumbering insects, they took to the air in a whirling cloud of fluttering *Lepidoptera*. The sound of a million tiny wing beats surrounded us, butterflies flitting past our ears with a breathy, half-heard whisper. It was a truly magical, meditative experience. Being immersed in this flickering veil of the world's best-travelled insect –

monarchs have even been known to cross the Atlantic – I felt as if we were among appreciative slow-travelling friends. The wild wonder of this moment was made all the sweeter by the fact that the enigma of where millions of Monarchs evaporated to each winter was only solved relatively recently, in 1975, when this elusive enclave was discovered.

In her award-winning book *Flight Behaviour*, novelist Barbara Kingsolver uses the monarch butterflies to great effect as a powerful narrative tool, in a book which artfully explores personal reactions to climate change, especially in the context of science and belief. In one passage, an entomologist character is being interviewed about climate change by a TV journalist, Tina, who challenges him on the evidence: 'Scientists of course are in disagreement about whether this is happening and whether humans have a role', she states. His reply is devastatingly crafted: 'The Arctic is genuinely collapsing. Scientists used to call these things the canary in the mine. What they say now is, the canary is dead. We are at the top of Niagara Falls, Tina, in a canoe. There is an image for your viewers. We got here by drifting, but we cannot turn around for a lazy paddle back when you finally stop pissing around. We have arrived at the point of an audible roar. Does it strike you as a good time to debate the existence of the falls?'

The disruption of the monarch's migration, the gentle fluttering of brightly coloured wings, by the 'audible roar' of the approaching climate catastrophe is aurally evocative. It adds to the climate-change soundtrack of rumbling, crumbling ice sheets and crackling, roaring bushfires. We can choose not to listen, but the music plays on, building to a crescendo around us. The answer, of course, is for us to change our tune.

Below the reserve, souvenir sellers hawked all manner of mariposa memorabilia, from jigsaws to lapel badges. Many stalls also sold toy wooden logging trucks. This was depressingly ironic in that perhaps the biggest threat to the butterflies is the ongoing and illegal deforestation of the unique arboreal habitat they have no doubt been returning to for countless millennia.

I later felt this same sense of timelessness under threat in a much more human fashion in Oaxaca. This is home to a heady mix of Mexico's indigenous peoples, nearly a third of the country's ethnic groups, and a riotously colourful melting pot of cultural diversity. The highlight, nestled amongst the cobbled streets and haughty colonial architecture, was the commercial chaos of the Mercado de Abastos, probably our favourite market from the many we'd visited on four continents over the last 11 months.

Fiery shafts of sunlight poured through the haphazard corrugated zinc roof of the vast bazaar and into the hot, shady, aromatic space below. Fist-sized spring onions, black, sticky tubs of *mole* paste, fly-blown meat stalls, sugary sweet-sour tamarind balls and curious unctions for local traditional beliefs seized our attention – including one potent potion cryptically called 'the lucky hunchback'. For back pain perhaps? We snacked on *chapulines*, the region's popular fried grasshopper delicacy – crispy bugs with an oddly metallic blood-like flavour – as we lost ourselves in the market's depths.

Scurrying through the dark passages between tables groaning with fresh produce, we stumbled on a Mexican one-man band amongst the fruit and vegetables. Playing an unlikely instrumental combination of drum kit and saxophone, the grizzled old dude was bashing out a beatnik-style rhythm on his bass and tom-toms. This he interspersed with funky saxophone noodling and bursts of hoarse song. We were mesmerised. As were the wee market kids. His rendition was complicated by having to use one hand to fend off unwanted percussive additions to the performance by the gaggle of giggling children darting in to beat his drum. Free-form market jazz. You don't get that in Sainsbury's.

Mindful of the threats creeping up on the magnificent monarch butterflies, I worried how long the assembly of aromas, attitudes and acoustic anarchy of the Abastos market might resist the encroaching corporatisation of Walmart and their ilk. With well over 2,000 stores and a turnover of 100+ billion pesos (£5 billion) and already Latin America's biggest retailer, WalMex is growing rapidly and aggressively. I hope that the people of Oaxaca, unlike the loggers merrily chopping down the butterflies' vital habitat, realise and appreciate what they have before it's gone. There is greater long-term richness and wealth in both Angangueo

*The coolest busker in the world. Full stop. Mercado de Abastos, Oaxaca, Mexico*

and Abastos as they currently stand than there can ever be in terms of simple timber or one-dimensional Walmart 'value'.

Finally, after two glorious months of cacti, culture, cowboy hats, *cervezas* and enough *frijoles* to sculpt a convincing scale model of Popocatepetl, we left Mexico. From our base in Palenque we took a swift, smooth *lancha* ride up through the fast-flowing, jungle-fringed and rock-strewn waters of the Usumacinta River and, landing on the far bank half an hour or so later, we were in Guatemala. Most conveniently, the familiar sight of a border money-changer clutching wads of alien currency greeted us, quickly converting our Mexican pesos into Guatemalan quetzales. Armed with a grubby stash of notes of strange denomination and uncertain value, we sped in a minibus along a dusty, unpaved road to Flores. A new town, new country, new money, but the same dirty, dishevelled and ever so slightly-delirious Us.

We'd headed to Flores for a jungle trek into Tikal, the huge city of Mayan skyscrapers jutting up through the rainforest canopy. This had been a lifelong ambition of mine, for reasons that will become clearer later. We'd assembled an intrepid band of fellow explorers from folk we'd become acquainted with whilst crossing the border into Guatemala.

Botz was a weathered-faced, long-haired British guy, with a terminally relaxed demeanour, calm, heavy-lidded eyes and humour as keen as a chef's prize knife. Appropriately he'd worked in kitchens in Amsterdam for fifteen years, sharpening his repartee, and now ran a hostel in the mountains of southern Spain. A veritable treasure trove of gags and anecdotes, every lurid story he told seemed to begin with a bottle of vodka and a handful of ecstasy tablets, and end in suitably lubricious fashion in a rubber fetish club.

Then there were two bubbly, worldly-wise, well-fed, late-20-something American blokes. Constantly chattering, when they weren't dissecting US politics or practicing psychoanalysis on each other they were trading trivia questions, creating cumulative general knowledge of brain-bogglingly colossal proportions. So relentless and voluble was their banter that, a couple of days into the trek, Botz drily observed *I never knew the jungle would be so full of two Americans.*

*Our Mayan guide, Cristobal. Tikal, Guatemala*

Finally there was a lean, softly spoken Canadian scaffolder who was working on the tar sands in Alberta helping to extract filthy hydrocarbons. He and I needed to talk about climate change. Seriously.

In the village at the start of the trek we met our Mayan guide Cristobal, a humble, self-effacing and quietly spoken 40-something, of deceptively diminutive but strong stature. We set off with our backpacks loaded onto a pair of mules and the usual entourage of yipping mutts. The canine escort included one particularly frail, meek and pathetic Chihuahua. You didn't really fancy its long-term prospects in what was, as it had been in Siberia, the often-literally 'dog-eat-dog' world of Guatemalan villages.

As we trotted along a dirt track into the jungle we passed the mangled remains of a – thankfully very dead – large black-and-orange tarantula that hordes of industrious ants were busily dismantling for dinner. Cristobal was merrily pointing out *plantas medicinales*, demonstrating a handy if potentially controversial 'baby sedative', a useful Immodium substitute that caused constipation quaintly called *tapaculo* (literally 'plugbottom'), and a quinine plant, from which we all nibbled bitter-tasting leaves and began hankering vainly for cool gin and tonics.

At dusk Cristobal led us, like Bruce Wayne's butler Alfred, to the Bat Cave at El Zotz. Just before dark, tens of thousands of webbed-winged beasts stream out of a crevice in the craggy white limestone cliff. There was an astringent aroma of ammonia from the bat guano on the ground as we watched hungry birds of prey gather on the rock face, ready to snack on the bats as they appeared. Cristobal informed us three bat species co-habited in the cave: nectar-drinkers, fruit-eaters and vampires. I immediately started mentally gauging the thickness and protective qualities of my mosquito net.

At first one or two earlyrising bats emerged, flitting off into the gathering gloom. Then the jerky trickle became a fluttering flood as the commune-like colony emptied from their grotto in a crescendo of high-pitched squeaks and leathery flaps: a nocturnal chiropteran commute of the planet's only truly flighted mammals. Taking to the wing, as we flightless humans took to our beds.

*Mayan Temple rising from the dense Peten jungle, Tikal, Guatemala*

After we'd spent a cold, awkward night's sleep bent like bananas in our hammocks, Cristobal indicated the highly venomous and strangely cute baby snake that was curled up near our camp. *Muy peligroso!* (Very dangerous!) he exclaimed in his loud, clear Spanish, which even linguistically-compromised dullards like us could understand. In fact, *muy peligroso* was the way Cristobal described most of the stuff we saw in the jungle, from viciously spiked vines and thorny creepers to hand-sized spiders and stinging ants. Obviously he was seeking to reassure us, but the constant reminders of how nasty and brutish everything was tended to have precisely the opposite effect.

We scrambled into the remnants of El Zotz, a satellite of the main city at Tikal, a sort of suburban ruin. It was entirely unrestored and, much like Ta Prom at Angkor Wat in Cambodia, almost completely over-run by the jungle. We clambered up the steep temples on ladder-like tree roots that gnarled over the rough stones. Looking over a lawn of leafy canopy, we could faintly see our final destination of Tikal. The centrepiece, Temple IV, was poking up above the trees, another long, hot sweaty 20 miles of hiking through insect-infested, jaguar-prowled, monkeyed-up jungle.

As we trekked, the intensely fecund jungle thronged around us. Howler monkeys growled and boomed out their territory, like the sound of tormented souls echoing through a long drain-pipe. Spider monkeys were more direct and lobbed sticks at us, shaking the branches overhead intimidatingly. Aerodynamically unbalanced toucans flitted from tree to tree, their heavy bills threatening to drag them into a dive on every other wingbeat, giving their flight a lightly lilting undulation. Below in the undergrowth red-wattle-throated pheasants clucked and scratched in the dirt, and snuffling coatimundi scuttled shyly away from us back into the dense foliage.

That night, in our deep jungle campsite, Cristobal told us some appropriate *historias de la celba* (stories of the jungle), of *malos espiritus* (evil spirits) and man-eating jaguars. David Quammen, in his powerful book *Monster of God: The Man-Eating Predators in the Jungles of History and the Mind*, visited the communities that live alongside some of humanity's last natural predators: a remote enclave of lions in Gujarat in India, villages in Siberian tiger territory, and Australian Aboriginals sharing their lives with the not-so-sentimental saltwater crocodile, among others. Quammen writes evocatively of our own possible psychological and philosophical fate, once our previously intermediate position in the food chain is irrecoverably altered by the final extinction of those beasts that eat us. He has empathy for those people who live, and often die, alongside these animals, juxtaposed by his concern for us as a species bestriding the global ecology and disconnecting ourselves to a position above it. We are increasingly ignorant of our place in the natural world, in assuming we are somehow apart from it, not a part of it.

The fire and candlelight flickered across Cristobal's charismatic and deeply creased, shadowy face, starkly lit even by the weak flames, against the impenetrable, foreboding darkness of the jungle just beyond. *El Jaguar* was still relatively common in this part of the forest, he explained, and going into the jungle alone or unarmed was a risky business. *Cuatro gente, cinco, ses – bien,* Cristobal explained, but *menos cuatro gente – quizás problema*. The Monster of God was still very much alive and well in both this part of the forest and in the minds and nightmares of the locals.

The slightly spine-tingling tales of lone forest workers attacked and devoured by big cats were tempered by the bizarre nature of Cristobal's supernatural stories. These seemed to involve the threat of being seduced by gorgeous ghosts who look exactly like your lover. So you embrace them, they disappear and you become lost in hopeless pursuit of a world of phantom love. Somewhat comedically, Cristobal illustrated this process by turning his back to us and hugging and stroking himself lasciviously in the way teenagers do to fake an embrace at the school disco.

Cristobal then tried to describe another jungle beast to us, which we attempted to visualise via our broken Spanish. The elusive *tepezcuintle* took mental shape as, after more hilarious miming, we established it was *sin cola* (tail-less), *como café* (coffee-coloured), was delicious to eat and rather surprisingly *gusto como pescado* (tasted like fish). We also discovered it was around a foot long, as Cristobal demonstrated with his hands apart in 'one-that-got-away' fisherman-style. *It's about this big,*

Botz, who'd been partially translating Cristobal's description through a haze of rum, offered rather superfluously whilst mirroring Cristobal's gestures.

The following night, safely back in Flores, we each drew our own interpretation of what we imagined a *tepezcuintle* might look like. The quality of artwork was highly variable. Later at dinner, we asked the taco restaurant owner if she had *tepezcuintle* on the menu. *No!* she exclaimed, *es muy caro!* (it's very expensive). We asked her to judge our drawings and, once she and her impressively moustachioed husband had wiped the tears of laughter from their eyes, she was only too happy to oblige.

A *tepezcuintle* turned out to be a large rodent.

Before the trek I'd been eager to explore the ruins of what for centuries was the heart of the once-thriving Mayan civilisation. Tikal, of which El Zotz was part, had once supported tens of thousands of people, but then quite suddenly and dramatically went into swift decline and ultimately abandonment. As Jared Diamond put it in his book *Collapse – How Societies Choose to Fail or Succeed*, the fate of Tikal was all too worryingly predictable: 'What happened? A major factor was environmental degradation by people: deforestation, soil erosion and water management problems, all of which resulted in less food. Those problems were exacerbated by droughts, which may have been partly caused by humans themselves through deforestation. Chronic warfare made matters worse, as more and more people fought over less and less land and resources.'

These threats all felt eerily familiar. The Peten jungle setting appears misleadingly wet. Yet the initial success of Tikal was based on Mayan ingenuity in capturing and storing rainwater for drinking and agriculture in an area naturally devoid of lakes and wells. All too relevantly, it was a cycle of climatic change and consequent shifts in precipitation that finally did for the Maya: 'Sunny days, in and of themselves, don't kill people. But when people run out of food and water, they die', wrote Richardson B. Gill in *The Great Maya Droughts: Water, Life, and Death*.

Cogitating on Jared Diamond's prescient book title, it had been unsettling to see the evidence of civilisational collapse first-hand. The concerns of the Survivalists I'd met in New Zealand came rattling

*A magnificent shining 'Chicken' bus, Antigua, Guatemala*

skeletally out of my mental cupboards. I wondered how much the Maya were aware of their own undoing. Did they understand and appreciate the forces and factors at play that were undermining their very existence? How conscious were they of the delicate ecological balances and their own innovations that had enabled such a large, densely populated community to exist? Did successive generations appreciate theirs was an environment with little water and low agricultural productivity? In short, did they understand how vulnerable their whole civilisation was to comparatively subtle changes in climate?

A great cultural empire that had grown and flourished for centuries simply fell apart. The Mayans themselves didn't disappear, of course, and, while many must have died in the violent resource clashes of the transition, others simply dissipated back into smaller, more sustainable jungle communities. By the end of the ninth century AD the Mesoamerican mega-cities of their time – Tikal, Caracol, Calakmul – collapsed in a few short decades after a long millennium of progress. It would be almost another thousand years before indigenous guides led astonished European explorers to the fabled 'lost' cities in the mid-19th century.

As we'd finally stood atop Temple IV, the efforts the Maya had gone to in constructing towers, some hundreds of feet tall, to rise above the thick, impenetrable crown of the forest, became clear. Little wonder that climbing such structures in the close, dark claustrophobia beneath the canopy and emerging into the bright, airy vista above felt like taking a few steps closer to heaven. It transformed one's perspective of context, location and clarity of position. In the forest below, disorientation for the dilettante was almost instant. All directions looked much the same. From the pinnacle, the panorama was complete and one's pathway obvious.

They say you can only recognise a paradigm shift in retrospect. As in the jungle, it's hard to see it when you're in the middle of it. Yet in our rapidly urbanising 21st century, when hundreds of millions of people have been, are and will be migrating into cities around the world, the lessons of the Maya gnawed at me. Our next generation of mega-cities face multiple issues: food security, water availability, adequate fuel and power, the maintenance of social order and community cohesion. This is a situation far more complex, interdependent and fragile than even the Maya's precarious positioning, and at a much, much larger scale. Are we sleep-walking into the darkness, I asked myself?

This thought occupied me as we arrived in Antigua, the picturesque former capital of Guatemala, all cobbled streets and red-tiled colonial courtyard houses. The horizon is dominated by the dark shadows of monstrous volcanoes that tower over the low-rise buildings. The scars of the earthquakes that accompanied previous eruptions are also evident in the numerous shells of shattered churches around the city. Symbols of seismic desecration.

We scaled nearby Mount Pacaya, involving a steep 90-minute climb to the crater, eventually scrambling over the rim and peering down through the passing clouds onto a scene of devastation below. The basin was a twisted mass of menacing black rock, riven by canals of bright orange lava pushing up through the splintered surface. As we marched merrily towards the red-hot action, the temperature soared and blasts of superheated, dry air swept up from the cracks beneath our feet. Gathered beside a lethargic tongue of oozing molten rock, the lava began to bulge threateningly, dislodging a cascade of half melted rocks in our direction and sending us scurrying backwards over the serrated surface.

It was like traversing the skin of a lethally-hot rice pudding; we were consumed by the fear that the brittle surface could crumble away at any second, dumping us all to a hideous fiery demise in the liquid hell bubbling away beneath. These fears were not unfounded, given that a subsequent eruption at Pacaya killed one of the first reporters on the scene, and the volcano is currently erupting again as I type. It struck me as a compelling metaphor for the thin veneer of civilisation on which humanity currently sits.

We are a generation that is more acutely aware of the scale and interconnectedness of our collective challenges than perhaps any other in history. Some argue this is depressing, dispiriting, demotivating. The world can feel like it's inevitably spiralling into decline. We'd seen plenty of evidence for such a defeatist hypothesis during the trip: Slavic stoicism in the face of climate science, yet another resource grab in Mongolia,

*The Agua volcano looms above Antigua, Guatemala*

*Getting the message, San Pedro de Laguna, Atitlan, Guatemala*

*Busy bus station, Panajachel, Atitlan, Guatemala*

and, in China, the state-run capitalism, explosive economic growth and historically unprecedented urbanisation. Our ability to eat the seas; our blue planet's 'inner space', empty; the vicious cycle of destructive droughts, bushfires and floods unleashed down under; permanent loss of incredible, irreplaceable biodiversity or the punishing prohibition policies against drugs, to name but a random few examples from our journey.

And yet I find this knowledge of the size and urgency of our problems empowering and inspiring. We cannot fix what we don't know is broken, reinvent the best of history or redesign and innovate for a better tomorrow, if we don't confront the facts, the evidence – no matter how negative, nagging and nerve-racking it may be in the short-term. The fear this knowledge potentially generates is formidable, enough to disempower us entirely if we allow it. But equally it can galvanise us to accept our responsibilities and, in doing so, grasp future opportunities our present imaginations struggle to even dream of.

As the potentially terrifying nexus of global overpopulation, climate change, grinding poverty and inequality converges, it can invoke a sort of *Apocalypso* party spirit. We're all buggered, so we might as well enjoy ourselves while it lasts, for however long it lasts. The very escapist nature of so much tourism fuels this fire with an irony-free 'last-chance-to-see' approach to low-lying paradise islands soon to be inundated by rising sea levels, or a 'fiddling-while-Rome-burns' promise of multiple mini-breaks. This is either a form of denial, as we confronted in Australia, or akin to the resigned climate fatalism of Russia.

But what if we were to act decisively, at scale, and together on this knowledge? What if we rose to the urgently pressing, convoluted and complex challenges we face, positively as the Vietnamese have done? Can we become the heroes by rewriting our own collective story? Mindsets matter. For if we believe we will fail, we set ourselves up to do so. Faith in our ability to deliver change is fundamental. The future sits on the edge of the knife. Early pioneer of sustainability, the inspirational polymath Buckminster Fuller, sums it up thus: 'Think of it. We are blessed with technology that would be indescribable to our forefathers. We have the wherewithal, the know-it-all to feed everybody, clothe everybody, and give every human on Earth a chance. We know now what we could never have known before – that we now have the option for all humanity to make it successfully on this planet in this lifetime. Whether it is to be Utopia or Oblivion will be a touch-and-go relay race right up to the final moment.'

In his *Operating Manual for Spaceship Earth*, Fuller describes us all as astronauts, piloting our planetary craft of finite resources that cannot be resupplied through the galaxy... and carelessly having lost the instruction guide! His thinking was radical, as the book was based on a talk Fuller first gave in 1967, a full year before the iconic 'Earthrise' photo taken from the surface of the moon and almost five years before the even more famous 'Blue Marble' shot of the whole earth from space. Both of these were hugely influential in inspiring the nascent environmental movement.

Real astronauts, in the NASA sense, frequently empathise with Fuller's analysis following their first hand experience of seeing our home from orbit, documented as 'The Overview Effect'; many of the hard-bitten former test pilots that joined the space programme have been deeply and profoundly moved by what they saw. Witnessing a powerful, perspective-altering epiphany, these tough men were transformed by the realisation of earth and all its biodiverse inhabitants' vulnerability, interconnectedness and, of course, beauty. Most of all, they felt a responsibility to share their insight and do something about it. Crucially, the solutions also felt achievable, our divisions and the barriers to change easily surmountable. How could they not be, given the stakes involved?

We were eating dinner in Altagracia on Ometepe, the world's biggest lake island, which sits in the choppy brown waters of Lake Nicaragua. Tucking into smoky slices of barbecued pork on a bed of chewy plantain strips, we were deeply nostalgic for something we hadn't quite yet lost. The simple pleasures of outdoor dining on dark, grubby lanes, watched hawkishly by plaintive mutts, were coming to an end. A world where food was more likely to be 'Tesco' than 'al fresco' beckoned. We were dragging our feet reluctantly and even more slowly than usual through our final days in Central America.

In the evening, a battered Land Rover with a Botswanan number-plate pulled up. Out stepped fellow slow travellers Jill and Paul, who'd left the United Kingdom 14 years ago, originally planning to drive from Cairo to Capetown. They'd ended up working on safari camps across Africa for a decade and had spent the last two years driving through South America. With them was their son Elliot, an earnest but charming lad of five years old, 'going on 45' chuckled Jill, and possibly one of the best-travelled pre-schoolers on the planet. *So which countries have you visited?* we asked Elliot. *Well I was born in Africa,* he clarified, *but I feel like I own the world.*

Part of the hacienda we were all staying at served as a classroom for local children, giving Elliot his first ever opportunity for a taste of formal tuition. *Would you like to go to school today?* Jill asked Elliot the next morning. *Yes,* he said thoughtfully, before firmly and precociously grasping the wrong end of the educational stick. *I think I have something to teach people.*

Did our experiences have anything to teach people? Our trip had in many ways inspired our own kind of Overview Effect. We hadn't achieved the high-altitude angle of the astronauts. But there was something special about the physical journey we'd made in continuous contact with the terrestrial and marine exterior of what cosmologist Carl Sagan called our 'pale blue dot'. It had connected us deeply with the diverse and wonderful land and seascapes we'd traversed, from the power of tempestuous oceans on which we'd tossed, to the gritty deserts, vertiginous mountains like nature's temples in the sky, and mysterious forests rich with folklore. We had genuinely been around the world, truly grounded and bound to its perilously thin life-filled surface. Beneath an equally slender atmosphere that, like our exploits on the Guatemalan volcano crater, mirrored the temporal fragility of our own ephemeral existence.

Our journey had been irrepressibly social. We'd skipped across the stepping stones that friends old and new represented in the streams of a much wider and deeper but still overwhelmingly benign and compassionate humanity. As we'd roved from Soviet apartment block to Mongolian yurt, Chinese courtyard to Mexican *palapa*, we'd been held

*Gentleman in contemplative mood, Guatemala*

in a mutual embrace with our fellow human beings. Understanding and celebrating the fact that what ties us, binds us, bonds us inextricably together is inestimably stronger and more powerful than the petty, pitiful, puerile things that might divide us. Our need for physical safety, desire for a sense of belonging, love and companionship, and a belief in hope, aspiration for a better future, a brighter tomorrow for us, our families and humanity's collective fate.

Interdependence was no longer just a notion, it was a principle of life so obvious, glaring, real and vital it made me want to shout as I had in China, David Foster Wallace-like, 'This is water. THIS IS WATER!' We need to remind ourselves of these evident truths daily. Over and over again, the timeless relationships forged between people, between them and the environments in which they live, between them and their fellow floral and faunal 'astronauts' were laid bare: our great big, co-evolved and co-dependent, terrestrial and aquatic family, in all its dysfunctional but magical glory.

The trip had made us eternally grateful for the fortunate privileges our accidents of birth had bestowed upon us: the relative comfort, safety and security of our lives, our health and the many opportunities – educational, professional, recreational – presented to us on a plate. To gripe and groan about supposedly blighted Blighty would now seem churlishly unappreciative in the extreme after all we had seen and experienced. We were excited to be heading back to friends and relatives, though like some roving rhizome we had now put down roots around the world.

With only days to go before we were due to board the *Horncap*, our banana boat back to the United Kingdom, we made for Cahuita on the Caribbean coast of Costa Rica. After four months of Spanish-speaking Latino Mexico and Central America, we found ourselves among English and Creole-speaking Black Caribs. The familiar accent and aroma of jerk spices helped us acclimatise for our impending return to Brixton. Home, though still several thousand miles away, suddenly felt a little closer.

In the fourth of his *Four Quartets*, 'Little Gidding', T S Eliot writes:

*We shall not cease from exploration*
*And the end of all our exploring*
*Will be to arrive where we started*
*And know the place for the first time.*

We were heading home with a fresh perspective, a renewed vigour and feelings of excitement. The pre-trip fatigue and frustrations of Brixton and professional urban life felt far behind us. We'd been around the whole world in order to change our view of our own little world.

We hiked through the Cahuita jungle, beside palm-fringed surf beaches. There, amongst the branches like a bundle of dead leaves, we spied the ultimate slow-travel icon, a three-toed sloth. An impossibly cute baby rested on her stomach, clinging tightly to her greenish fur. Sloths are host to a blue-green alga that grows on their pelts, providing essential camouflage; when you're this sluggish, elusion is better than escape. Moving at a deliciously slow pace along her branch, she turned to survey us. Her expression was unfazed, slightly distant, almost smiling and lazily benevolent. As if to say 'What, precisely, my friends is all the rush?' Reaching the end of the woody limb, she leisurely extended a long clawed arm to hook around the creeper of the next tree. Via a process of spectacularly unhurried manoeuvring she placidly made her way across the intervening gap. No grabbing, seizing, or snatching, just a gentle exploratory feel, confident clasp and languorous swing. We can learn a crucial lesson or two from this cool, calm and contented creature.

Firstly, the sloth's appropriate pace seemed to epitomise our journey, embodying the idea that faster isn't necessarily better, and that our experience at speed is often dramatically diminished. Or as Victorian aesthete John Ruskin advises: 'No changing of place at a hundred miles an hour will make us one whit stronger, happier, or wiser. There was always more in the world than men could see, walked they ever so slowly; they will see it no better for going fast. The really precious things are thought and sight, not pace'.

The slow movement has ironically picked up speed in recent years. Or perhaps 'gathered momentum' would be a better way of putting it. From slow food to fashion, money to media, art to parenting, and so on to travel, conscious consideration is delivering a more mindful, meaningful approach to the way we live, work and play. As Carl Honore, who captured this zeitgeist paradigm shift in his bestseller *In Praise of Slow* says, 'In the war against the cult of speed the frontline is in our heads'.

Secondly, as one of the seven deadly sins, 'sloth' gives its eponymous animal a bad name. Whilst widely interpreted as being about physical laziness, torpor or downright bone-idleness, sloth is actually as much about a spiritual laziness as it is about an inability to get out of bed. It's a failure to do what you're supposed to, ought to, could do, and underpins the thinking behind the oft-quoted line 'All that is necessary for the triumph of evil is that good men do nothing'. In this sense, the 'sin' of sloth is a failure of potential, to be the best we can be, to do what's right and make best use of the talents, gifts and opportunities at our disposal. We can change the world tomorrow. The bigger question is: will we?

I could conclude this book by telling you that awareness of climate change should compel you to give up flying as we did. I could lay on you a thick layer of avoidable guilt around personal carbon emissions, individual greed and self-centredness. I could write about blame, culpability and short-term thinking. I could, in short, finish by justifiably being a right royal depressing pain in the arse. And I'd arguably be telling the truth in doing so!

However, that would be playing into the misconception that slower travel necessarily involves some form of sacrifice. That saying farewell to flying is a devastating loss. And that would be wrong. I won't brandish the stick of limiting potential and attempt to browbeat you with the evidence against aviation. Apart from creating massive cognitive dissonance, it is also highly unlikely to work.

Instead I will dangle the carrot of unfulfilled possibility. The idea that flight-free travel is revelatory and transformative in a way that air travel never can be. As the world and its wonders peel off their protective layers in a profoundly provocative striptease before you, revealing things that the 'knee-trembler behind the bike sheds' of a cheap flight rarely, if ever, will. You have nothing but the false gods of cost and convenience to lose and, literally, the real wealth of the world to gain. We'll change the world because we want to, not because we have to.

Journalist Tom Brokaw's book *Greatest Generation* eulogised the US cohort which grew up during the hardship of the Great Depression, fought and helped win the Second World War, and went on to give birth to the Baby Boomers and, ultimately, the American Dream. They were, in Brokaw's own words: 'The greatest generation any society has ever produced. [These] men and women fought not for fame and recognition, but because it was the right thing to do. When they came back they rebuilt America into a superpower.'

Let's be clear about this: we are not being asked to make the ultimate sacrifice for the causes we believe in or the very real challenges we face, as those who stood up to and ultimately defeated the Nazis had to. Or as those who struggle in war zones around the world currently are. Rather than give up our lives, we are being asked to change our lifestyles so that we, and others, may live, thrive and aspire too. It is a humbling comparison, but one that should energise us. It certainly energises me.

Travel is a gifted privilege not a given right. Think about this next time someone argues they 'deserve' a holiday. It should be, as American suffrage movement writer and activist Miriam Beard writes, '...more than the seeing of sights; it is a change that goes on, deep and permanent, in the ideas of living'. This was the lasting legacy of our trip. The simmering insights gleaned on and off the dusty roads, iron rails and salty seas. Designs for life to help us redesign the world.

What would it mean for us to really live up to Brokaw's *Greatest Generation* moniker? Actually not that much: some smart behavioural substitution, perhaps, in the way we generate energy, eat and get around. Being a little less selfish in the way we prioritise what's important to us. Considering the bigger picture more in how we work, where we invest and what we buy. Reaffirming our relationship with our vast genetic family that is all life on earth. And in doing so, we might just generate a greater sense of solidarity with each other and our one and only, lonely planet.

# BOOKS READ

The Long way round – Ewan MacGregor & Charlie Brookman

Lanzarote – Michel Houellebeq

Whatever – Michel Houellebeq

Fresh Air Fiend – Paul Theroux

The Worst Journey in the World – Apsley Cherry-Garrard

South – Ernest Shackleton

Pecked to Death by Ducks – Tim Cahill

Dr Zhivago – Boris Pasternack

The Master and Margarita – Mikhail Bulgakov

In the Empire of Genghis Khan – Stanley Stewart

Genghis Khan, Life, Death & Resurrection – John Man

Gullivers Travels – Jonathan Swift

My Invented Country – Isabel Allende

Joy Luck Club – Amy Tan

Whisky Galore – Compton MacKenzie

Time Travellers Wife – Audrey Niffenegger

Never let me go  – Kazsuo Ishiguru

A prayer for Owen Meaney – John Irving

A Cook's Tour – Anthony Bourdain

The God Delusion – Richard Dawkins

Amsterdam – Ian McEwen

The Devil in Amber – Mark Gatiss

Steal You Away – Niccolo Ammanitti

Catfish & Mandala – Andrew X Pham

The Quiet American – Graham Greene

The Wrong Doyle – Robert Girardi

The Picture of Dorian Gray – Oscar Wilde

You shall know our velocity – Dave Eggers

Roadkill – Kinky Friedman

Lunar Park – Bret Easton Ellis

A Widow for One Year – John Irving

Kite Runner – Khalid Hosseini

Burmese Days – George Orwell

The Shipping News – E. Annie Proulx

Cats Cradle – Kurt Vonnegut

On Mexican Time – Tony Cohan

A Thousand Splendid Suns – Khaled Hosseini

The Shock Doctrine – Naomi Klein

Made in America – Bill Bryson

One Hundred Years of Solitude – Gabriel Garcia Marquez

Of Love and Shadows – Isabel Allende

The Road – Cormac McCarthy

Bel Canto – Ann Patchett

The Mosquito Coast – Paul Theroux

Incidents of Travel in Central America, Chiapas & Yucatan – John Stephens

The woman who waited – Andrei Makine

The Stories of Eva Luna – Isabel Allende

Captain Alatriste – Arturo Perez-Reverte

The Deceiver's – John Masters

We need to talk about Kevin – Lionel Shriver

Patchwork Planet – Anne Tyler

Zanzibar – Giles Foden

The Rum Diaries – Hunter S. Thompson

The Virgin's Lover – Phillipa Gregory

Tennyson's Gift – Lynn Truss

Midnight in the Garden of Good & Evil – John Berendt

And then we came to the end – Joshua Ferris

Monster of God – David Quammen

The Fourth Hand – John Irving

Waterland – Graham Swift

# MILES AND CARBON TRAVELLED

| Day | Journey | Miles | CO2/Kg |
|-----|---------|-------|--------|
| 1 | 59 bus to Waterloo | 2 | 0.1 |
| | Train to Portsmouth Harbour | 63 | 4.1 |
| | Number 5 bus | 1 | 0.1 |
| | 23.59 delayed ferry to Bilbao | 628 | 2.0 |
| 3 | Finally arrive in Bilbao! | | 0.0 |
| 4 | Train to Salamanca | 209 | 13.5 |
| 6 | Train to Porto | 156 | 10.0 |
| 7 | Train to Lisbon | 170 | 11.0 |
| 8 | Train to Faro | 293 | 18.9 |
| | Train to Vila Real | | 0.0 |
| | Ferry to Ayamonte | | 0.0 |
| | Bus to Seville | | 0.0 |
| | Train to Malaga | | 0.0 |
| 12 | Train to Valencia | 291 | 18.7 |
| 13 | Train to Barcelona | 189 | 12.1 |
| | Sleeper train to Paris | 517 | 33.3 |
| 16 | Train to Brussels | 163 | 10.5 |
| 17 | Train to Amsterdam | 108 | 6.9 |
| 19 | Train to Middleburg | 81 | 5.2 |
| 21 | Train to Grevesmuhlen | 357 | 23.0 |
| 24 | Train to Berlin | 131 | 8.4 |
| 25 | Train to Prague | 174 | 11.2 |
| 27 | Train to Vienna | 245 | 15.8 |
| | Train to Graz | | 0.0 |
| 30 | Train to Ljubljana | 82 | 5.3 |
| 32 | Train to Zagreb | 73 | 4.7 |
| 33 | Train to Budapest | 187 | 12.1 |
| 38 | Train to Krakow | 182 | 11.7 |
| 39 | Train to Warsaw | 157 | 10.1 |
| | Bus to Vilnius | 244 | 15.7 |
| 40 | Bus to Riga | 163 | 10.5 |
| | Train to Moscow | 522 | 46.0 |
| 43 | Train to irkutsk | 2617 | 168.4 |
| 49 | Train to Sludlyanka | 62 | 4.0 |
| | Train to Port Baikal | 62 | 4.0 |
| 50 | Ferry to Listvyanka | 1 | 0.0 |
| 51 | Bus to Irkutsk | 44 | 2.8 |
| 52 | Bus to Caijka | 155 | 10.0 |
| | Hovercraft to Olkhon | 2 | 0.0 |
| | Jeep to Khuzhir | 23 | 1.5 |
| 57 | UAZ to Olkhon coast | 23 | 1.5 |
| | Hovercraft to Caijka | 2 | 0.0 |
| | Bus to Irkutsk | 155 | 10.0 |
| 58 | Bus to Arshan | 99 | 6.4 |
| 60 | Bus to Ulan Ude | 124 | 8.0 |
| 62 | Train to Ulaanbaatar | 272 | 17.5 |
| | Gobi trip | 625 | 40.0 |
| | Khovsgul trip | 938 | 60.0 |
| 87 | Train to Beijing | 727 | 46.8 |
| 92 | Train to Shanhaiguan | 169 | 10.9 |
| 94 | Train to Beijing | 169 | 10.9 |
| 97 | Train to Tianjin | 167 | 4.3 |
| 98 | Ferry to Kobe, Japan | 1038 | 3.3 |
| 100 | Shinkasen to Tokyo | 269 | 17.3 |
| 105 | Shinkansen to Kyoto | 186 | 12.0 |
| 106 | Shinkansen to Osaka | 83 | 5.3 |
| | Ferry to Shanghai | 856 | 2.8 |
| 110 | Train to Xiamen | 502 | 32.3 |
| 114 | Bus to Hong Kong | 291 | 18.7 |
| 119 | Train to Guangzhou | 81 | 5.2 |
| 122 | Train to Pingxiang | 313 | 20.2 |
| 123 | Bus to Hanoi | 679 | 43.7 |
| 126 | Bus to Halong Bay | 112 | 7.2 |
| | Ferry to Cat Ba | 9 | 0.0 |
| | Ferry Cat Ba to Halong Bay | 9 | 0.0 |
| 128 | Train to Lao Cai | 137 | 8.8 |
| | Bus to Sapa | 24 | 1.5 |

| Day | Journey | Miles | CO2/Kg | Day | Journey | Miles | CO2/Kg |
|-----|---------|-------|--------|-----|---------|-------|--------|
| 132 | Bus to Bac Ha | 68 | 4.4 | 281 | Bus to Hildago de Paraal | 133 | 8.6 |
| | Bus to Lao Cai | 45 | 2.9 | 282 | Bus to Durango | 210 | 13.5 |
| | Train to Hanoi | 137 | 8.8 | 283 | Bus to Zacatecas | 158 | 10.2 |
| 133 | Bus to Hoi An | 390 | 25.1 | 286 | Bus to Guanajuato | 149 | 9.6 |
| 137 | Bus to Da Lat | 167 | 10.7 | 289 | Bus to Morelia | 94 | 6.1 |
| 141 | Cycle to Mui Ne | 53 | 0.0 | 290 | Bus to Zitacuaro | 59 | 3.8 |
| 144 | Bus to HCMC | 111 | 7.1 | 292 | Bus to Mexico City | 79 | 5.1 |
| 148 | Bus to Phnom Penh | 135 | 8.7 | 294 | Bus to Martinez de la Torre | 141 | 9.1 |
| 152 | Bus to Battambang | 156 | 10.0 | | Drive to Monte Gordo | 30 | 1.9 |
| 153 | Boat to Siem Reap | 162 | 0.5 | 304 | Bus to Mexico City | 171 | 11.0 |
| 156 | Bus to Bangkok | 335 | 21.6 | 305 | Bus to Zihuatanejo | 199 | 12.8 |
| 158 | Train to Butterworth | 573 | 36.9 | 310 | Bus to Angangueo | 159 | 10.2 |
| 159 | Ferry to Georgetown | 5 | 0.0 | 312 | Bus to Mexico City | 79 | 5.1 |
| 161 | Ferry to Butterworth | 5 | 0.0 | | Bus to Oaxacca | 227 | 14.6 |
| | Train to Kuala Lumpur | 179 | 11.5 | 315 | Bus to San Cristobal | 270 | 17.4 |
| 162 | Train to Singapore | 197 | 12.7 | 321 | Bus to Palenque | 67 | 4.3 |
| 165 | Cargo ship to Brisbane | 3819 | 4.3 | 324 | Bus to Flores | 145 | 9.3 |
| 173 | Campervan to Sydney | 1118 | 72.0 | 330 | Bus to Rio Dulce | 110 | 7.1 |
| | Bus to Wagga Wagga | 238 | 15.3 | 331 | Bus to El Estor | 24 | 1.5 |
| | Train to Melbourne | 229 | 14.8 | 333 | Bus to Coban | 69 | 4.4 |
| 213 | Ship to Napier, New Zealand | 1723 | 1.9 | 334 | Bus to Santa Cruz del Qiche | 59 | 3.8 |
| 219 | Bus to Rotarua | 96 | 6.2 | 335 | Bus to Panajachel | 27 | 1.7 |
| 221 | Bus to Wellington | 231 | 14.9 | 336 | Boat to San Pedro | 7 | 0.0 |
| 223 | Ferry to Picton, South Island | 45 | 0.1 | 344 | Boat to Panajachel | 7 | 0.0 |
| 224 | Bus to Christchurch | 171 | 11.0 | | Bus to Antigua | 32 | 2.1 |
| 226 | Train to Greymouth | 103 | 6.6 | 348 | Bus to San Salvador | 117 | 7.5 |
| 228 | Bus to Queenstown | 217 | 14.0 | 350 | Bus to Managua | 225 | 14.5 |
| 230 | Hike to The Divide | 19 | 0.0 | 351 | Bus to Granada | 27 | 1.7 |
| 233 | Bus to Milford | 31 | 2.0 | 354 | Taxi to Lago de Apoyo | 6 | 0.4 |
| 235 | Bus to Te Anau | 31 | 2.0 | 356 | Bus to Granada | 6 | 0.4 |
| 236 | Bus to Queenstown | 31 | 2.0 | 357 | Bus to San Jorge | 36 | 2.3 |
| 238 | Bus to Christchurch | 222 | 14.3 | | Ferry to Moyagalpa | 10 | 0.0 |
| 239 | Campervan to Auckland | 474 | 30.5 | | Bus to Finca Magdalena | 18 | 1.2 |
| 248 | Cargo ship to Tahiti | 2546 | 2.9 | | Bus to San Jose | 198 | 12.7 |
| | Cargo ship to Ensenada | 4055 | 4.6 | | Bus to Cahuita | 125 | 8.0 |
| 263 | Buses to La Paz (x 6) | 657 | 42.3 | 367 | Cargo ship to Dover | 5415 | 6.1 |
| 276 | Ferry to Topolobampo | 300 | 0.9 | 381 | Home | | |
| | Bus to Los Mochis | 12 | 0.8 | | **Total Miles** | **44545** | |
| 278 | Train to Creel | 160 | 10.3 | | **Total Carbon / Kg** | | **1569.0** |

Khovsgol Lake, Mongolia

# ACKNOWLEDGEMENTS

I'm indebted to all who have given so generously of their time and opinions in the appropriately slow process of writing and publishing this book. Thanks to the editors whose constructive critiques of my prose have proved so invaluable in shaping the narrative, Emily Walmsley, Nicky and Susanne at Hidden Europe, Michael Lee and Candida Thriff-MacDonald. Thanks to my Futerra Co-Founder Solitaire Townsend, 'Foundette' Lucy Shea, 'Daddy' Dave Willans and all the other Futerrans who helped hone the text. Thanks to the brilliant Nick Hayes for his beautiful illustrations, and to the tireless work of Warren Beeby and Heather Knight in making the designs 'sing'. A massive cheer to my pals and publishers Dan and Tania of Wild Things, whose belief and faith in the book from Freshford in 'The Shire', have finally made it happen.

Thanks to my Mum and Dad whose own intrepid travelling adventures - working on cruise ships and traversing Europe in a jigsaw patterned Austin with ladybird hubcaps in the late sixties - have undoubtedly inspired mine. And of course thanks to Fi my travelling companion, the joy and pleasure of sharing this journey with you will never be forgotten.

Thanks also to all the amazing, interesting and inspiring people whom I've met both on the trip and in the longer journey of this life. Some of you are in the book, many of you are not, but all of you are in the thoughts, hopes and dreams that have shaped me and this story as it has unfolded.

This book is dedicated to all those who dare to travel differently.

# ABOUT THE AUTHOR

*Lake Baikal, Siberia*

Born in Norfolk and trained as a marine biologist Ed concluded he was going to spend the rest of his life saying 'if you don't stop catching all the fish, there won't be any fish'. So in 2001 he co-founded **futerra.co.uk**, a communications company with a mission to make sustainable development so desirable it becomes normal. Ed advises businesses, campaigners and governments on sustainability, and besides circumnavigating the world for this book has also worked all over it. Ed is a London Sustainable Development Commissioner and Chairman of specialist European rail booking business **loco2.com**. He lives in Brixton, South London. **ed@futerra.co.uk**  **@frucool**

hello@wildthingspublishing.com